STREETS &
PATTERNS

STREETS & PATTERNS

STEPHEN MARSHALL

Spon Press
Taylor & Francis Group

LONDON AND NEW YORK

First published 2005
by Spon Press
2 Park Square, Milton Park, Abingdon, Oxon OX14 4RN

Simultaneously published in the USA and Canada
by Spon Press
270 Madison Ave, New York, NY 10016

Reprinted 2006

Spon Press is an imprint of the Taylor & Francis Group

Typeset in Univers Light and Interstate (T) by
Florence Production Ltd, Stoodleigh, Devon
Printed and bound in Great Britain by
Cromwell Press, Trowbridge, Wiltshire

British Library Cataloguing in Publication Data
A catalogue record for this book is available from the British Library

Library of Congress Cataloging in Publication Data
Marshall, Stephen, 1967–.
  Streets and patterns/Stephen Marshall. 1st ed.
       p. cm.
    Includes bibliographical references and index.
  1. Streets – Design.   2. City planning.   3. Traffic engineering.
  I. Title.
  NA9053.S7M37 2004
  711'.41 – dc22   2004006474

ISBN 0–415–31750–9

CONTENTS

Illustration credits   ix
Preface   xi

1   **Introduction**   **1**
     Revolution   3
     Counter-revolution   9
     Transport and urban design   10
     This book   15

2   **The challenge**   **21**
     Streets   22
     Highway layout   27
     Desired patterns   29
     Complexity and contradiction   34
     Conclusions   40

3   **Street type and hierarchy**   **45**
     Principles of hierarchy   46
     Street type and classification   52
     The strategic structure   58
     Street type revisited   63
     Conclusions   67

4   **Pattern type**   **73**
     Classification of pattern   74
     Developing typologies of pattern   83

Quantifying pattern 97
Conclusions 101

5 Route structure 107
Network representation and analysis 108
Route structure 115
Route structure properties 120
Route type 123
Conclusions 130

6 Connectivity and complexity 133
Example networks 134
Connectivity analysis 138
Complexity analysis 145
Characteristic structure 151
Conclusions 154

7 The constitution of structure 159
Hierarchical structure 160
Composition, configuration and constitution 165
Constitutionally defined street type 169
Types of constitutional structure 171
The structure of car orientation 178
The structure of disurban creation 181
Conclusions 186

8 Modes, streets and places 191
The modal kaleidoscope 192
A new formulation for route hierarchy 200
Streetspace classification 210
Urban street typology 214
Conclusions 215

9 From streets to patterns 221
Design approaches – generative processes 222
A street-based constitution 228
Example patterns 235
Conclusions 241

10   **Conclusions**   **245**
          Tottenham Court Road revisited   246
          Coding for streets and patterns   248
          Implications for practice   250
          The future   254

          Appendices   261
          Glossary   291
          Bibliography   297
          Index   315

0.0 • Semmel weis Utca, Budapest

ILLUSTRATION CREDITS

PREFACE

This book originated in the desire to understand the relationships between transport and urban design and, in particular, how certain aspects of transport provision – such as the layouts of routes, streets and networks – could contribute to better urban design.

In the course of researching this book, it became clear that the most pressing unresolved issues for transport and urban design were not so much to do with the destructive impact of modern transport infrastructure on the urban fabric, but with the formative role of streets and street layout in structuring the setting for urban design.

In the past couple of decades at least, it has not been so clear what the 'ideal' form or structure of transport layouts might be, whether applied to existing urban areas or as a basis for forming new urban structures. That is to say, it is no longer considered ideal for urban areas to be structured on a road system optimised for traffic circulation. Rather, there has been a return to favour of traditional mixed-use streets, which has precipitated the need to consider what kinds of streets best meet today's needs, and how these streets might form different kinds of urban pattern.

The contemporary movements of New Urbanism and sustainable development have stimulated new ideas and imperatives in this area, but there is still, effectively, a mismatch between the urban design-led agenda based on mixed-use grids of streets and the conventional Modernist-grounded system based on hierarchies of roads and land use zones. These two systems are not easily compatible, with the result that there is a kind of uncomfortable accommodation, with roads-grounded theory having grafted-on bits of urbanism here and there, and urban design theory having bits of engineering retrofitted here and there. We almost find ourselves faced with two rival programs or operating systems updating each other in parallel – but where we are never quite sure which is the latest or best version. It is not always clear how to reconcile the different points of view; whether to decommission some of the conventional approaches, and, if so, which ones; or to replace them with something new, and, if so, what?

To tackle these issues, this book has looked behind and beyond immediate policy and design conventions, revisiting a range of first principles, to inform a conceptual framework that may be used to underpin today's streets-oriented urban design agenda.

Although in the first place oriented to supporting urban design aspirations, the research for the book has required a particular appreciation of some of the 'nuts and bolts' of transport planning and engineering, in order to get to the heart of some of the problems of urban layout, since urban structure in its physical sense is significantly influenced by the structure of movement and access.

In effect, good urban structure is necessary to create good urbanism – just as good engineering structure is necessary to create good architecture. However, although structure is necessary, it is not sufficient. Good engineering cannot rescue bad architecture. Engineering supplies, at least, some of the most basic functional requirements of a building – that it stands up – even if the rooms don't properly function for human occupation and use. Similarly, a good urban structure supplied by a functional transport system cannot on its own create good urbanism. Modern urban layouts have often been designed in the most limited functional sense – a certain number of housing units connected to the right kinds of access road, plugged into a superstructure of main roads. But the wider functions of urban 'placemaking' have sometimes suffered; the result has not been the most attractive places for human occupation and use.

The challenge, then, is to rethink how transport may better serve urban design; how urban layout may be improved towards better 'placemaking' without compromising the basic functionality of circulation and access. This implies adapting structures to be more sympathetic to urban design ends, rather than simply throwing away the engineering altogether.

This book does not attempt to address all aspects of transport and urban design, but through a focus on streets and patterns and how these are tied up with urban structure, it is hoped that it can contribute to the creation of better urban places, that are 'functional' in the widest sense.

The creation of this book has, in a sense, encompassed a series of journeys. The research has involved a chronological journey going back 40 years to some of the seminal works of the 1960s, which in many respects still provide the key foundations and reference points for today's urban debates, and that still seem to have a strong and prevailing influence, for better or worse, on our thinking about design and layout today.

Then, there has been a disciplinary journey in and around the fields of transport and urban design, exploring not only the territories of planning and engineering, but touching here and there on aspects of urban morphology, geography, geometry, topology and typology.

There has also been a journey to complexity and back. In the course of the research, the topic of 'structure' seemed to expand progressively under examination, revealing new layers of complex detail, almost like an unfolding fractal. While the research process has involved visiting some distant points of abstraction, the book itself has attempted to bring out some clear messages which can be used to inform ongoing practice.

The writing of this book has also involved many physical journeys over the past few years – from the journeys along the Circle line in central London between places of work, to longer journeys to and from Scotland and Japan, where some parts of the book have also been written. I would like to thank those who have accompanied or hosted me over different parts of these journeys for their support and encouragement.

The book as a whole draws on two or three streams of research, including research originally carried out at the Bartlett School of Planning, University College London, subsequent research carried out at the Transport Studies Group, University of Westminster, and dedicated research undertaken directly for the purposes of the book. I would like to thank David Banister, Peter Hall, Peter Jones and Ian Plowright for their constructive discussion and feedback on parts of the original research that have fed into this book.

As to the creation of the book itself, I would like to thank Nick Green, Neil Johnstone and Ming Wai-Cheng for invaluable, thought-provoking comments on the draft manuscript.

I am grateful to all those individuals and organisations which have permitted the use of their graphic material in the book (see Illustration credits); and especially to those who took original photographs for inclusion in this book: John Eden, Nick Green and Treasa Creavin.

Stephen Marshall
London, 1 March 2004

1 INTRODUCTION

The change from horse-drawn to motor traffic was a revolution, and nothing less than a corresponding revolution in roads and road user will suffice to put things right.
Alker Tripp, *Road Traffic and Its Control*[1]

In 1963, the UK Buchanan Report on *Traffic in Towns* laid out a vision of urban design for the motor age. This envisioned cities of multi-lane motorways and multi-storey car parks, with tower blocks and pedestrian decks set above labyrinthine systems of distributor roads and subterranean service bays. Central London was shown transformed into a vast megastructure complex sprawling across Fitzrovia and Bloomsbury, vividly demonstrating the 'radically new urban form' demanded by the motor vehicle.[2]

The image opposite was merely intended as an *illustration* of the Report's implications – demonstrating what *could* be required if society chose to take the accommodation of motor vehicles to its logical conclusion. Had this choice been taken up, the result would have been a dramatic transformation of towns and cities – and not least of the portion of inner London illustrated.

A bustling commercial street, Tottenham Court Road, would be transformed into a multi-lane motorway, terraced and flanked on either side by parallel collector–distributor roads, forming a traffic canyon some 100 m wide, accommodating a dozen lanes of traffic. Its four-level intersection with Euston Road would occupy an area that could accommodate a hospital or university (Figure 1.1).[3]

Such surgery would scarcely be contemplated today. Already, by the early 1960s, the wisdom of highways-driven city redevelopment was being

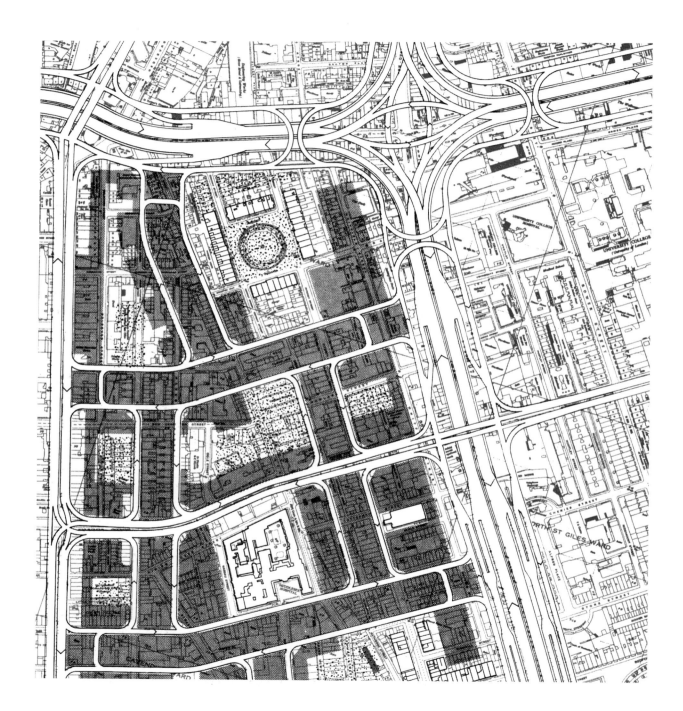

questioned by radical urban writers such as Jane Jacobs, who saw streets as the lifeblood of cities rather than mere traffic channels; and subsequently by Christopher Alexander, who saw streets as multi-functional urban 'patterns'.[4]

But, in the vision presented in *Traffic in Towns*, the role of Tottenham Court Road as an urban 'seam' between Fitzrovia to the west and Blooms-bury to the east would disappear as those districts became separated, insular precincts. Shops would be marooned on the pedestrian deck, away from passing trade. Buses would be abandoned in the limbo of the district distributor level. The familiar urban 'patterns' of the grocery store by the bus stop, and the pub on the street corner, would be lost. There would be no pub on the corner, since no building would interfere with the requisite junction visibility requirements. There would be no crossroads, since these would be banned on traffic flow and safety principles. Indeed, there would be no 'streets': just a series of pedestrian decks and flyovers.

The vision was more than a fleeting urban hallucination from the 1960s. It expressed principles that were to become the prevailing norm for urban road layout, not only in Britain, but around the world. It was no less than a snapshot of an unfolding urban revolution.[5]

REVOLUTION

What was this urban revolution all about? At heart, the traditional pattern of urban structure constituted by streets was swept away by a brave new system of vehicular highways separate from buildings and public spaces. Richard Llewelyn-Davies called this the 'revolutionary, even cataclysmic, impact of modern transport planning on the form of towns'.[6] In the second half of the twentieth century, as the car and the modern highway took a grip on urban design, city form underwent perhaps its most dramatic transformation in thousands of years.[7]

The cataclysm of Modernism was not just about comprehensive redevelopment and the introduction of a new kind of infrastructure – that had happened before, when the railways entered the Victorian city. What modern road planning did was to alter the fundamental relationship between routes and buildings. It effectively turned cities inside out and back to front.

The cataclysm of Modernism

Over the course of history, all sorts of urban activities have taken place on the main streets: they were not just for through passage, but for meeting, trading, hawking, busking, bear-baiting, public speaking and pillorying. If anything, there seemed to be a natural relationship between the busiest, most vital streets and the most significant urban places (Figure 1.2).

1.1 • Inner London transformed. In this illustration from *Traffic in Towns*, the north–south commercial street Tottenham Court Road is replaced by a multi-lane motorway, severing the Fitzrovia district (west) from Bloomsbury (east).

1.2 • Dunbar in 1830. The high street is the widest street and the most significant urban space in the village. The main street has wells and a weigh-house – this hints at the variety of urban activities present.

Modernism not only broke this relationship between movement and urban place: it reversed it. It proposed an *inverse* relationship between movement and urban place. The movement would now be the movement of fast motor traffic; the urban places would become tranquil precincts.

In the UK, Alker Tripp had already promoted the idea of turning existing arterial streets into segregated highways for motor vehicles, like railways, barred to public access. The main streets would have their buildings turned back to front, and side roads disconnected. As Tripp calmly put it: 'Roads-ends need not be closed up with bricks and mortar; a row of posts will suffice for the present.'[8] Colin Buchanan later commented:

It is when one considers carefully the full implications of Alker Tripp's theory – the searing of the town with a railway-like grid of roads and the literal turning of the place inside out – that the first qualms arise and one asks whether, if this is the price to be paid for the motor car, it is really worth having.[9]

Despite these qualms, Buchanan made the founding principle of *Traffic in Towns* the distinction between roads for traffic and those providing access to buildings. This directly echoed the approach of Tripp two decades earlier, who asserted that these two functions were 'mutually antagonistic', and must be separated in two kinds of urban road.[10]

This, in a sense, turned the road system itself upside down. Formerly major streets became backwater access roads or pedestrian precincts. The most important traffic routes were no longer streets. The relationship between main routes and central places was reversed (Figure 1.3).

The historic pattern of accessibility focused on the centres of settlements became replaced by accessibility distributed around the urban periphery. Whole settlements became, in the words of the writer Alex Marshall,

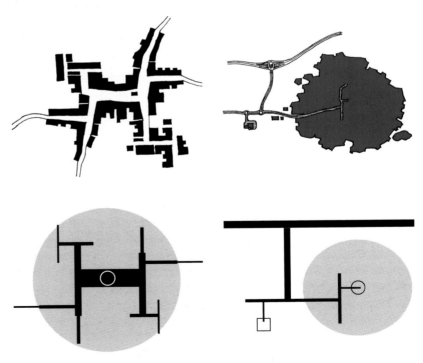

1.3 • Caricature of historic and modern settlement structures. (a) The market square is centre stage, and the intensity of circulation dissipates outward from this core. The routes out of town are of a relatively low standard. (b) The main flows and highest standard routes are on the national network outside the town. The relationship between notional centre and main routes is reversed.

(a) Historic structure

(b) Modern structure

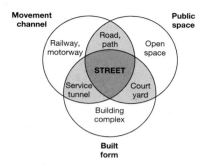

1.4 • Elements of the street.

'appendages off a freeway ramp'.[11] At the scale of urban streets and blocks, modern road systems also turned pockets of the urban fabric 'inside out', inverting streetspace as the focus of public space.

Tripp prefaced his comments on how streets should be redesigned with the telling phrase 'from the traffic point of view'. With hindsight, this point of view seems to have been built into much of urban planning policy in the second half of the twentieth century, often appearing to have priority above all others. And as a central plank of Modernist policy it was adopted enthusiastically by engineers, architects and planners alike. The circulation system has always formed the 'backbone' of settlements; but traditionally it was streets that performed this spinal role. In contrast, Modernism filleted the city – stripped the spine and ribs out from the urban flesh, and set up the road network as a separate system.

The dissembly of the street

The urban street had traditionally united three physical roles: that of circulation route, that of public space, and that of built frontage. These three elements may be loosely equated with the linear concern of the transport engineer (the street as a one-dimensional 'link' in the traffic network), the planar concern of the planner (streetspace as land use) and the three-dimensional concern of the architect or urban designer (Figure 1.4).

However, the revolutionary rhetoric of Modernism passed a death sentence on the street. Modernism set up a new urban model that liberated the forms of roads and buildings from each other. Rather than being locked together in street grids, the Modernist model allowed roads to follow their own fluid linear geometry, while buildings could be expressed as sculpted three-dimensional forms set in flowing space (Figure 1.5).[12] Each

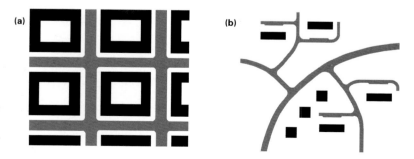

1.5 • Traditional versus modern layouts. (a) Fit of roads and buildings. (b) Roads and buildings follow their own dedicated forms.

form could follow its own dedicated function, resulting in a divergence of forms and quite separate geometries for buildings and roads. The street, in official vocabulary, ceased to exist.[13]

The schism of Modernism

This effectively amounted to a schism in urban design between the treatment of roads as movement channels, and the treatment of buildings and public space. It led to a deconstruction and separation of the elements of the street (Figure 1.6). What applied to the product also applied to the process, resulting in a division of labour between the design professions. Road layout became the preserve of highway engineers and traffic engineers, specialising in the sciences of traffic flow and the engineering design of infrastructure. Meanwhile, the architects concentrated on the buildings, creating new works of 'urban sculpture'.[14]

The result was that street design became subsumed within the rather specialised discipline of road design – based on the scientific considerations of traffic flow and the kinetics of vehicular motion, practised by engineers trained in hydraulics and mechanics, rather than architects trained

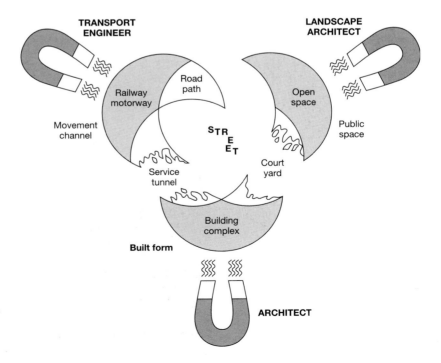

1.6 • The schism of Modernism. Modernism saw the deconstruction of the elements of the street (Figure 1.4) and the separation of professional roles in the design of its different facets.

in spatial form and aesthetics, or planners versed in the arts of the public realm.

The single-minded pursuit of traffic-driven approaches almost reduced the whole 'town planning' process to an elaborate and obscure mathematical calculation to optimise a very limited number of variables – such as the 'peak hour passenger car unit flow rate' – to which everything else was subordinated.

Following the modernist paradigm, each road would have a function and would be designed accordingly. The fastest, highest capacity roads would be segregated from pedestrians and non-motor traffic, with a minimum of intersections and no direct frontage access. Existing streets would be shorn of buildings, and converted into distributors or expressways. The body of the street was dismembered, evacuating its soul.

The disurban legacy

This roads-and-traffic-driven approach proved 'disastrous'.[15] This is because the impact of highway engineering in urban areas is not limited to the physical intrusion, severance, demolition and blight that can collectively be referred to as *urban destruction*. It also includes the negative effects of

1.7 • Disurban creation.

1.8 • Hulme, Manchester. Patterns of revolution and counter-revolution.

highway engineering as a formative influence on urban layout, in effect, *disurban creation*.[16]

Disurban creation refers to the tendency of highway-led approaches to result in dull or dysfunctional layouts, where new development is lacking identity, vitality or urbanity (Figure 1.7). While the cost of urban destruction is tangible, disurban creation is more of an opportunity cost; the opportunity lost for creating good urban places. While less immediately pathological than urban destruction, the problem of disurban creation would have to be faced up to, sooner or later.

COUNTER-REVOLUTION

The historical transformation from traditional streets assembled in street grids to modernist point blocks set in open space and then back to street grids again must be one of the most significant reversals in urban design history. An observer from space could read the morphological volte-face in the classic image of the redevelopment and re-redevelopment of Hulme in Manchester between the 1960s and 1990s (Figure 1.8).[17]

Since the early 1990s, movements such as New Urbanism have drawn attention to the problem of roads-driven disurban creation, and have taken the initiative towards solving it. The rhetoric of the 'motor age' has been replaced by the rhetoric of sustainability and neo-traditional urbanism. Compact, dense, mixed-use neighbourhoods are back in fashion, with a new breed of traditional-style buildings and street patterns to choose from. The street itself, once seemingly in terminal decline, has undergone something of a renaissance. Street grids are back in vogue.

Hand in hand with this neo-traditional urbanism are what we could call neo-traditional transport policies. That original form of transport – walking – is now lauded as the most favoured mode of movement, followed closely by cycling, with both complemented by public transport for longer journeys. Traffic engineers trained to squeeze the maximum traffic flow out of city streets are now urged to 'calm' those streets, slowing down traffic and giving space back to the pedestrians. The 'monolithic modernism' of highway engineering and car-oriented urban 'solutions' are on the back foot.[18]

However, it has taken some time for the curbing of the worst of roads-driven urban destruction to be followed through by tackling roads-driven disurban creation. Efforts do not seem to have got far beyond recognition of the symptoms of the problem.[19] And, despite increasing recognition of streets as 'people places', on closer scrutiny, we find some familiar Modernist principles still exerting a powerful influence on the layout of our towns and cities.

The Buchanan Report was not just an exercise in accommodating traffic in towns, nor a showcase for the possibilities of 'traffic architecture'. It presented a fundamental 'code' for urban structuring, based on the road system. While plans for superhighways and slab blocks have long fallen by the wayside, Buchanan's basic code remains: the core principles for the layout and 'hierarchy' of roads, and their relationship with building frontages and urban structure, live on in current theory and practice. In a significant sense, we still build towns this way.

Therefore, despite present good intentions to prioritise sustainability, and the desire for a return to more traditional urban forms, achieving these is not straightforward. While the destruction of central London might no longer be contemplated, it would be difficult to actually *create* a Fitzrovia or a Tottenham Court Road today. According to the prevailing legacy of the Buchanan Report, we could build any number of bland housing schemes or metropolitan megastructures. But we could not create the exemplary urbanism of traditional cities such as London.[20] This represents the basic stimulus and the challenge of the book; at the heart of which is the relationship between transport and urban design.

TRANSPORT AND URBAN DESIGN

There has been a distinguished tradition of architects, urban designers, planners and landscape architects – quite apart from transport planners and engineers – who have recognised the significance of transport for structuring cities. This recognition was particularly evident in the era of Modernism, where transportation efficiency was considered the 'prime shaper of urban space'. According to the canons of the Athens Charter, 'traffic flow and its design was the primary determinant of city form'. The central transport spine of the linear city became the 'symbol of modernity'.[21] According to Paul Spreiregen, the architect should consider the circulation system as a 'total urban concept'. Edmund Bacon describes various ways in which 'shafts of space', 'simultaneous movement systems' and grand axes – or their modern equivalents – may be used to structure cities. Both theorists and practitioners have actively considered the transport system, and particularly the street system, in its role as the primary structural element of the city.[22]

The significance of transport

The significance of transport for the formation and growth of cities is well established – from the ability of ancient city-size settlements to feed themselves, to the creation of modern cities like New York or Los Angeles that are significant products of their transport system.[23]

1.9 • Transport and urban character. (a) Rue des Pucelles, Strasbourg. (b) Century Freeway, Los Angeles.

(a)    **(b)**

Transport infrastructure has had a particular influence on the fabric of cities, as a physical presence and as a land use (Figure 1.9). The amount of urban land occupied by transport-related land uses, including streets, lanes, car parks, highway intersections, railway yards, and so on, can easily account for a third of the total land areas of cities.[24] Hence, the influence of transport on urban design, for better or worse.

Problems with transport

Since the 'schism of Modernism', increasingly the finger of blame for bad urbanism has been pointed in the direction of the transport professions. Highway promoters and transport departments have been described as being 'fanatical' and 'sinister', responsible for 'tearing the environment to bits and encouraging its most cancerous aberrations'.[25]

However, the negative influence of transport is not just one of urban destruction, but also disurban creation. What is at stake is not simply the scale and impact of insensitive transport engineering. After all, this may be no worse than the impact of destructive if well-intentioned planning –

described by the Prince of Wales as 'war by other means'. Rather, critics may envy or resent the way that transport-related concerns – bound up and defended by seemingly unchallengeable principles relating to traffic flow and safety criteria – seem to have ultimate supremacy over all other influences on the form and structure of urban layout.[26]

In particular, the blame is pointed at the rigid application of highway engineering standards that seem to control much of urban layout (Figure 1.10).[27] These rigid highway conventions and standards have often led to 'a sense of sprawl and formlessness and development which contradicts some of the key principles of urban design'. Highway engineers have been caricatured as the pariahs of the urban design professions. Indeed, it has been suggested that 'Almost all the blame for the amount of disappointing bland housing estates can be laid at the door of highway engineers.'[28]

Of course, it is not all one-way traffic; and Robert Cowan points out that the architecture and planning professions have to take their own share of the blame.[29] The issue of street design and street pattern is not necessarily one of inevitable inter-professional conflict. After all, disciplinary boundaries are somewhat fuzzy – even arbitrarily drawn in the first place – and different professions could be in charge of the different aspects of design.[30]

In effect, then, urban designers and planners do not wish to claim the territory of the design of streets and patterns simply as a matter of

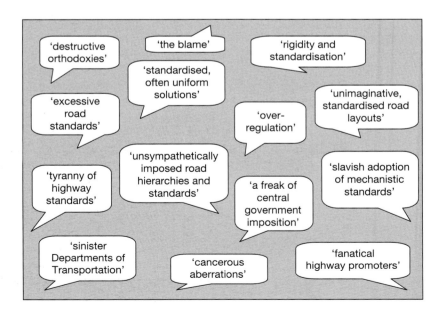

1.10 • Criticisms of the highway engineering influence on urban layout. For full citations, see Appendix 1.

professional 'poaching' – to break the engineers' monopoly on transport issues, to claim a share of highways-dominated infrastructure budgets, or to strengthen their role as project managers. It is not as if urban designers and planners particularly desire to perform traffic flow computations or design roundabouts.

In effect, the desire to control streets and street pattern is because of the way that transport provision significantly influences the structure of urban layout.

Transport and urban structure

Transport is not just another land use. In other words, transport infrastructure and streetspace are not just any arbitrary part of a two-dimensional tessellation of land use parcels. The design of street pattern is not just a matter of distributing the land use labelled 'transport' here and there to fit within a patchwork of other urban spaces and places. To a significant extent street pattern is – and must be – influenced by the geometry of movement and the topology of route connectivity.

The 'movement space' constituted by streets forms the essential connective tissue of urban public space – from the micro scale of circulation within buildings to the macro scale of whole cities. Buildings are commonly discrete objects, but even when conjoined to form terraces – or mega-structures – sooner or later they tend to be separated from other buildings by public thoroughfares. Similarly, plans showing plot boundaries reveal that agglomerations of plots tend to form insular blocks separated by blank spaces which represent access routes (Figure 1.11).[31]

So streetspace forms the basic core of all urban public space – and by extension, all public space – forming a contiguous network or continuum by which everything is linked to everything else. This continuum is punctured by plots of private land. The plots of private land surrounded by public streets are like an archipelago of islands set in a sea of public space.[32] Just as every sea port, no matter how large or small, is directly connected to every other sea port, every access point to a plot of land or urban block leads to every other access point essentially through the medium of the public street system (Figure 1.12).

The ancient Romans called their urban blocks *insulae*, or islands, reflecting the topological containment of buildings and land parcels – howsoever nested or subdivided – within an all-embracing common continuum of public space. This public space is primarily constituted by the system of public streets.

1.11 • The 'access archipelago'.

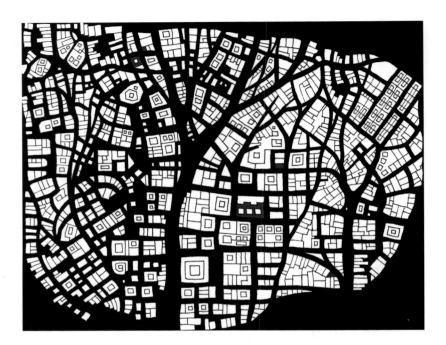

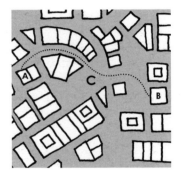

1.12 • Navigating the 'archipelago' from A to B. All ports of call are connected by the continuum of public space, C.

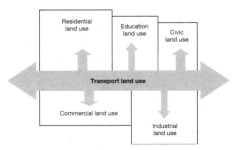

1.13 • The topological significance of the transport land use. The 'transport land use' of public streetspace is contiguous and connects all other land uses.

This contiguity is a basic topological property which sets apart the access network – the 'transport land use' – from other land uses. This makes transport a fundamental organising feature, and gives it an importance that transcends the direct travel or traffic function of routes. In effect, transport *topology* has an importance and influence that goes beyond the concerns of transport *policy* (Figure 1.13).

To say that transport is key to urban structuring does not imply that 'transport' as an urban function or land use is more important than 'housing' or 'open space'. Nor does it mean that transport is the only influence on the pattern of streets and land parcels: clearly, these patterns will be influenced by topography, land ownership, land value and other social, economic and physical factors. However, it does mean that close attention to the structural logic of the access network is important for understanding how existing cities are structured and how new ones may be designed.

So, although a street is much more than an urban road, the movement function is in a sense central to the street function from the point of view of spatial organisation. Consequently, those responsible for catering for the movement of people and vehicles – of whatever profession – will necessarily have a strong influence on the design of streets and street patterns.

This is why the street may be regarded as a fundamental building-block of urban structure. The public street system forms the principal part of the urban transport system, and is therefore pivotal to our story. This explains why a change in transport mode (from horse power to the internal combustion engine) was more than just a technological regime change, but more like an urban revolution – and why it might seem to need a 'counter-revolution' to put it right.

THIS BOOK

The challenge is now to devise or adapt for today's needs a system of urban design that can retain the benefits of safety and efficiency of transport flows, while also accommodating the diversity of modes, urban uses and frontage functions that were traditionally reconciled in the form of the urban street. The challenge is to address the street as an urban place as well as a movement channel, and how to make this conception of the street work – not just as an isolated architectural set piece, but as a contribution to wider urban structure.

While there is nowadays a strong aspiration to integrate the urban design and engineering aspects of laying out buildings, streets and urban development, the realisation of this aspiration must go beyond the rhetoric of good intentions. We must go beyond the recognition that 'streets are for people' – the recognition that streets are the subject of a variety of urban design professions' concerns – and the consensus that 'something needs to be done'. Basically, we have to be clear about where the outstanding ambiguities and conflicts lie, and tackle the kinds of 'unchallenged truths' referred to by Kelvin Campbell and Robert Cowan in their urban manifesto *Re: Urbanism*.[33]

This book aims to tackle these unchallenged truths. This implies something more than a facelift for design guidance, but some deeper surgery. It implies that we have to go back to first principles; it means getting to grips with issues such as circulation, spatial organisation and underlying structures, and not just superficial form. This necessarily means tackling a series of rather abstract and technical issues, from basic geometrics and mathematical abstractions such as graph theory to practical traffic engineering concerns (Figure 1.14).

For example, in the course of the book we shall revisit the issue of hierarchy as set out by Colin Buchanan in *Traffic in Towns* in 1963, the structure of transport networks as studied by K. J. Kansky in the same year, and another kind of network property – 'arteriality' – that links hierarchy and

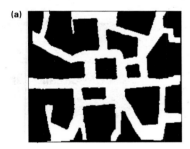

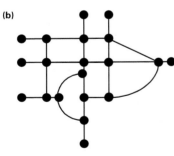

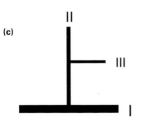

1.14 • Patterns of streets. (a) Geometric patterns. (b) Topological patterns. (c) Hierarchical patterns.

network structure, identified by Alastair Morrison in 1966. This book necessarily goes into some depth and detail on some of these issues, but the effort can bear fruit, by tackling certain problems at source.

To do so, this book combines two basic strands: the 'design debate', which is most directly related to the outward orientation of the book, and the 'nature of structure', which represents the theoretical 'interior'.

The first strand – 'the design debate' – relates to professional concerns about how the roles of the street may be reconciled, what forms of street pattern are desirable, and how they might be designed to create desirable functional urban layouts. The challenge of the design debate is introduced in Chapter 2.

The second strand is an in-depth investigation into 'the nature of structure', and how various structures may be described and analysed, and how such abstract structures underpin the urban and street patterns built out on the ground. The investigation of the nature of structure includes scrutiny of types of *street*, and the basis for their arrangement in 'hierarchies' (Chapter 3), types of *pattern*, and how they may be classified (Chapter 4); how streets may be represented and analysed as *routes* (Chapter 5) and as assemblies or patterns of *route structure* (Chapter 6). The different kinds of structural issue are then drawn into a single conceptual framework (Chapter 7), which in a sense represents the convergence and conclusion of the core research content of the book.

From here, design concerns phase in again, with advocacy for possible applications to practice, in terms of systems of *streets* (Chapter 8) and how these may be used to generate *patterns* (Chapter 9). The book ends with consideration of how the system developed can both support the existing 'good practice' of functional urbanism, as well as pointing towards the city of the future (Chapter 10).

BOX 1. ORGANISATION OF THE BOOK

A series of Boxes, one per Chapter, is used to highlight some key points or concepts that support the understanding of the rest of the book.

Chapters 1 to 7 each have a corresponding Appendix in which supporting material is presented.

Key terms are presented in a Glossary.

To get to there from here, the first task is to articulate the terms of the design debate: just what are the rigid engineering standards and tyrannical highway rules that seem to bedevil urban layout? And what actually are the urban designers' preferred alternatives?

NOTES

1. Tripp (1950: 297).
2. MoT (1963, p. 142, other pages).
3. MoT (1963: 147). The estimate is based on visual inspection of the land area occupied by the main buildings of University College London and University College Hospital.
4. Jane Jacobs indicted the 'failure of town planning' in her classic work of 1961; while Alexander laid out a conceptual critique that questioned the rigid simplisticity of hierarchically planned urban systems (1966a).
5. The approach of *Traffic in Towns*, by its own reckoning, was 'almost revolutionary'. Ashton also describes *Traffic in Towns* as 'a revolutionary solution to the nightmare of traffic congestion that now faces us in this country' (1966).
6. Llewelyn-Davies (1968: 46).
7. This was in some ways the most dramatic transformation since the dawn of urbanism, and the invention of the street in the first place (Marshall, *Cities Design and Evolution*).
8. Tripp (1942). Tripp was an assistant traffic police commissioner, road safety pioneer and urban 'seer' (Hall, 2002: 39).
9. Buchanan (1958: 153).
10. Tripp ([1938] 1950).
11. Alex Marshall (2000). See also Garreau (1992) on Edge Cities; Marshall (2003a) on urban settlement hierarchy.
12. The buildings have been variously characterised as stand-alone 'pavilions' (Martin *et al.*, 1972) or 'isolated monuments' (Oc and Tiesdell, 1997) forming 'still life' set pieces (Southworth and Owens, 1993). Bacon (1975: 231) described the separation of buildings from the landscape as 'the great amputation'.
13. In the UK, streets became 'distributors' or 'access roads' (MoT, 1963).
14. This professional schism is likened by Robert Cowan to the Big Bang, with the professions marooned on receding galaxies, each incomprehensible to the other (1997: 12). On inter-professional relationships, see also Sabey and Baldwin (1987); Hebbert (2003).
15. Punter and Carmona (1997: 178); Cowan (1995: 13).
16. 'Disurbanisation' may be related to the loss of the urbanity and sense of place associated with traditional cities (Oc and Tiesdell, 1997: 15); with the 'centrifugal tendency' of spatial distribution generated by the motor car (Cooke, 2000: 37); 'disurbanism' is associated with the breaking of traditional relationships between buildings, public space and movement (Hillier, 1996: 174).

17. For references relating to New Urbanism, streets and street grids see, for example: Krieger and Lennertz (1991), Calthorpe (1993), Murrain (1993), Katz (1994), Ryan and McNally (1995), Morris and Kaufman (1998), Leccese and McCormick (eds) (2000), Greenberg and Dock (2003); for an overview, see Hebbert (2003).

18. Newman and Kenworthy (1999: 288).

19. Although some progress has been made, there has perhaps been a lag of a couple of decades between the recognition and absorption of the need to avoid urban destruction – say, from the early 1970s – and the recognition and absorption of the need to avoid 'disurban creation', which has perhaps only managed to get underway from the 1990s.

20. Campbell and Cowan (2002: 40) put it this way: 'Unfortunately the rules do not allow a high street to be built today.'

21. Lang (1994: 171); Kostof (1991: 154); Gold (1997: 31); Bacon (1975); Spreiregen (1965: 157).

22. Hilberseimer (1944: 104); Smithson and Smithson (1967; 1968: 42); Trancik (1986: 106); Brett (1994: 71); Friedman (1998); Roberts et al. (1999: 55); Roberts and Lloyd-Jones (2001); Erickson (2001); Lillebye (2001: 5).

23. Clark (1958); Hall (1999: 754); Marshall (2000).

24. Southworth and Ben-Joseph (1997); Alexander et al. (1977); Mumford (1961). The exact proportion of land consumed, and how it is defined, are open to a variety of interpretations. Lewis Mumford described this as 'space-eating with a vengeance' (1961: 510); Allan Jacobs sees the proportion of public space taken up by streets as a chance for street design to positively influence the design of cities (1993).

25. Mumford (1964: 180); Scully (1994: 225); Cowan (1997: 7).

26. In his notorious Mansion House speech, Prince Charles implied that planners did more harm to parts of London than the *Luftwaffe*'s bombing raids (Prince Charles, 1987). Professional power relationships are discussed by McGlynn (1993); Punter (1996: 264); Punter and Carmona (1997: 86); Campbell and Cowan (2002).

27. Carmona (1998: 180); Davies (1997: 27); Schurch (1999: 5); Punter and Carmona (1997: 23). The criticism also comes from engineers themselves (Jenkins 1975: 17).

28. DTLR and CABE (2001: 41); Cowan (1997: 8), Thorne (LTT, 1998).

29. Robert Cowan points out that the architecture and planning professions have tended to claim pre-eminence in the development process, but 'They could not claim convincingly to be simultaneously in charge and guiltless' (1997: 6). Conversely, Cowan recognises that there are highway engineers 'who believe that there is more to cities than traffic flows and road hierarchies, and who use their skills and experience to subvert the destructive orthodoxies of their profession' (1997: 8). Indeed, many transport and engineering professionals welcome the progressive accommodation of urban design principles as an opportunity, not a threat (Hazel, 1997: 22; Fowler, 2003).

30. Southworth and Ben-Joseph (1997) suggest that residential streets could fall under the jurisdiction of the architect, landscape architect and planner. Rosenkrantz and Abraham have suggested the need for 'a new profession combining skills of traffic network management and urban design' (1995). Abbey (1992) would have the whole business of designing highways orchestrated by 'highway architects'. Bartlett (1995) also suggests a role for 'urban architects'. See also Campbell and Cowan (2002: 24) on disciplinary boundaries.

31. See Krüger (1979) for analysis of the connectivity of built form in contradistinction to the connectivity of the movement network.

32. The term archipelago in its original sense – applying to the Aegean Sea – referred to a sea sprinkled with islands, although contemporary usage tends to emphasise the meaning of a collection of islands.

33. Campbell and Cowan (2002: 40).

2 THE CHALLENGE

The image opposite shows the abrupt halt that urbanism faces when it meets the disurban territory of the distributor road: in this case, in the form of a prosaic roundabout. What happens when the irresistible force of New Urbanism meets the immovable object of 'road hierarchy'? This is a question that lies at the heart of the challenge of this book.

On the one hand, we have plenty of ideas, guidance and consensus on what urbanistic grids of streets might look like. On the other hand, we have plenty of principles and conventions on how distributor roads should relate to each other in a road hierarchy. But the two do not necessarily match up.

The mismatch is currently exemplified in the way that the UK design guide *Places, Streets and Movement* – which is intended to address the design of streets in mixed use areas – is a companion to *Design Bulletin 32*, which is a guide to the design of *roads* in residential (i.e. mono use) areas.[1] Falling between the cracks, as it were, is a fair amount of urban design territory, not least the traditional main street, which is not comfortably addressed by either guide. And yet these guides perhaps represent one of the closest points that the two traditions approach each other – that most closely span between the extremes of streets as architectural ensembles and streets as trunk roads.

Accordingly, although there is increasing recognition of the significance of the street to urban design – by engineers as well as urban designers and planners – the streets often seems to somehow 'float free' of any clear or consistent conceptual framework. To fit engineering convention the street has to be conceptualised as an urban 'access road', that belongs in a 'road hierarchy', not a 'street grid'. In a sense, we have to suspend our belief in

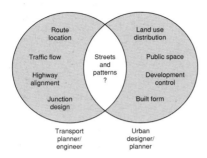

2.1 • Streets and patterns as overlap or void between design professions.

the existence of streets when submitting design concepts to fit the realm of conventional engineering practice, or suspend belief in the existence of those conventions at the creative stage of envisioning urbanistic grids of 'streets', 'mews' and 'boulevards'. And so, although there may be a consensus that there is a need for reform, it is not so clear what exactly should be reformed and what should be retained.

For a start, we seem to have lost the art of designing street grids. The street grid lies in a disputed territory between the spheres of influence of the transport and urban design professions. For many years, while Modernism held sway, this territory became a kind of no man's land in design terms, since streets themselves – and hence street grids – were out of favour. In the ensuing theoretical void, engineers simply got on with designing layouts of 'roads in urban areas' (Figure 2.1).

The advent of neo-traditional urbanism and the revival of the street have changed all this. Urban designers and planners are showing renewed interest in both streets and street patterns; they may rue the ceding of this design territory, and wish to 'reclaim the street', and with it, street pattern. These now represent an overlapping area and a potential area for conflict. The reconciliation of this conflict – or the filling of the 'void' with something positive – represents the challenge tackled by this book as a whole.[2]

Chapter 1 set out in a broad sweep the general challenges of transport and urban design. This chapter now focus on the specifics of the challenge of urban layout constituted by streets and patterns, by looking in more detail at key areas of the professional design debate. It examines existing priorities and issues for design guidance, demonstrating the lack of clear articulation of desired street types and patterns from an urban design perspective. In doing this, it sets out the different areas of confusion and conflict between different aspects of street pattern, structure and hierarchy. This stimulates the investigation into the nature of street type and pattern that forms the core part of the book.

STREETS

The types of street to be included in a scheme are the key to its overall character.

Urban Design Compendium[3]

A street can be seen as a road that happens to have an urban character; or as an urban place, that happens to serve as a right of way.

The first view is typically the starting point of the transport planner or engineer, who would see street design as a specialist aspect of road design – one that has to deal with several urban 'complicating factors' that get in the way of designing a good road.

The second view is perhaps more like the starting point of the urban designer, who will conceive of ensembles of buildings, sequences of spaces, and their associated functions, one of which is the specialist concern of movement – which becomes a transport 'complicating factor' that gets in the way of designing a good place.

Under the system of Modernism, the view of the street as an urban road prevailed; but increasingly the recognition of the street as a multi-functional urban place has been gaining ground. This book addresses the tension between the two. It does not attempt to deal with all aspects of street design across the spectrum of engineering and urban design concerns, but focuses on the interface between the two points of view.[4]

Street type

The issue of street type is important because it leads from description of type to prescription of type. In other words, the types of street that are systematically recognised in design guidance will influence the types of street that are designed and built. If certain types of street are not recognised, and do not feature in design guidance, then these types may disappear, there being no adequate guidance or specifications available for employing them. Even the street itself – as an urban route type in the first place – might be in danger, if the category 'street' is denied in official guidance geared to the design of 'urban roads'. Therefore, in order to meet today's needs for streets-oriented urban design guidance, we need to be aware of what kinds of urban route and street are potentially available.

Street roles and classification

Any particular street will tend to have 'multiple personalities', that is, have a variety of different characteristics that are present simultaneously.[5] For example, Marylebone Road in London is a major traffic route and bus route; it serves as a ring road and bypass to central London; it has the form of a dual carriageway boulevard; it is designated a Red Route and part of the Transport for London network; it is the A501 (Figure 2.2).[6]

Any particular street is likely to have a variety of official designations, as well as any number of other possible bases for distinction. The Institution of Civil Engineers has noted this as a confusion of different systems of road classification, that are each directed towards different purposes. Those

2.2 • The multiple personalities of Marylebone Road. Marylebone Road is a boulevard, a traffic route, a ring road, a primary route, among many roles.

purposes include distinguishing administrative responsibility for routes (e.g. national trunk road), assisting with information (e.g. route signing), or distinguishing road standard (e.g. dual carriageway) or construction criteria (e.g. based on the design life measured in 'millions of standard axles').[7]

Particularly influential has been the idea of a 'functional' classification, in which roads are classified according to their (intended) function, rather than their (present) form.[8] An example of conventional 'functional' hierarchy is that given in the UK professional manual *Transport in the Urban Environment* (Table 2.1).

This kind of classification is not just a description of possible types, but it is a prescription for ongoing management and future design, that

Table 2.1 **The road hierarchy of Transport in the Urban Environment**

Road type	Predominant activities
Primary distributor	Fast moving long distance through traffic. No pedestrians or frontage access
District distributor	Medium distance traffic to primary network. Public transport services. All through traffic between different parts of the urban area
Local distributor	Vehicle movements near beginning or end of all journeys
Access road	Walking. Use of highway by frontagers. Delivery of goods and servicing of premises. Slow moving vehicles
Pedestrian street	Walking. Meeting. Trading
Pedestrian route	Walking. Some cycling in shared space
Cycle route	Cycling

Source: IHT (1997: 146).

implies that these are ideal types, or the only allowable types. It is also significant, because this is not just a linear listing, but is an ordered 'hierarchy' that is linked to allowable connections between street types, as well as binding together the distinction of different types of movement and frontage function.

The *Transport in the Urban Environment* hierarchy has only four types of road which accommodate vehicular traffic, and only one type – the access road – which is dedicated to providing a full multi-functional role for any vehicle type and frontage access. In other words, it only has one type of road that fits the description of a street.

This has meant in practice that a diversity of actual streets has had to be shoehorned into a narrow range of categories apparently dominated by traffic function. An arterial street like Marylebone Road has to be forced into a category either as a distributor road – placing vehicular movement ahead of other considerations, and in denial of its pedestrian and frontage roles – or as an 'access road', which is not meant as a strategic traffic conduit (Figure 2.3).

Urban design and street type

Clearly, the above situation is at odds with the urban design view of streets. The *Urban Design Compendium* suggests that 'A new terminology is required to describe all the roles that streets can play in making successful places.'[9] Whatever kind of terminology is advocated, it is likely to involve some recognition of streets that combine through movement and local use

(a)

(b)

2.3 • Denial of the traditional arterial street. Under the current system, traditional arterial streets such as Marylebone Road (Figure 2.2) are not recognised as such; only the separate roles of (a) primary distributor or (b) access road (frontage street).

Table 2.2 **Suggested street types from** *The Urban Design Compendium*

Conventional	Suggested street types that combine capacity and character
Primary distributor	Main road – routes providing connections across the city
District distributor	Avenue or boulevard – formal, generous landscaping
Local distributor	High street – mixed uses, active frontages
Access road	Street or square – mainly residential, building lines encouraging traffic calming
Cul-de-sac	Mews/courtyard – shared space for parking and other uses

Source: Llewelyn-Davies (2000: 75)

or frontage activity. This wider view of streets is also echoed by the Institution of Civil Engineers and Urban Design Alliance, whose recent *Designing Streets for People* report suggests the need to balance the traditional 'right of way' with a sense of 'right of place'.[10]

Urban design approaches to street type often tend to focus on physical form, such as the street cross-section (including width of carriageway and building type), or the kind of streetspace on plan (e.g. square, mews) or perhaps land use function (e.g. residential, commercial). One possible approach is given in the *Urban Design Compendium* (Table 2.2). However, although this is a step in the right direction from the urban design point of view, it remains to be seen how to reconcile these types with conventional hierarchy, which for better or for worse prevails as a key influence on structuring urban layout.

Another approach to street type is suggested by Peter Calthorpe, who advocates the use of 'connector streets' in his influential work *The Next American Metropolis* (Figure 2.4). Connectors are supposed to carry 'moderate levels of local traffic smoothly, in a way that is compatible with bicycle and foot traffic'.[11] While associated with traffic function, the connector itself is significantly defined by its position in a particular kind of connective network. That is, the connector street's distinctive character is owed significantly to the structure of the road network, rather than to its physical form or its traffic function. While Calthorpe's 'connector street' is clearly demonstrated on plan, the limits of what is or is not a connector street are not defined; this could merit further attention.

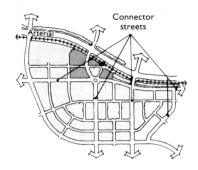

2.4 • Calthorpe's connector streets.

Overall, there is a need to address the issue of street type by considering the full variety of possible kinds of form and function: how should street types relate to each other within a given typology (e.g. how a connector street might relate to an arterial or cul-de-sac)? How might street type relate to pattern type (e.g. Calthorpe's connector street with connective network)? How might different types relate to each other within a 'hierarchy' (e.g. how street types are related as a 'hierarchy')? Finally, how might these notions of street typology be reconciled with conventional road hierarchy, addressing different modes of movement and traffic functions?

HIGHWAY LAYOUT

The nature of the hierarchy of the elements of the network and the elements themselves are what gives any urban design its character . . . The geometry of the road network . . . and the manner in which the elements are linked together are all the subject of urban design.

Jon Lang[12]

Just exactly how the urban design of streets and spaces may be reconciled with road network structure is a central concern of the design debate addressed in this book. As we have seen earlier, highway engineering layout standards are perceived to be part of the disurban problem. Therefore, we need to explore the kinds of highway layout guidance to see more clearly where the problem lies in terms of street pattern.

Highway layout guidance

It is conventional for highway design guidance to specify road standards in terms of design components such as link alignment, carriageway layout, junction type and construction standards. For example, when we look at the aspects of streets to which regulation applies in the USA, we find that these include the relation of proposed streets to adjoining street systems, rules for street intersections and rules for dead-end streets.[13] However, whatever else highway layout standards control, there is little that specifies actual street pattern.

This is a general trend among transport engineering and policy texts, where street or road network pattern structure may be alluded to here or there, but only mentioned in passing, or not treated at all. For example, some texts refer to very general kinds of pattern (such as radial or gridiron) but these relate more to the description of typical forms already existing, than to target patterns intended for network design application. When we look for any detailed guidance on specification of pattern, we do not find any explicit prescription.[14]

For example, in the UK, the general reference work *Transport in the Urban Environment* says little explicitly on the matter of network pattern. In the USA, the American Association of State Highway and Transportation Officials' 'Green Book' has no guidance on street pattern. In its opening chapter, indicative street layouts are shown, for the purposes of demonstrating the role of typical street types, but, throughout the rest of this comprehensive and authoritative volume, there is no suggestion of what a desirable or optimal street pattern should be.[15]

The UK design guide for residential roads and footpaths, *Design Bulletin 32*, alludes to a variety of kinds of layout, including 'hierarchical layouts' and 'network configurations', but it is not possible to infer exactly what is meant by these, as there are no accompanying diagrammatic examples. Therefore, although this kind of layout guidance has been accused of giving rise to 'a plethora of standardised housing layouts', in DB32 itself there is virtually no explicit guidance on overall street pattern. In other words, any 'monotonous' effect is surely the result of lack of imagination on the parts of the designers (of whatever profession). This hints that the highway engineering rules *per se* do not necessarily preclude good design, nor inevitably create 'bad urbanism'.[16]

In the USA and elsewhere, the New Urbanist movement and associated neo-traditional approaches have brought much creative effort to bear on the issue of street pattern. The principle of having interconnected streets is central to traditional neighbourhood design (TND).[17] However, even the Institute of Transportation Engineers' *Traditional Neighborhood Development Street Design Guidelines* have no explicit guidance on the overall form of street pattern – other than the general suggestion that 'TND streets are interconnected'.[18]

The elusive issue

Despite criticism of engineering standards in general, we look in vain for the actual traffic or highway engineering specification indicating what overall form street pattern should take. This is curious, since it implies that there is – if anything – a lack of guidance on the highways approach to pattern, rather than a straitjacket of authoritarian prescription.

In practice, highway and traffic engineering tends to deal with component parts rather than wholes. That is, they deal with the design of links,

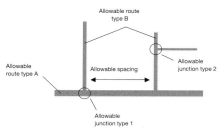

2.5 • Highway guidance for layout structure. Despite criticism of 'standardised' layouts, highway guidance tends to address individual components, not prescribe overall pattern.

junctions and their relationships (e.g. junction spacing). They do not prescribe the resulting pattern (Figure 2.5).

The road network is effectively like a kit of parts, chiefly conceptualised as links and nodes (junctions), joined together like an engineering structure. The road links and junctions – like structural members and joints in a building structure – are designed to carry so much capacity, in the fulfilment of such and such a function. Individual junction types might be recommended or discouraged. But as for overall pattern, this appears to be left open.

This lack of prescription and indeterminacy actually allows a certain amount of flexibility. However, it may also result in a feeling of lack of control; or may leave a creative vacuum. Given the lack of explicit guidance on pattern, there may be a *de facto* tendency to use 'hierarchical' systems to generate only 'tree-like' or 'loop and cul-de-sac' road patterns on the ground. Yet, although commonly associated, 'hierarchical' and 'tree-like' are, as we shall see, not necessarily the same thing.

To get a fuller grasp of the nature of the challenge, we turn to look at the elusive issue of street pattern from the point of view of those advocating alternatives to the status quo, and expressing a variety of desired patterns.

DESIRED PATTERNS

What are those qualities? Easier to recognise than describe, and easier to describe than prescribe with any precision . . .
Urban Villages[19]

Such guidance as exists on overall street pattern tends to come not from highways or traffic engineering conventions, but from the urban design and planning traditions. Unlike the definite, often quantified standards of highway engineering, urban designers' and planners' expressions of desired patterns are often couched in terms of verbal descriptions of properties, or demonstrated by means of illustrative plans.

The quest for clarity

I would give each path an *identifiable* character and make the network *memorable* as a *system of clear and coherent sequences* . . . Each road could be given a *coherent form*, and the intersections with other paths made *clear*.
Kevin Lynch[20] [emphasis added]

2.6 • Examples of desired properties of urban structure. A fuller list of desired properties and sources is given in Appendix 2.

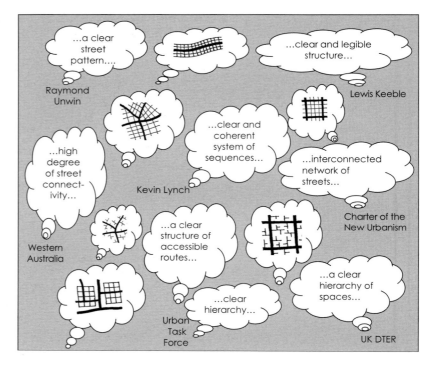

Terms such as coherence, clarity and legibility permeate planning literature and recur frequently in works of design aspiration and guidance. They are often used liberally to describe the desired qualities of urban structural features such as street patterns and networks of spaces (Figure 2.6).

The selection of examples – listed fully in Appendix 2 – is not exhaustive, and one could surely point to more cases in a similar vein. Nevertheless, the haul of concepts from even a preliminary trawl can be illuminating, in this case with regard to the recurrence of the terms: 'legible' appears five times, 'coherent' appears ten times, and 'clear' or 'clearly' appear over twenty times (Appendix 2).

It is not always obvious, however, what is meant by these terms, especially since, more often than not, the statements are not accompanied by diagrams to illustrate patterns with (or without) these qualities. For example, Lewis Keeble is one of many advocates of a 'clear pattern', but warns against 'artificial symmetry or factitious order'.[21] The lack of a definition or demonstration of the clear pattern makes it difficult to know at which point clarity might become factitious. Meanwhile, the idea of a 'connected network' is almost tautological, since any given network should be, by definition, connected up. And when the Urban Task Force calls for 'a clear structure of accessible routes . . . which lead from one destination point to another', we are left none the wiser as to what is envisioned.[22] These statements could apply to almost any pattern, from a rural patchwork of pathways to the spatial blueprint for a modernist megastructure.

Yet there is clearly *something* of significance that is trying to be articulated. Although there may be a confusing profusion of terms, there must be something 'there' that is being referred to. This reflects the fact that patterns cannot be concisely described with words alone.

It seems that if 'legible' and 'clear' and 'coherent' are to be treated seriously as design qualities, then they must be capable of adequate specification. Instances of street patterns that are clear and unclear, coherent and incoherent, and legible and illegible should be distinguishable. This suggests that they should be demonstrable on plan.

Pattern demonstrations

A desired pattern may be depicted on plan, which can be more structurally demonstrative than a verbal description. That said, a single diagram on its own may not necessarily isolate the key 'active ingredients' of a desired design. A more effective method is to contrast 'preferred' and 'discouraged' diagrams, to help demonstrate the key properties (Figure 2.7).[23] Current urban design guidance typically depicts a grid-like pattern as the preferred case and a tributary pattern of loops and culs-de-sac as the discouraged one – although in the past the reverse was the case.[24]

However, in presenting a simple polarisation, even the use of paired diagrams may only be able to demonstrate rather crudely the difference between extreme types, such as between grid and cul-de-sac systems. In reality, there will be a range of types spanning between these extremes; although as yet design guidance tends not to draw or define finer distinctions.

A second problem is that illustrative diagrams in general tend to bind together different connotations in a single layout depiction – and it may not be known which connotations are essential and explicitly intended, or which are incidental features that are not supposed to be a definitive part of the demonstration. For example, a 'preferred grid' may be depicted as orthogonal (right-angled) and rectilinear (straight-lined), whereas a simple topological connectivity might be all that was intended. Conversely, there is no way of knowing if a 'preferred grid' that happens to depict a loose 'organic' pattern expressly implies that rigid rectilinearity is to be rejected or not.

2.7 • Examples of 'preferred' and 'discouraged' layouts.

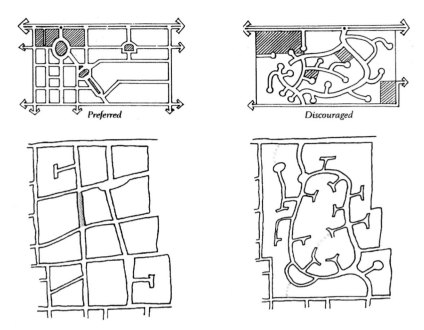

Preferred   *Discouraged*

This tells us that while the depiction of a plan is in one sense useful by being structurally explicit, in another sense, it may also be open to mis-interpretation, since it is not necessarily clear which parts of the plan are essential properties, intended to be taken literally as generalised principles. In other words, the use of plans has advantages from the point of view of description, but may have disadvantages from the point of view of prescription.

Problems of prescription

There appear, therefore, to be some problems with the prescription of patterns for design guidance. First, we have seen verbal descriptions of properties which do not clearly specify geometric patterns that could be followed (Figure 2.6). Second, we have seen explicit graphical presentations of 'preferred' and 'discouraged' patterns (Figure 2.7), which might be ambiguous from another point of view. These might be too *specific*, by including incidental detail that is not explicitly intended as part of the prescription. This detail may inadvertently suppress other possible variants, inhibiting creativity.[25]

There is also a further problem, relating to how desired exemplars may be followed by practitioners. For example, the design guide *Places, Streets*

2.8 • Poundbury as a 'good practice' exemplar.

2.9 • Poundbury's typology of streets and spaces.

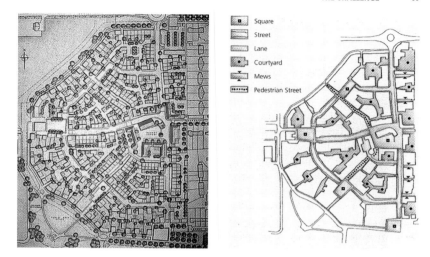

and Movement depicts the layout of Poundbury as an exemplar for good design (Figure 2.8). The development is laid out around 'a network of spaces' where 'primacy is given to the creation of coherent, attractive neighbourhoods'. The Poundbury example includes a typology of streets and squares (Figure 2.9).

While the Poundbury example is an interesting illustration of a 'hierarchy' of street types, there is no explicit theory of hierarchy accompanying it, nor generalised guidance on overall patterns, that might allow one to repeat the exercise to achieve the desired 'coherence'. Similarly, the *Essex Design Guide* demonstrates graphically that areas should be focused on 'cores' from which the street system should radiate – but it is not so clear how a general 'theory of cores' might directly translate into an actual design approach.[26]

Indeed, *Better Places to Live* asserts that there is 'no standard formula' for designing the well-connected layouts it advocates. The Urban Task Force recommends that design guidance should provide good practice examples, rather than the 'prescription' associated with conventional roads-oriented design guides such as DB32.[27]

While these approaches may be welcomed for getting away from 'rigid prescription' and 'standard formulae', they also both seem to suggest abandoning an attempt at generalised principles that may easily be adopted by design practitioners up and down the country. Both imply looking at good practice exemplars; but this on its own might yet have less flexibility, and

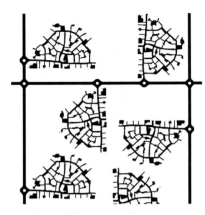

2.10 • A plethora of Poundburys.

could in itself be seen as a kind of standardisation – the 'typecasting' of pattern, perhaps.

That is, there could be an over-reliance on employing specific master designers to weave their design magic in the creation of their own 'signature' patterns, which could generate their own coherence internally, but without any transparent means of transferability. Or, taken to another extreme, it could lead to a plethora of 'Poundburys' marching across the countryside, as the present exemplar is replicated mechanistically by others, within the existing framework of engineering convention (Figure 2.10).

And aside from *this* issue of standardardisation – as the form of Figure 2.10 hints – there is still no resolution of the issue of what happens when the exemplary urbanism of Poundbury hits the distributor road network.

COMPLEXITY AND CONTRADICTION

While we have an emerging impression of desirable features such as connective, walkable street grids, and apparently undesirable properties such as road hierarchy, it is not wholly clear what kind of connectivity or hierarchy is meant. This section deconstructs five key areas of confusion which this book as a whole aims to clarify:

1.   street type and hierarchy;
2.   'bad' versus 'good' hierarchy;
3.   hierarchy versus pattern;
4.   preferred versus discouraged patterns;
5.   pattern versus process.

Street type and hierarchy

Systems of road hierarchy which specify a limited typology or 'hierarchy' of allowable street types – typically expressed as road types – have been criticised for being apparently based on traffic flow or road capacity.[28] The classification may appear to be a rather narrow ranking, which appears to prioritise vehicular traffic over other modes.

In fact, the basis for specification of type is not clear or consistent. Although conventional road hierarchy is based on 'functional' classification, there is ambiguity about whether the function refers to what a street 'functions as' (e.g. a rat run) or refers solely to its intended function is (e.g. street for local traffic). There is also ambiguity as to whether the functional basis for the classification is 'trip function', 'traffic function', 'road function' or 'network function'. A variety of trip, traffic, road or network-related parameters could be used to specify the function of any given road or street, but the definitions are not necessarily clear or consistent. Ray Brindle comments on the ambivalence as to 'whether we are specifying design characteristics to help define road types, or vice versa'. Meanwhile, Phil Goodwin has suggested that a functional hierarchy of roads is simply a 'fantasy'.[29]

Exploring the characteristics of classification and hierarchy will require consideration of the meaning of 'function', how function is allocated, how street type relates to position in the street pattern, and to hierarchical structure. Getting to the bottom of the issue of street type will be a full analysis in its own right (Chapter 3).

'Bad' versus 'good' hierarchy

Although conventional road hierarchy is often criticised, sometimes urban designers and planners themselves appreciate *some* kind of hierarchy, based on distinguishing different kinds of street type. Design guides will call for a network that 'clearly distinguishes between arterial routes and local streets', a 'clearly recognisable hierarchy of streets', a 'hierarchy of clear connections' or a 'hierarchy of routes and places'. Earlier, we saw the case of Poundbury (Figure 2.9) where a hierarchy of street types was presented. [30]

So, some kind of hierarchy can be 'good' from an urban design point of view – although it is not necessarily clear or consistent what this 'good hierarchy' entails. It might be contrasted with 'bad' hierarchy of conventional engineering approaches, but even here, the distinction is not necessarily clear.

For example, in the USA, the ITE's *Traditional Neighborhood Development Street Design Guidelines* suggest that 'While TND street networks do not follow the same rigid functional classification of conventional neighborhoods with local, collector, arterial, and other streets, TND streets are hierarchical to facilitate necessary movements.'[31]

The *Essex Design Guide* is confusing in a slightly different way. It explicitly rejects having a 'hierarchy of road types', but this appears to be contradicted by the depiction and listing of road types which appear to be controlled in a way indistinguishable from conventional road hierarchy[32] (Figure 2.11).

There is surely something going on here. There is evidently something 'good' about a hierarchy of different kinds of street that may be desirable from the urban designers' and planners' point of view. Yet this is not clearly articulated in the examples discussed. Nevertheless, the urban designers seem fairly sure that it is not the conventional engineers' hierarchy that is desired. What is needed is, in effect, a clearer deconstruction of hierarchy and how this relates street type to street pattern (Chapter 7).

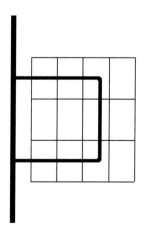

2.11 • Diagram demonstrating layout of three types of route (redrawn from the current *Essex Design Guide*).

Hierarchy versus pattern

Hierarchy and pattern are often confused: the terms are often used ambiguously and apparently interchangeably. Table 2.3 gives some examples of the mix of uses of the terms.

In effect, the term 'hierarchical' is commonly used to denote a tributary ('loop and cul-de-sac') layout, in contradistinction to traditional grid layouts, even though grid layouts may also be hierarchical in nature, either by design or emergence. In other words, the adoption of a particular layout (e.g. grid) does not preclude the retention of a particular kind of hierarchy. Indeed, the kind of 'integrated grid network' envisaged by advocates of neo-traditional urbanism may well have greater differentiation of route types than conventional 'hierarchical' road networks (Chapter 6).

Design guidance may inadvertently reinforce the confusion of the verbal descriptions by use of graphic depictions. The expression of a desired hierarchy may suggest a diagram depicting a particular pattern. As Ray Brindle points out, conventional road classifications typically 'depict roads as forming a tributary (i.e. tree) system, each road picking up traffic from less important roads and channelling it to more important roads'.[33] While this is indeed often the case, the depicted *pattern* does not necessarily follow from the underlying rules of *hierarchy* (Figure 2.12).

This gives us an inkling of the kind of richness of possibility that we need not lose: we can have layouts that are both 'hierarchical' and 'grids' – such as the case of the Craig Plan of Edinburgh (Figure 2.13)

Part of the challenge of this book, therefore, is to sort out the different meanings and implications of different kinds of tree or grid patterns and different kinds of hierarchy, 'tree-like' or otherwise (Chapter 7).

Preferred versus discouraged patterns

The ongoing debate on street pattern often boils down to a simple polarity between 'grid' network forms versus 'tributary' (or 'loop and cul-de-sac') forms. But justification of these preferences is a complex and to some extent contradictory issue.

1. *What kind of pattern?* A pattern of streets may comprise any or all of: a pattern of roads, a pattern of paths, and a pattern of blocks or plots of land. While in some cases these may be coincident, in other cases there may be different patterns serving different purposes (Figure 2.14).[34]
2. *Clarity, identity and legibility.* Conventional tributary (loop and cul-de-sac) networks may be criticised on the basis that they lack a 'clear structure and identity'. However, a grid is not necessarily 'clearer' or more 'structured' than a tree pattern. Some research results suggest that grids may have fewer

Table 2.3 **Contradistinctions of hierarchy and pattern**

Conventional (problem)	Neo-traditional (solution)
'hierarchy of roads'	'network of spaces'
'hierarchical street networks'	'reduced street hierarchy'
'sparse hierarchy'	'dense network'
'hierarchical street networks'	'highly connected gridded streets'
'a highly differentiated street hierarchy'	'an integrated grid network'

Sources: Llewelyn-Davies (2000: 76); Kulash (1990); Kulash (in Ewing, 1996: 16); McNally and Ryan (1993); Banai (1996: 183)

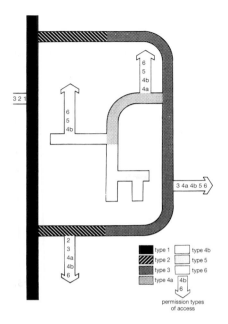

2.12 • Hierarchical layout prescription. A descending hierarchy of route types (1, 2, 3 etc.) is here depicted in a tributary pattern of loops and culs-de-sac. But the 'permissible types of access' do not themselves preclude more grid-like configurations.

■ type 1	□ type 4b
▨ type 2	░ type 5
▓ type 3	type 6
▒ type 4a	4b / 6

permission types of access

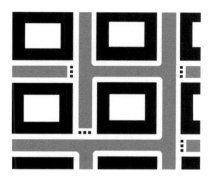

2.14 • Superimposed patterns. The pedestrian network is a grid but the vehicular network is discontinuous.

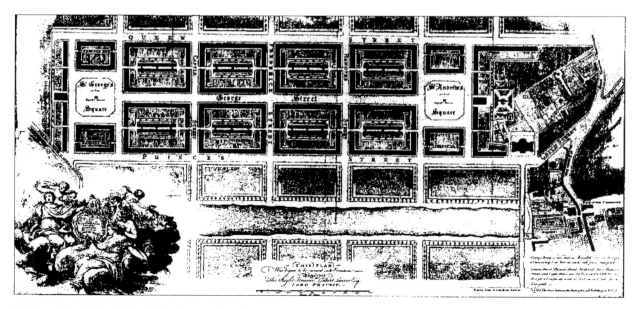

2.13 • Craig Plan, Edinburgh. This traditional street grid could meet the caricature of 'good hierarchy' admired by urban designers. It is a planned layout with a clear hierarchy of streets and lanes that connect together in a systematic manner. It is therefore 'hierarchical', but in a way unlike Figure 2.12.

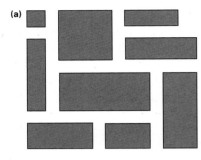

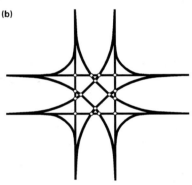

2.15 • Camillo Sitte's layout considerations. Sitte favoured T-junctions (a) over crossroads (b) primarily for urban reasons.

'identifiable' districts than curvilinear suburban patterns. And the *Urban Design Compendium* promotes a 'hierarchy of routes and places' to assist the objective of legibility. Perhaps it is more the differentiation or regularity of pattern, rather than whether this is a grid or a tree, that is at stake.[35]

3. *'Traditional' versus 'neo-traditional'*. Although neo-traditional design may favour permeable street networks, it is not uncommon to see neo-traditional designs with liberal use of culs-de-sac. Indeed, Michael Southworth has demonstrated that some neo-traditional designs may resemble conventional 'auto-oriented' suburbs as much as traditional grid-based neighbourhoods, in terms of proportions of crossroads and culs-de-sac.[36]

4. *'Concentration' versus 'dispersal'*. One of the neo-traditionalists' arguments in favour of 'permeable' street networks is that the route options offered by the grid 'disperse' traffic, 'rather than forcing all traffic onto increasingly crowded collector and arterial streets'.[37] However, these oversimplify the dynamics of traffic networks. Ray Brindle observes that 'Recently there has been much talk of the "permeability" of networks which has, in part, generated mischievous theories about the ideal structure of local networks.' He warns of the dangers of transport planners and traffic engineers being seduced by the rhetoric of neo-traditionalist planners with their preference for the grid.[38]

5. *'Geometric' versus 'organic'*. Finally, even the merits of the grid from an 'urbanist' point of view cannot be taken for granted, and have for long enough been subject to criticism from a variety of quarters. Camillo Sitte, perhaps one of the most famous pioneers of a 'neo-traditional' approach, was certainly against rigid engineering solutions. However, he also strongly argued against the use of crossroads, grid planning and monumental symmetrical layouts – three of the characteristic hallmarks of many of today's New Urbanist designs. We could say that Sitte's brand of neo-traditional design was 'organic' rather than 'geometric'.

Ironically, the systematic purge of crossroads by late twentieth-century traffic engineers has often been supported by the use of a much propagated diagram, depicting the disproportionate number of crossing conflicts involved in crossroads layouts, which appears to have descended from Sitte (Figure 2.15).[39]

The last two cases (points 4 and 5 above) share another irony: in both cases the neo-traditionalist viewpoint is ostensibly arguing for *better traffic circulation*. Sitte was using the claim that crossroads impede vehicular flow to help to back up his main argument, which was for more irregular street patterns (which would be based on T-junctions). The Urban Task Force is using the argument that tree-like patterns are supposedly inferior to grids – on the grounds of *traffic* flow and congestion – to support its (convincing enough) arguments against tree-like patterns for pedestrians and public transport.[40]

As a whole, the arguments presented above point to the lack of a consistent theoretical justification for 'grids' over 'culs-de-sac'. Part of the reason for their inconsistency is that there is an underlying problem of in-adequate specification of the alternative patterns being debated. This illustrates the need to be explicit in description, in order to be clear about what aspects of structure we are arguing about. What would be useful, therefore, is the separate articulation of these kinds of structural issue. Better description can in turn be used to support whatever kind of justifi-cation is being made for different kinds of urban space or network pattern. In other words, clear prescription first requires adequate description of pattern (Chapters 4 and 6).

Pattern versus process

Finally, there is the issue of pattern versus process. Neo-traditional design, which has been one the main stimuli behind this book, is to a significant extent associated with the desire to replicate traditional street patterns. As alluded to earlier, these neo-traditional patterns are not necessarily struc-turally faithful to actual traditional patterns.[41] Moreover, these neo-traditional patterns are not necessarily created in a 'traditional' manner – in other words, how those original patterns themselves developed – but may be imposed in a rigid manner of formal design.

For example, the design of Poundbury was inspired by neo-traditionalist and, indeed, organic ideas. The master plan for Poundbury forms a kind of pseudo-organic pattern, and was partly aiming to 'complement' or emulate the historic core of Dorchester.[42] However, on inspection, the layout appears not exactly similar to the centre of the town, which contains a grid of streets.

Moreover, the layout appears to be simply imposed on the existing site, oblivious to the existing pattern of fields and farms. The master plan for Poundbury – perhaps ironically for a development so closely associated with the traditionalist Prince of Wales – has boldly proposed a full build-out that would obliterate an existing Roman road that runs through the site. Where once there was a dead straight, historic route running out from the town, there would now be a 'village' of houses arranged around a street pattern of contrived irregularity. Despite its success in integrating architec-tural and highway forms internally, Poundbury is hardly an 'organic' extension of the town of Dorchester. It is a design conceived elsewhere, and parachuted down, as it were, from the drawing board.

Therefore, when considering what is an 'organic' or 'geometric' pattern, it is necessary to consider also process, and how different generative processes may give rise to different patterns (Chapter 9).

CONCLUSIONS

This chapter has demonstrated some of the current confusion and inconsistency regarding the specification of desirable street types, patterns and hierarchies that influence the form and structure of urban layout. This effectively expresses the design debate as a research agenda for the remainder of the book (Box 2).

BOX 2. KEY ISSUES FOR RESOLUTION
1.   The basis for street type.
2.   The connection between street type and hierarchy.
3.   The identification and justification of 'good' and 'bad' hierarchy.
4.   The distinction between hierarchy and pattern.
5.   The identification of 'preferred' and 'discouraged' patterns.
6.   The relationship between pattern and process of generation.

The first key issue is that of street type: there is no place in conventional road hierarchy for the traditional urban street. Then, there is no clear or consistent basis for reconciling the street of the current urban design agenda with the 'link' in conventional transport analysis, or road type in conventional hierarchy. The basis for conventional hierarchy itself seems somewhat unclear – whether regarded as 'good' or 'bad' hierarchy by engineers or urban designers.

We have also seen that there is a lack of clear and consistent guidance on the overall form that a street pattern should take. On the one hand, highway engineering approaches are criticised for being too rigid, and yet these do not seem to prescribe any particular pattern; on the other hand, there is a rather diverse range of urban design and planning aspirations, which are either expressed too unclearly – for the purposes of description – or perhaps too specifically, for the purposes of prescription. For those approaches departing from conventional engineering principles, it is sometimes difficult to grasp what kind of theory might be underlying the rhetoric. Where a certain kind of desired pattern *is* clearly graspable – the simple rectangular grid, for example – its theoretical justification is not at all clear or consistent.

In general, design guidance has to maintain a careful balance between being too nebulous and being over-prescriptive. Bill Hillier points out that the drawback of many normative theories of design is that they are over-specific where they should be permissive, and vague where they should be precise.[43]

In the case of street pattern design guidance, the problem is partly caused by the fact that patterns are difficult to describe verbally. As we have seen, a verbal description typically runs the risk of being too vague, whereas an illustrated pattern may appear too specific, too limiting. The result tends to be a polarisation – between grids and culs-de-sac – which is unable to handle the possibility of alternatives in between. Without descriptors of urban structure of sufficiently high resolution, the debate over street pattern is likely to remain entrenched as a battle between the extrema of endlessly permeable grids and terminally tributary culs-de-sac.

Effectively, what we need is a better specification of street type, pattern and hierarchy in order to have a firmer and more consistent basis upon which to suggest 'preferred' options. The issue of street type will be investigated in Chapters 3 and 5, while the characterisation of patterns will be investigated in Chapters 4 and 6. Ultimately, these will be drawn together in a single framework in Chapter 7, from which recommendations for onward design processes will subsequently flow.

Overall, this chapter has to some extent 'softened up' what might before have been perceived as firm, clear-cut matters of unquestioned orthodoxy. We can now proceed to the main assault on the topic.

NOTES

1   DoE/DoT (1992); DETR (1998a).
2   On reclaiming the street for people, see, for example, Jacobs (1961), Rudofsky (1969), Appleyard (1981), Moudon (1987), Engwicht (1993, 1999), Chorlton (2003), Hazel (2003), Rook (2003). On issues of inter-disciplinary territory, see also Scully (1994: 225); Cowan (1995, 1997); Campbell and Cowan (2002: 24). Dunnett also describes the street as a 'battleground' (2000: 78).
3   Llewelyn-Davies (2000).
4   Rykwert (1978) and Rook (2003) discuss the different meanings of 'roads' and 'streets'. Streets may be analysed from a variety of historical, anthropological, sociological and cultural perspectives (Anderson, 1978; Moudon, 1987; Kostof, 1992; Fyfe, 1998; Gehl, 1998); from urban design perspectives (Moughtin, 1992; Jacobs, 1993; Southworth and Ben-Joseph, 1997; Jacobs et al., 2002) and from the perspective of sustainability (Jefferson et al., 2001).
5   ICE (1996: 8).
6   Marshall (2002a).
7   ICE (1994: 22). For further discussion of street classification from the point of view of road classification, see Morrison (1966); Jones (1986); ICE (1996); AASHTO (2001); Bartlett (2003a, 2003b).

8   Some would stress the importance of this classification by function, e.g. Tripp (1950); ICE (1996: 1, 2, 9, 11); AASHTO (2001: 1, 4, 13). See Chapter 3.

9   Llewelyn-Davies (2000: 75).

10 ICE (2002: 11).

11 Calthorpe (1993: 99).

12 Lang (1994: 201).

13 Southworth and Ben-Joseph (1997).

14 O'Flaherty (1986); Banks (1998: 286) and Bell and Iida (1997) refer to patterns but not in a prescriptive sense. Explicit reference to or guidance on pattern is also absent in texts by Oglesby and Hicks (1982); Macpherson (1993); DoE (1994); Wright (1996). These comments are intended as a demonstration of the extent to which the specific issue of pattern guidance is absent from mainstream transport and highway engineering literature; it is not otherwise a criticism of these particular works, which serve their own purposes satisfactorily. (In any case, see Chapter 9.)

15 IHT (1997); AASHTO (1995, 2001).

16 DB32: DoE/DoT (1992). This guide does give some graphic examples of street grids – including several incorporating crossroads – but with the caveat that they are not necessarily supposed to be interpreted literally. 'Plethora of standardised layouts' – from *Local Transport Today* (LTT, 24 September 1998). The lack of imagination is suggested by the need for the creation of *Places, Streets and Movement* (DETR, 1998a), which principally contains guidance on creative interpretation of the existing layout rules, rather than being a new set of rules.

17 Crane (1996); ITE (1999: 6).

18 ITE (1999: 6). The only street layouts shown are referring to identity of streets and use of T-intersections, not to actual pattern.

19 Aldous (1992: 17).

20 Lynch (1990: 93–94).

21 Keeble (1983: 25).

22 DETR (2000: 26); Urban Task Force (1999: 90).

23 Similar kinds of 'preferred' and 'discouraged' examples are found in Bentley *et al.* (1985); Katz (1994); Leccese and McCormick (2000), Carmona *et al.* (2002: 31).

24 Burdett (1998) has drawn attention to the fact that previously these roles were reversed, juxtaposing two plans explaining the Abercrombie plan for London: one showing the problematic 'jumble' of the old street pattern, the other the orderly solution of Modernism (Carter and Goldfinger, 1945: 72–73). Burdett interprets this juxtaposition as the fearless assertion of 'wrong' and 'right'. Today, of course, these labels would be reversed. See also reference to 'bad' gridirons and 'good' loop and cul-de-sac systems recommended by the US Federal Housing Administration (Southworth and Ben-Joseph, 1997: 85).

25 This is echoed by Cowan (2002: 21) of design guidance in general.

26 Essex Planning Officers' Association (1997: 12); DETR (1998a: 30).

27 DTLR and CABE (2001); Urban Task Force (1999).
28 For example, *The Urban Design Compendium* suggests that the UK street classification of distributors and access roads is based 'solely on vehicle capacity' (Llewelyn-Davies, 2000: 75; also Thorne and Filmer-Sankey, 2003: 29).
29 Goodwin (1995: 7); Brindle (1996: 69).
30 Ross (1997: 23); Western Australia (1997: 20); DTLR and CABE (2001: 25).
31 ITE (1999: 21).
32 Essex Planning Officers' Association (1997: 55).
33 Brindle (1996: 55).
34 This kind of arrangement has also been suggested by the *Essex Design Guide* (Essex Planning Officers' Association, 1997: 11) and Southworth and Ben-Joseph (1997: 126).
35 Southworth and Ben-Joseph (1997: 122) refer to the lack of legibility of cul-de-sac layouts but also point out that grid patterns may be monotonous. Research results on lack of identity of grids are reported by Rapoport (1977). The *Urban Design Compendium* suggests that permeability assists the urban design objective of circulation, while hierarchy assists the urban design objective of legibility (Llewelyn-Davies, 2000).
36 Southworth (1997); Southworth and Ben-Joseph (1997: 105–107); Southworth (2003).
37 Rosenkrantz and Abraham (1995). Similar arguments are proffered by Morris and Kaufman (1998), the Urban Task Force (1999) and DTLR and CABE (2001: 25).
38 Brindle (1995: 9.8).
39 In presenting his diagrams, Sitte remarks that the issue of conflicting paths at crossroads 'seems to have been overlooked heretofore' (Sitte, [1898] 1945: 60). Similar 'conflict' diagrams recur in traffic and planning literature, for example, Ritter (1964: 79); MoT (1966: 57); Alexander *et al.* (1977: 264); Keeble (1983: 43); McCluskey (1992: 62); Leleur (1995: 38); Behrens and Watson (1996: 127); O'Flaherty (1997: 453); Ben-Joseph and Gordon (2000: 250); Bird (2001: 401); also alluded to by Campbell and Cowan (2002: 40).
40 The Urban Task Force claims that 'tree-like networks' are unfavourable to cars, since they 'concentrate congestion' (1999: 91). This begs the question as to why such layouts – by this logic disadvantageous to all transport modes – were ever built. In fact, the same layouts are elsewhere criticised for being *car-oriented*. The technical issues of safety of crossroads and congestion versus dispersion themselves lie outside the scope of this book.
41 Also Chapter 2, following from the work of Michael Southworth (2003).
42 Thompson-Fawcett (2000); DETR (1998a); Krier (1993a; 1993b).
43 Hillier (1996: 67).

3 STREET TYPE AND HIERARCHY

We must kill off the street . . . We shall truly enter into modern town-planning only after we have accepted this preliminary determination.
Le Corbusier, 1929[1]

Le Corbusier was one of the most creative and influential architects of the twentieth century, and perhaps Modernism's foremost architect–planner. Among other things, he was a painter, sculptor, furniture designer, architect and planner, famous for his boldly sculpted buildings, minimalist furniture, and megalomaniac master plans. A visionary who understood the potential of contemporary technology, Le Corbusier was in awe of the speed and power of motor vehicles, and envisioned the consequences for the city of the future. It was a city without streets (Figure 3.1).

Le Corbusier's vision had no need for traditional main streets such as avenues or boulevards – so no pavement cafés, and no Champs-Elysées. This was not an oversight: the demise of the traditional street was Le Corbusier's express intention. He intuitively knew the logistical power the street had in binding up cities in their old ways. So when he attacked the traditional city, he went for the jugular.

To expedite traffic flow in his brave new world, Le Corbusier later proposed a route hierarchy – la règle des 7V – in which traffic was channelled from inter-urban highways (V1) down to local roads, until finally the last route type V7 was for pedestrian circulation in and around buildings (Figure 3.2).[2]

The issue of road hierarchy goes to the heart of the 'revolution' introduced at the beginning of this book. Although hierarchy is a rather abstract concept, it can have very concrete consequences: it has been implicated

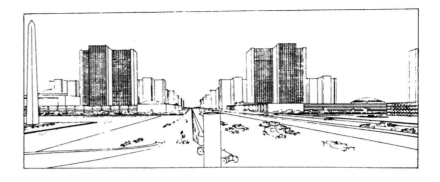

3.1 • Le Corbusier's futuristic vision (1922). This city of crystalline skyscrapers and superhighways was dreamed up when the streets of the day were choked with horses and carriages.

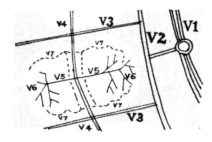

3.2 • An interpretation of Le Corbusier's *Règle des 7V* (law of seven routes) – the architect's greatest contribution to road hierarchy.

both in urban destruction (aiding and abetting demolition and severance by urban motorways) and in disurban creation (giving rise to the car-oriented townscape of bleak distributor roads).

Yet, as we have also found, architects and planners in the modernist mould have embraced the use of highways and their hierarchies for urban-structural purposes (Chapter 1). Moreover, *some* sort of hierarchy may be proposed by contemporary urban designers and planners as a positive formative device, as in their advocacy for a 'clear hierarchy of spaces' (Chapter 2). It seems that it is not inevitable that hierarchy should be synonymous with disurban creation. After all, ancient Roman cities effectively had 'hierarchies' of streets; in the Middle Ages, Leonardo da Vinci proposed a system of traffic segregation involving different street types. The reconstruction of London after the Great Fire of 1666, and the laying out of Edinburgh's Georgian New Town, were both based on the adoption of a 'hierarchy' of discrete street types.[3] Despite these traditional exemplars, nowadays we often associate hierarchy with something apparently engineering-dominated, traffic-oriented and anti-urban. We need to pin down why.

This chapter sets out to examine the workings of hierarchy, to unravel the fundamental relationships between street type and hierarchy: where do street types come from, how are street types related to each other in hierarchies, and how do these relate to network patterns?

PRINCIPLES OF HIERARCHY

Road classification has become established as a dominant consideration in the design of any road network, urban or inter-urban. For many years the classification of roads has formed the starting point for the American Association of State Highways and Transportation Officials' *Policy on*

Geometric Design of Highways and Streets.[4] In this thousand-page 'bible', the concepts of functional classification and 'hierarchies of movement' are introduced on page 1.

Road *hierarchy* is a particular form of classification of roads in which each type has a ranked position with respect to the whole set of types. Understanding the meaning of this ranking will be a key concern of this chapter. To do this, we start in this section by exploring conventional road hierarchy from first principles.

Conventional road hierarchy

Conventional road hierarchy is not only to do with the functional efficiency of traffic flow, but is also concerned with the safety, amenity and the environmental quality of urban areas.[5] It therefore does take account of non-traffic considerations in the urban context, although it often appears to do so by putting the traffic first, and fitting the other concerns around that.

The kind of road hierarchy in the UK is typical of many kinds of road classification and hierarchy in use around the world. Table 3.1 shows a range of formal classification systems used in institutional standards, such as national guidelines or local authority codes of practice.

While the terminology differs in each case, the basic principles follow the same general pattern, with a spectrum from major roads to minor roads. Major roads tend to be associated with strategic routes, heavier traffic flows, higher design speeds, with limited access to minor roads with frontage access. Minor roads tend to be associated with more lightly trafficked, local routes, with lower design speeds and more frequent access points and with access to building frontages.

The consequences of these associations are as follows.

1. Roads designated as 'streets' – implying built frontages and public space – are normally found at the lower end of the spectrum.
2. There tends to be greatest segregation of transport modes implied at either extreme of these hierarchies: segregated vehicular traffic at one end and segregated pedestrians at the other, with all-purpose roads in between.
3. Most route types appear to be designated according to transport or traffic function, although some at the lower end (e.g. street, mews, etc.) also imply relationships with buildings.

Table 3.1 represents a diversity of different terminologies, but the types often seem to be relating to the same kinds of street, and arranged in similar kinds of hierarchical sets. To gain an appreciation of how these kinds of classification came to be the way they are, and a general understanding of road hierarchy, it will be useful to examine the background to the concept.

Table 3.1 Examples of institutional hierarchies

Traffic in Towns, UK	ITE, USA
Primary distributor	Freeway
District distributor	Expressway
Local distributor	Major arterial
Access road	Collector street
	Local street
	Cul-de-sac

Essex Design Guide, Essex, UK	VicCode, Victoria, Australia
Local distributor	Major arterial
Link road	Arterial
Feeder road	Sub-arterial
Minor access road	Trunk collector
Minor access way (2 types)	Collector street
	Access street
Mews (2 types)	Access place
Parking square	Access lane

Belgium, functional classification	India
1. Motorway	National highways (NH)
2. Metropolitan road	State highways (SH)
3. Trunk road	District roads (DR)
4. Inter-district road	Major district roads (MDR)
5. Through street	Other district roads (ODR)
6. Local street	Village roads (VR)

Note: for sources and more examples, see Appendix 3.

Hierarchical antecedents

Conventional systems of road hierarchy in many countries have evolved from principles stretching back over many decades. For example, today's hierarchical approach in the UK, in *Transport in the Urban Environmen*t, can be related back directly through *Roads and Traffic in Urban Areas* to *Traffic in Towns*.[6] *Traffic in Towns* built on previous principles set out by Alker Tripp, who was himself influenced by ideas from the USA, where the development of the notion of a road 'hierarchy' was advanced in Olmsted's design of Central Park, New York.[7]

Both Tripp and Buchanan were concerned with the issue of road safety, and both proposed solutions involving pedestrian–vehicular segregation of one sort or another. Buchanan himself emphasised environmental quality as his starting point in *Traffic in Towns*, with traffic in a subservient role. But despite this good intention, when applied in practice the result often appeared to be traffic-dominated outcomes (see Figure 1.1).

To understand how hierarchy came to be the way it is, it will be revealing to take a closer look at Buchanan's original propositions, which have been influential in the design and management of road networks to this day.

Traffic versus towns

Buchanan's thesis is founded on a basic principle:

> Basically, however, there are only two *kinds* of roads – *distributors* designed for movement, and *access roads* to serve the buildings. [original emphasis][8]

In effect, this 'basic principle' – that lies at the heart of *Traffic in Towns* as a whole – is a division between a system of traffic distributors, where the needs of movement are prioritised, and a system of 'environmental areas' where environmental considerations are prioritised. In a sense, this is a division of 'traffic' and 'towns' into separate areas of priority. The spatial consequence of this is a cellular approach to urban structure, where environmental areas – likened to 'urban rooms' – are connected by a complementary network of roads – 'urban corridors' (Figure 3.3).

In Buchanan's system, effectively the 'traffic' forms the main superstructure, while the 'town' is fragmented into separate subdivisions. This system was influenced by considerations of hospital layout, where circulation takes place on main arteries (corridors) and areas of work and repose take place in more secluded areas (rooms).[9]

3.3 • Buchanan's cellular concept. Environmental areas (incorporating minor roads) are plugged into a superstructure of main traffic distributors.

Problems with rooms and corridors

A problem with the 'rooms and corridors' analogy is that it only recognises two possible types of space – polarised between the corridor, emphasising circulation (usually connoting an impersonal, transient space), and the room for occupancy (usually connoting safety, comfort, ownership, identity). While these may reflect the extreme of the motorway and the precinct, this leaves no place for the traditional mixed function urban street which serves both as a circulation artery and as an urban 'place' in its own right. Under Buchanan's clinical division, these varied urban activities – social, political, commercial and ceremonial – would all be shunted aside into the 'urban rooms', while the main streets would become bare corridors reserved for circulation.

Buchanan's prescription may be quite appropriate for private motor traffic, but it leads to a separation of roads intended for use by public transport (the distributors) and those expected to be used by pedestrians (access roads). The megastructure of *Traffic in Towns*' Fitzrovia case study (Plate 1 in Chapter 1) is a particularly stark example – where the buses are separated from the pedestrian deck by up to two escalator flights[10] – but the basic problem of spatial separation still applies in more mundane examples of 'prairie planning' up and down the country.

This kind of road hierarchy might once have represented an ideal system for urban road management – indeed, it still represents a possible idealised system for the distribution of motor traffic. But it no longer represents what is today considered an idealised system for urban street management, suitable for catering for a diversity of urban uses and transport modes.

Diagnosis

Buchanan subdivided distributors into primary, district and local distributors, which, together with access roads, gives a simple system of four types of road. But these four types seem too few and too narrow to reflect the rich diversity of actual road and street types existing on the ground.

On closer inspection, the reason why there is a lack of fit between the idealised classification and the reality is not just because there is a small number of types, nor because these types are narrowly defined in terms of a single function. It would be quite possible to have a workable if limited classification that simply divided all streets into wide versus narrow, or public versus private, or 'streets' versus 'squares'. Each of these examples only considers one theme as a basis for classification (e.g. width), and within that theme presents only a choice of two categories. Yet, these cases would still serve for their own particular purposes.

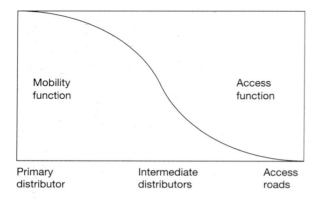

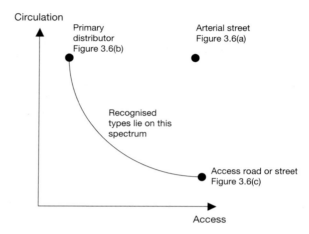

3.4 • The classic inverse relationship between mobility and access. The two variables are *dependent*: hence effectively only one 'dimension' of classification.

3.5 • The conventional classification has no place for the traditional arterial street. The traditional arterial street does not lie on the spectrum from primary distributor to local access road.

The problem with the conventional hierarchy is that it imposes an *artificial* relationship between 'mobility' and 'access'. In effect, there appear to be *two dimensions*, but these are bound together in a *single, inverse relationship* (Figure 3.4).[11] This means that any street that does not fit onto this 'idealised' relationship does not fit into the classification (Figure 3.5). The result is that the classification cannot represent the actual street types found on the ground. This means that not only is the classification no longer a reflection of today's aspirations, but it is not capable of representing the range of existing street types – and never was.[12]

This causes problems on the ground, as it has required the shoehorning of all sorts of real, functional and perfectly good streets into inappropriate kinds of distributor or access road categories that deny their actual multi-functional role. To reiterate: this is not so much a result of the limited number of types available, but the artificiality of the inverse relationship, which cannot accommodate a whole range of traditional street types, in particular, the traditional arterial (Figure 3.6).

The formulation of road hierarchy based on the inverse relationship between mobility and access has aided and abetted a lot of urban destruction, as well as being a root cause of disurban creation – hence its association with 'bad' hierarchy. That this relationship turns out to be something rather artificial helps to explain why some might intuitively suspect hierarchy of harbouring 'unchallenged truths' which could now be ripe for change.

(a)

(b)

(c)

3.6 • The misfit arterial. (a) Traditional arterial street combining traffic movement and frontage access. (b) Distributor road – dedicated to traffic movement. (c) Access road – combines traffic and pedestrian movement with access to buildings.

In order to start exploring alternative ways in which hierarchy might be reformulated towards today's streets-oriented urban design agenda, we can take a look at a wider range of kinds of classification used in a broader range of contexts, and explore further the concepts of 'function' and the basis for hierarchical ordering.

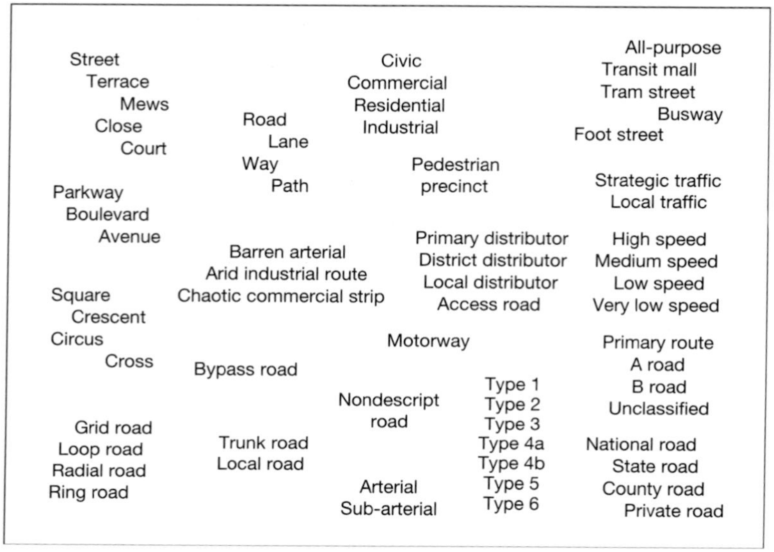

3.7 • A diversity of types of street. For a fuller catalogue of street types and sources, see Appendix 3.1.

STREET TYPE AND CLASSIFICATION

A glance at a city street atlas can reveal a diversity of labels associated with different kinds of street – from the humble lane and place to the grander boulevard and piazza. Overall, a wide variety of street types is observable across a variety of contexts, from architecture to urban morphology (Figure 3.7).

In practice, these street types do not float loosely in typological space, but tend to be systematically recognised and ordered in definite sets. This section reviews a variety of street typologies and classification systems, which will lead to a wider exploration of the 'problem' of hierarchy, and provide some insights into how alternatives to conventional hierarchy might be constructed.

Street typologies

Table 3.2 shows a range of typologies, representing an eclectic catalogue based on both historic examples and contemporary advocacy, often proffered by individuals rather than institutions.

Unlike the hierarchies shown in Table 3.1, which tended to be based on the same general spectrum of mobility–access, the selection in Table 3.2 offers a variety of types, shapes and sizes. In other words, 'urban roads with frontages' are not necessarily limited to one particular part of the

Table 3.2 **Examples of range of street typologies**

Act for the Rebuilding of the City of London (1667)	**A Pattern Language (Alexander et al.)**	
1. High and principal streets (40 ft wide)	Ring roads	
2. Streets and lanes of note (35 ft wide)	Parallel roads	
3. By-lanes (14 ft wide)	Promenade	
4. Narrower alleys (9 ft wide)	Shopping street	
	Looped local roads	
Edinbugh New Town (Figure 2.13)	Green streets	
1. Square	Bike paths	
2. Major street	Pedestrian street	
3. Transverse street	Arcade	
4. Minor street	Trellised walk	
5. Mews lane		
	The Next American Metropolis (Figure 2.4)	
Urban function	Arterial streets and thoroughfares	
1. Civic street	Connector streets	
2. Commercial street	Commercial streets	
3. Residential street	Local streets	
4. Multi-function street	Alleys	
Poundbury (Figure 2.9)	**Avalon Design Code**	
Square	Width	'More urban'	'More rural'
Street	160 ft	Boulevard	Parkway
Lane	100 ft	Boulevard	Highway
Courtyard	80 ft	Main street	Avenue
Mews	70 ft	Street	Road
Pedestrian street	54 ft	Minor street	Minor road
	44 ft	Court	Lane
	24 ft	Alley	Way

Note: for sources and more examples, see Appendix 3.

hierarchy, but can form either major arteries or minor routes. Especially at the lower end of the scale, there is often a wide variety of types. The key point is that streets are explicitly present; and not systematically subordinate in the ranking.

Poundbury's 'hierarchy of spaces' appears to place the most prominent 'place' (i.e. Square) at the 'top'. However, as discussed in Chapter 2, there is no explicit spatial organisation associated. In the case of Edinburgh's New Town, the 'road hierarchy' was class-coded to reflect an intended 'social hierarchy', where the grand Squares were intended for persons of highest social rank, the streets were for persons of intermediate rank, and the mews

(a)

(b)

(c)

(d)

3.8 • A four-level 'hierarchy' of streets in Edinburgh's New Town. See also Figure 2.13. (a) Main street. (b) Transverse street. (c) Minor street. (d) Mews lane.

were intended for persons of lowest rank – and horses (Figure 3.8). This hierarchy was clearly connected with the layout, which was configured partly in order that the genteel inhabitants of the Squares need never come into contact with the lower orders in the lanes. Here, the hierarchy is not just in terms of streets of different width or building type, but implies a definite spatial or structural organisation. This gives a clue to another way that street type may be specified.

Analysis of classification themes

We saw in Chapter 2 how any particular street will tend to have 'multiple personalities' – which may be equated with different roles or characteristics. Each characteristic of a street – such as width, frontage type or traffic type – suggests a *theme* by which it could be classified and ordered in relation to other street types. A selection of themes is shown in Table 3.3.

When creating a typology of streets, the set of types could be classified by a single theme, or a variety of themes. In practice, classifications

Table 3.3 **A taxonomy of road types, classification themes and theme types**

Set of road types	Classification theme	Type of theme
Square, circus, crescent, cross	Shape of space	Form
Dual 3-lane, dual 2-lane, single carriageway	Carriageway standard	
Limited access road, distributor, access road	Access control	
Street, terrace, mews, court	Built form/frontages	
Narrow street, wide street	Width	
Civic, commercial, residential, industrial	Urban building type	
Shopping street, living street, etc.	Urban uses and users	Use
High volume road, low volume road	Traffic volume	
Long distance traffic road, local traffic road	Trip length (origin and destination)	
Road type used by any mode	Transport modes	
High speed road, low speed road, etc.	Traffic speed (observed)	
Route used by tourist traffic, works traffic, etc.	Road users	
Spine road, connector street, cul-de-sac	Structural role	Relation
Strategic route, link road, local route, etc.	Strategic role	
National road, regional road, municipal road	Ownership/management	Designation
Special road, principal road, A road	Statutory designation	
70 mph, 60 mph, . . ., 20 mph road	Speed limit (designated)	
Bus only; pedestrian only; etc.	Vehicle or user permission	
'Avenue', 'Street', 'Lane', 'Mansions', etc.	Nominal	
Designated route for tourists, works traffic, etc.	Designated route	

3.9 • Four categories of classification theme. See Table 3.3. (a) Types defined by form. (b) Types defined by use. (c) Types defined by relation. (d) Types defined by designation.

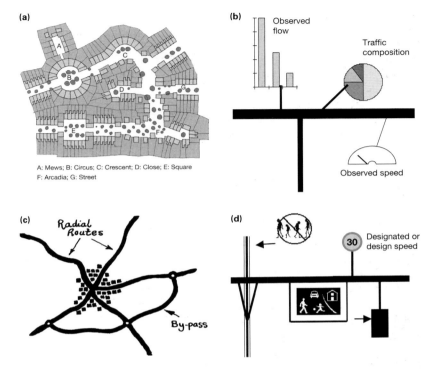

(a)

A: Mews; B: Circus; C: Crescent; D: Close; E: Square
F: Arcadia; G: Street

(b) Observed flow

Traffic composition

Observed speed

(c) Radial Routes

By-pass

(d) Designated or design speed

tend to bind in more than one theme within a single type. For example, a 'local access street' implies something short (or used for local trips), that is used for access; and that has the built form of a street. The themes in Table 3.3 are shown grouped for convenience into four main categories: Form, Use, Relation and Designation (Figure 3.9).[13]

Form here refers to the physical characteristics that, in principle, can be described or recorded for any section of street. *Use* refers to the activity on a street; again, in principle, this could be described or recorded for any section of street, although in this case it is likely to vary significantly by time as well as space. We could say that form relates to supply and use relates to demand. Form and use are quite straightforward and could be observed empirically by an outside agency (such as an observer from space), oblivious to the supposed 'purpose' of the street.

The third main category is termed *Relation*. This refers to the relative position of a street with respect to other urban or network elements, rather than (solely) referring to characteristics of a particular street section under consideration. For example, a 'radial' is essentially defined in relation to a set of routes converging to a centre, and is in principle independent of road form or patterns of use. A radial could be a quiet lane or a bustling boulevard.

Relation must therefore be seen as a category separate from form or use, since either form or use could change while the structural relation remained the same (or vice versa). For example, a 'radial route' could acquire a row of shops and double its traffic volume, but still be a radial route; conversely, it would no longer be a 'radial' if the other spokes in the network were removed – even if the physical form and use of the street itself remained unchanged.

The final category – *Designation* – refers to classification themes determined purely by allocation or assignation: it relates to properties that could be applied abstractly to a map of a road network. A typical example would be administrative status (e.g. ownership) or recommended traffic route (e.g. tourist route). Such properties might relate to form, use or relation, but in principle need not be fixed to these. Changes to these types of designation can take place without any change on the ground, and vice versa. (An observer from space could not directly detect a change in designation.)

The kind of theme(s) chosen to classify streets will depend on the purpose to which the classification is to be put. The question arises: why are some themes chosen rather than others? In particular, why are conventional road classifications arranged the way they are?

The meaning of function

Conventional hierarchical road classifications of the type shown in Table 3.1 are classically regarded as being 'functional' classifications, meaning roads are classified according to their function, rather than their form, use or ownership. The importance of function was recognised by Alker Tripp, and has been promoted, among others, by the Institution of Civil Engineers in the UK and the American Association of State Highway and Transportation Officials in the USA.[14]

But what exactly is 'function'? At first sight, function might be regarded as coming somewhere between Designation and Use – function reflects actual use to some extent, but is also directed towards future needs and uses, and therefore need not reflect present conditions (a route could be designated 'tourist route' even if little tourist traffic materialised).

Strictly speaking, however, we really have to consider this kind of 'functional classification' as a classification by designation. A route whose so-called function is to carry, say, 'long-distance traffic' is really simply a *designation* of intended purpose, not an observation of actual use. The so-called function would not change except by official recognition or decree, and therefore is indistinguishable from designation. Therefore, by this argument, so-called functional classification is just as much a designation as the kind of administrative classification based on ownership or management.

Official classification systems such as those in Table 3.1 tend to use only a limited number of classification themes. In a study of twelve street classification systems in nine European Union countries, for example, it was found that, from a range of 39 potential classification themes, only six were used systematically in practice, on which hierarchies were effectively organised. Of those six classification themes, five are nominally functional, and the sixth administrative. But all are effectively capable of being allocated by designation (Table 3.4).[15]

Classification by designation is convenient for a variety of practical reasons. First, as alluded to earlier, changes of designation can be unrelated to circumstances on the ground. This somewhat detached relationship could be interpreted as a form of inflexibility, since the status of a street may stay the same long after its form or use has changed. Alternatively, this could be interpreted as a form of flexibility, precisely because the label can cover a variety of forms or uses as they change over time, without requiring continual updating. This means that classification by designation finds favour as a practical method for roads authority use.

This flexibility means that a hierarchy can be laid out in advance, and is not intrinsically subject to too much fluctuation. Unlike physical width,

Table 3.4 **Themes used systematically in a study of twelve classification systems in nine European countries**

Classification theme	Interpretation
1. Traffic speed (designation)	Road sections are designated an intended speed
2. Trip length	Designated, based on assumed origin and destination distance
3. Destination status	Designated, based on assumed origin and destination status (city size for strategic road; size of development served for a local road)
4. Strategic role	Street types assigned as forming part of strategic network or local network
5. Circulation versus access	Designated function to cater for through traffic or local access
6. Administration	Designated legal responsibility for management or ownership

which may be inconsistent over the length of a route, or traffic volume, which would vary over both distance and time, a designation can stay stable indefinitely. Designating status according to function effectively builds in flexibility: because future function is being specified, any particular route or street can be expected to grow into its intended role. The functional designation need never be out of date, whatever the conditions on the ground, as long as it remains a future target.

If function is a designation, on what basis is it designated? The basis for designation does not always appear entirely clear or consistent: it seems to be a mix of parameters such as traffic flow, speed, design standard, strategic function and 'movement function' (as opposed to 'access function'). But these do not automatically correspond, either in theory or practice. How then is a particular section of road designated a particular status, when this status is not systematically related to form or use?

THE STRATEGIC STRUCTURE

We usually know a main road when we see one, and it may seem academic as to whether this main road is so called because it is a 'big road', a 'busy road' or a 'strategic road'. The correlation between road standard, flow and strategic status seems intuitively simple. Even if national road networks tend to be organised by designation, it appears to be a simple reflection of form or use. However, things are not necessarily as straightforward as this. If we look more closely, we find that designation is, generally speaking, not by form or use – but by *relation*. And this is not a trivial academic distinction; it provides a key to understanding hierarchy and the structure of urban layout.

Basis of designation

In the UK, 'A' roads may take the form of a narrow old street in a town, or a lightly trafficked cross-country road.[16] The A960 in Kirkwall town centre is a single lane paved street with priority to pedestrians. The A830 between Lochailort and Mallaig – a trunk road – still has a single track section (Figure 3.10).

If roads were classified by form, then the classification of a route might change along its length each time there was a change in some physical property. For example, every point at which the width of the road changed or a frontage type changed or a bus or cycle lane started or stopped would be a potential point at which the classification could change. While classification by form can be useful for an urban design appreciation of a street as an urban space, it is not that typically used for route classification,

(a)   (b)

3.10 • Two trunk roads. (a) The A5 near Shrewsbury is a high standard dual carriageway with high traffic flow, (b) The A830 near Lochailort is designated a trunk road despite being single track with relatively light traffic flows.

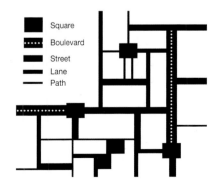

3.11 • Pattern of street types defined by form. There is no consistent structural organisation. Note the resonance with Poundbury typology (Figure 2.9).

otherwise the road atlas would be a multi-coloured patchwork of different segments representing a diversity of shapes and sizes of road (Figure 3.11).

If classification were by use, the classification would in principle change not only over space but over time, as over the course of a day or year the road would become a 'busy road' or 'less busy' road. Were roads classified systematically by use, the road atlas might in principle need to be an interactive, real-time device, where road status fluctuated with every seasonal or daily variation, with every change of traffic lights, or every passing footstep (Figure 3.12).

Even when classifications are ostensibly founded on some criterion such as 'trip length', there is no suggestion that each section of road is systematically monitored in terms of actual trip patterns as different journeys pass over its length. Were this case, the resulting pattern would be likely to fluctuate over space and time, with a major road becoming a 'local traffic route' as it passed through an urban area, picking up a high proportion of local traffic during the day, and then perhaps reverting to being a 'long distant traffic route' at night.[17]

Nor can classification relate directly to population size served, otherwise the set of major roads would be monopolised by the most populous corners of a country, and in principle would fluctuate over time as populations rose and fell. In practice, roads in the highest classification tier often serve relatively lightly populated parts of the country.

There is, nevertheless, a pattern to road classification, which *is* stable over time. When the status of a road does change, it tends to change not

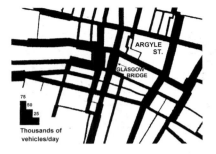

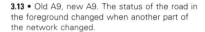

3.12 • Pattern of street types defined by use. There is no necessary spatial contiguity of the 'main routes' defined by flow.

3.13 • Old A9, new A9. The status of the road in the foreground changed when another part of the network changed.

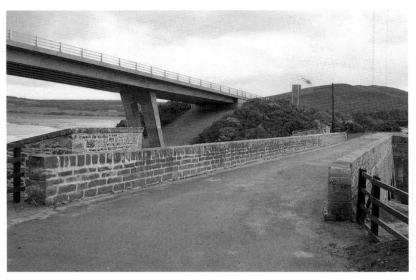

directly with fluctuations in traffic flow, trip length or population, but with changes in the road network itself. In other words, as new links are added to the network, route designations may shift to make use of the new links, and existing sections of route are reclassified in turn. If this is classification by function, it is classification by network function, not traffic function. The classification changes when the network changes. This time, the road atlas *is* updated (Figure 3.13).

In this case, the classification of an individual section of road refers to its relationship with the rest of the network. In other words, this is designation by relation. But what is the basis of this designation by relation? The answer can be found by looking again at the structure of the road network – the pattern formed by the different types of road on the map (Figure 3.14).

In other words, the actual classification is so arranged that it makes for a certain kind of pattern on the map. It is as much to do with geographical coverage – serving a spread of territory – as it is to do with road form or traffic use.[18] More particularly, it is to do with the topological contiguity of strategic routes. The choice of what are the strategic routes will undoubtedly be informed by other factors, but the clinching evidence is seen in the map itself, which shows all strategic routes connecting up in a particular way. This is based on a specific structural property known as 'arteriality'.

3.14 • Patterns formed by top tier of roads. (a) If designated according to highest traffic flows. (b) If designated according to size of cities linked. (c) If designated by longest route length or trip length. (d) As actually designated, Great Britain (A1–A9).

Arteriality

The outstanding feature that the national road network possesses is that strategic routes all connect up contiguously.[19] This is a property identified by the cartographer Alastair Morrison as 'arteriality', by which the 'pattern of arterial roads is the only one which necessarily forms a complete network' (Figure 3.15).[20]

Arteriality is a property typical of road networks around the world – although it is not limited to the road network context. It is a pervasive property – but an almost invisible one, intuitively built into road systems without conscious prescription (Box 3). Arteriality is a key property of structure whose significance will resonate – and be revisited – in the rest of this book, as it can be used to spatially organise routes and structure hierarchies.

Overall, arteriality is an important underlying structural property – 'underlying' in the sense that it is not normally explicitly expressed, such as in design guidance. It is usually taken for granted that roads of one level connect at least with roads of the same level or the level above.[21] Arteriality effectively underlies the kind of institutional hierarchies seen in Table 3.1 – but does not necessarily apply to those in Table 3.2 based on form or use.

We can conclude, then, that classification themes in conventional hierarchies may *appear* to be based on 'functional' criteria such as trip length, traffic flow or mobility function. But in fact, generally speaking, they only do so to the extent that such criteria fit the pattern of arteriality set out here. A hierarchy based on form or use *might* link up contiguously to some extent, but would not *necessarily* do so. Rather, it could end up with a non-contiguous 'mosaic' of route segments across the country. In other words, if designation were not based on arteriality, then road classification would not form the typical 'road-pattern-shape' of the road atlas.

3.15 • Typical road network possessing arteriality. For a given frame of reference, arteriality applies if the set of routes from the top down to any given level forms a complete, contiguous network. See Box 3.

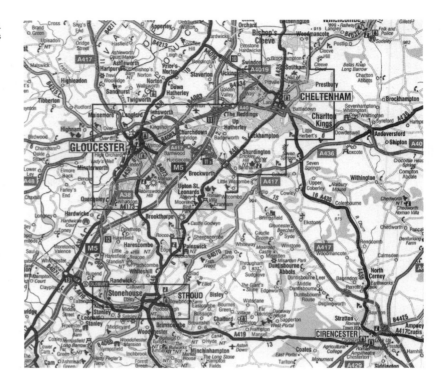

BOX 3. ARTERIALITY

Arteriality is a form of strategic contiguity whereby all 'top tier' elements join up contiguously. Arteriality can apply at any scale: for any given level or area there may be locally strategic elements which are locally contiguous.

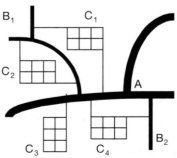

For a road network, arteriality implies that each route must connect to either a route of the same status or higher status. The result is that the highest status routes all form a single contiguous system (A), but sets of lower level elements are not necessarily contiguous (B, C). For any given level, the set of all elements from the top down to that level will form a single contiguous system (A + B; or A + B + C).

The term 'strategic contiguity' could be used to refer to arteriality in a more general sense, such as when applying to other contexts of organisational structure.

(a)

(b)

3.16 • Where to end the A9? The A9 used to go to John o'Groats, but now goes to Scrabster. From John o'Groats, ferries go to Orkney and Stroma (seen in distance). From Scrabster, vehicle ferries link in a chain to Orkney (seen in distance), Shetland, Faeroes, Norway and Iceland. The status of the roads reflects the strategic status of the destinations. (a) John o'Groats. (b) Scrabster.

Overall, conventional urban road classification or hierarchy is therefore effectively based on network topology, according to the property of arteriality, such that there is a contiguous network of the most strategic routes.

The designation of the 'most strategic routes' will itself depend on a combination of route characteristics and destination characteristics. Ultimately, the choice of end points and strategic routes is a matter of judgement. In the original road classification for Great Britain, the primary single-digit trunk roads were designated to radiate from London and Edinburgh, to Dover, Portsmouth, Avonmouth, Holyhead, Carlisle, Gourock and John o' Groats – subsequently Scrabster (Figure 3.16).[22]

Each of these places is strategic in its own way, but the choice of these particular locations rather than others must be considered subjective, or at least determined by factors far removed from supposedly unassailable engineering concepts of traffic flow and road safety. A 'functional' road classification is therefore no more or less subjective than any other kind of classification – like classifying a tree-lined urban road as a 'street', 'avenue' or 'boulevard'.

STREET TYPE REVISITED

> **It is therefore now generally accepted that the main roads ... should run between the areas leaving them as great islands free of fast through-traffic. Each built-up area will be sub-divided by the roads giving access to its principal parts ... There is thus a series of islands, each one being free of traffic having no purpose in it, and, as they get smaller having less vehicles on their roads.**
>
> Frederick Gibberd, *Town Design*[23]

(a)

(b)

(c)

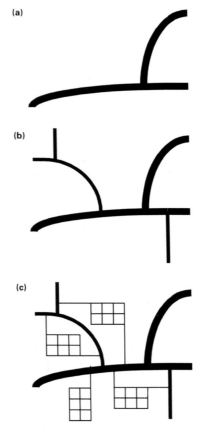

3.17 • The nesting of arterial networks. (a) A roads. (b) (A + B) roads. (c) (A + B + C) roads.

Having explored the length and breadth of national and inter-urban road networks, we can now return to the urban scale of traffic and towns, and re-interpret conventional hierarchy in the light of what we have learned in the course of the chapter as a whole. This will cement the interpretations of street type based on arteriality.

Strategic and local routes

Buchanan sub-divided distributors into three types: primary, district and local. Unlike the distinction between distributors and access roads – effectively a distinction of kind – the distinction between distributors is one of degree. The relationship between these distributors is 'hierarchical', but the basis of distinction is not essentially one of traffic flow or trip length or so on. Rather, the distinction is defined by arteriality.

For any network of routes, we can allocate a series of tiers such that arteriality applies: starting from the top tier, the set of any routes down to a given level forms a complete contiguous network (Figure 3.17(a)–(c)). However, lower tiers do not themselves necessarily form a complete contiguous network, but rather tend to form separate sub-networks (Figure 3.18(a)–(c)).

As a first act of reformulating street classification, we can define an *arterial* as a route or street that forms part of the top tier in an arterial network (A). The label 'arterial' is purely defined by relation to strategic level in the network; an arterial may take on different forms (e.g. arterial road or street) or configurational roles (e.g. arterial connector, arterial collector).

In the interstices between arterial routes, there will be a series of sub-networks (B, C). For each sub-network, we could identify 'sub-arterials', which are subordinate to the arterials (A) but which possess arteriality at the level of the sub-network level (i.e. they locally form the top tier route). We can define as many 'sub-arterial' tiers of 'sub-arterial' routes as desired, to generate a multi-tier hierarchical typology.[24] For a district level sub-network, B roads form a complete contiguous network. At this scale, the B roads are 'arterials' (district arterials). Similarly, for a local sub-network, the set of C roads could be arterials (local arterials) (Figure 3.19).

Each tier in the hierarchy therefore tends to equate to a different geographical extent: the major routes are the strategic routes and the minor routes are the local routes (where 'local' means routes forming networks of local extent, not routes used for local trips). Hence, we have created a 'hierarchy of arterials', where primacy is determined by the scale of area of coverage – for example, national or regional arterial, city arterial, district arterial, local arterial (Figure 3.20).

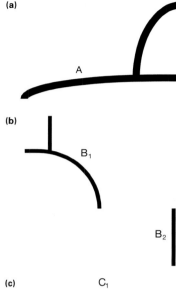

(a)

A

(b)

B₁

B₂

(c)

C₁

C₂

C₃

C₄

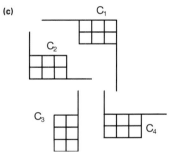

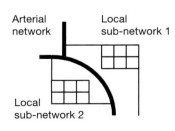

Arterial
network

Local
sub-network 1

Local
sub-network 2

▬▬▬▬ Tier II

─────── Tier III

This accords directly with Buchanan: 'The number of stages required in a distributory hierarchy will depend upon the size and the arrangement of the town'. This clearly shows that the division and sub-division of distributors are based primarily on the network area served, rather than traffic flow or road form. Quite explicitly, Buchanan refers to the '*town* or *primary* network'. This confirms that the 'primary' in Primary Distributor relates to geographical scale (meaning the primary system at the scale of a town); and that route type is defined in relation to *networks*. Overall, Buchanan actually suggests a full spectrum from national to local distributors, within which – in the urban context – the primary distributor is the top tier.

Similar systems of national road classification appear in many countries around the world, such as Japan with its National, Prefectural and Municipal roads, or India with National, State and District roads.[25] These may normally be regarded as 'administrative' rather than 'functional' designations, but effectively both systems are related significantly to geography and spatial nesting: one from the perspective of territorial jurisdiction and the other relating to network topology.

This brings home the point that even 'functional' classification has more to do with geography and network topology than with traffic function. It relates to dividing up the country into roughly equal areas of significance. Even Tripp, who was principally concerned with traffic flow and control, states: 'An adequate sub-arterial system has been created by the selection of suitable roads *conveniently spaced* to serve the whole *area*' (emphasis added).[26]

We can note in retrospect that the term 'distributor' connotes the idea of serving an area, or dividing or distributing within an area, rather than essentially implying a kind of movement (unlike 'drive', 'expressway', or the word 'road' etymologically speaking[27]). Indeed, the function of all public roads is ultimately to serve land: even at the national scale, all roads are 'access roads' – that is, they give access to the territory they pass through (Figure 3.21).

Buchanan's Venice

In fact, to illustrate the concepts of different kinds of route system, Buchanan applies the principles of *Traffic in Towns* to Venice. Here, the Grand Canal is the 'primary distributor', the next level of canals (used by

3.18 • Arterial network and non-contiguous sub-networks. (a) A road network. (b) B road sub-networks. (c) C road sub-networks.

3.19 • Sub-arteriality. The sub-network of B and C roads locally possesses arteriality.

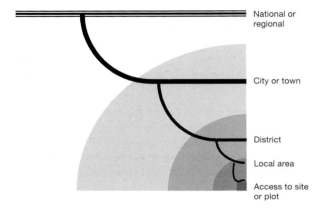

National or
regional

City or town

District

Local area

Access to site
or plot

3.20 • A hierarchy of roads and areas. Road types
are closely associated with the spatial scale of
the area they serve.

3.21 • The 'arterial' pattern of a leaf. We can
recognise that the pattern of veins on a leaf
possesses arteriality although we may know
nothing of the 'flows' along them. The
assignation of links to the strategic road
network is similarly abstract.

3.22 • Buchanan's Venice. The canals form a
three-tier 'hierarchy of distributors' based on
arteriality, carving Venice up into successively
smaller subdivisions. The routes suggested as
'principal pedestrian ways' all form a contiguous
network, implying that the designation of this
principal network is determined by arteriality
rather than form (e.g. width) or use (e.g.
pedestrian intensity).

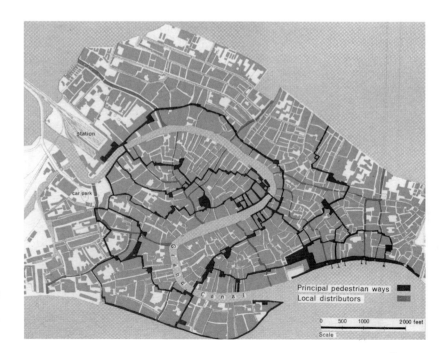

Principal pedestrian ways
Local distributors

0   500   1000   2000 feet
Scale

vaporetto waterbuses) are the set of 'district distributors', and the smallest canals used only by smaller boats are 'local distributors'[28] (Figure 3.22).

In invoking the Venetian example, the primary point Buchanan is making is that there is a completely separate (segregated) system of vehicular and pedestrian routes. Buchanan is also effectively demonstrating that distinctions between types need not be tied to a particular form or mode: a 'vehicular distributor' may as well be a canal plied by *vaporettos* as a street plied by Routemaster buses.

But Buchanan's Venice also supports the significance of arteriality as the basis for route classification. Buchanan notes in passing that the 'district distributor' canals divide the city into some 14 areas (islands). This is resonant with the idea of a hierarchy of route types (arterial, sub-arterial and local) serving different geographical territories. Perhaps most significantly of all, Buchanan's map shows 'principal pedestrian ways' drawn as a single contiguous system. This system includes all kinds of 'ways' from narrow alleys to Venice's main square, Piazza San Marco – a span that clearly represents a disparate collection of forms and uses. Since these 'principal ways' also happen to join up contiguously – that is, after all, what a network *is* – this reinforces the suggestion that the hierarchy is not essentially based on form or use, but network topology.

CONCLUSIONS

In this chapter, we have seen how and why road hierarchy is viewed negatively by some urban designers and planners, especially those who favour traditional urban design. First, conventional hierarchy contains a reduced diversity of route type, which has no place for the traditional mixed-use urban street. Second, it appears to be geared to (and ordered by) traffic function, at the expense of pedestrians, and public transport. These kinds of ideas were set out as early as the 1920s by the architect–planner Le Corbusier, but have been adopted and pursued with rigour and vigour by generations of engineers since.

Despite the range of classification systems and diversity of street types studied, the rationale behind those used in official designations tends to be remarkably consistent. Conventional street classifications are typically based on a spectrum of types which imply an inverse relationship between 'traffic function' and some kind of 'urban function'. This chapter has argued that this relationship was always 'unrealistic' (as the basis for the classification of actual road types) as well as today being considered 'unidealistic' (in the sense of no longer representing a desired future set of types). It is therefore a 'dysfunctional' classification.

It has also been argued that, despite the conventional emphasis on 'functional' classification, the 'function' is not in essence based on traffic flow, traffic speed, traffic purpose, trip length, population served or road standard – despite what official definitions may state. The so-called 'function' is in essence a *designation*, and although this designation is likely to take account of form and use, it is effectively a network function, based not on aspiration but actual position of routes within a network. This is no more or less a designation than any 'administrative classification' which may divide roads up into different jurisdictions for the purposes of management.

The designation of network function is based on a topological property known as arteriality. Arteriality is a form of strategic contiguity, which simply ensures that all strategic roads (regarded at whatever scale) connect up in a contiguous network (contiguous at that scale). This embeds urban route classification within the national network context, which in practice will tend to be geared to longer distance and hence motor traffic.

Since designation according to arteriality is based on selecting links to form a strategic network, it is liable to be as subjective as any other kind of qualitative classification. For example, a traffic engineer designating a route as a 'district distributor' in the road hierarchy is no more or less subjective than an urban planner designating a 'district centre' in the urban hierarchy. Both designations may be supported by quantitative factors (e.g. trip generation), but in essence both are ordinal assignations. Therefore, although road hierarchy assists application of sound engineering principles relating to traffic flow and safety, hierarchy itself is not in essence a traffic engineering concept; and the allocation of route types within a network must be seen as to some extent subjective and potentially open to challenge, or renegotiation.

Taken together, the foregoing represents a departure from conventional interpretations of road hierarchy. It explains why conventional hierarchy does not really work the way it is supposed to work. This means that the application of road hierarchy in practice is dysfunctional because design professionals may treat it too rigidly, as if based on 'sacrosanct' principles of traffic flow, and a 'logical' inverse relationship between mobility and access, when in fact it is based on a relatively subjective designation of strategic route status according to the topological pattern of arteriality.

If anything, the hierarchical ranking is actually based on a straight-forward relationship between strategic and local routes, relating to lengths of road and areas served. The type of hierarchy proposed by Le Corbusier was after all something organised according to plain old dimensions of space, rather than any avant-garde metric of traffic motion.

In the end, the analysis of this chapter suggests that hierarchy need not be a 'tyranny of traffic regulation', but a spatial or structural logic that could bridge the professional divide (just as Buchanan and Le Corbusier did personally). The issue of hierarchical structure will be revisited in Chapter 7. For now, we turn from an elementary scrutiny of street type to an elementary scrutiny of pattern type.

NOTES

1   Cited by Moholy-Nagy (1968: 274).
2   Le Corbusier (1955: 99). Different versions of la règle des 7V have different descriptions of the types; in some there is express provision for traditional 'streets' (V4 = Grand Rue). See also Spreiregen (1965: 171); Gerosa (1978).
3   Lillebye (2001: 20); Anderson (1978); Hebbert (1998); Brogden (1996).
4   AASHTO (1990: 1; 1995: 1; 2001: 1). The first two run to over 1000 pages; the third to around 900 pages.
5   IHT (1997: 145, 147).
6   IHT (1997); DoT/IHT (1987); MoT (1963).
7   Tripp (1942; 1950); Gold (1997: 175); Southworth and Ben-Joseph (1997: 64).
8   MoT (1963: 44). Tripp also made a two-fold division between traffic conduits and local roads in *Road Traffic and Its Control* (2nd edition, 1950) although in *Town Planning and Road Traffic* (1942) the sub-arterial category is presented separately as a third type. Kulash refers to the mobility function of arterial streets as 'the movement of as much traffic as possible as fast as is reasonable' (2001: 10).
9   MoT (1963: 42).
10   MoT (1963: 140). Also discussed in Marshall (2003b).
11   A version of the inverse relationship is expressed in AASHTO (2001: 7).
12   Strictly speaking, the classification can apply to any street in principle, by being purely a classification of 'intended function' rather than 'existing reality'. But if this intended function is so remote from the existing reality that few roads fit it, it puts into doubt the value of having such a hierarchy in the first place.
13   The terms 'form type' and 'use type' are discussed by Franck (1994) and Brill (1994).
14   Tripp (1950: 331); ICE (1996: 1, 2, 9, 11); AASHTO (2001: 1, 4, 13).
15   From the EC project ARTISTS (Marshall, 2002a). See Appendix 3.2.
16   ICE (1996: 8); also O'Flaherty (1997: 19).
17   Alker Tripp expressly rejected trip length as a criterion for road classification (1950: 303–304). For an example of a pattern of routes classified by speed, see Morrison (1981).
18   DETR (1998b: 7). Criteria for the core trunk network are (1) link main centres of population; (2) provide access to major ports, airports and rail terminals; (3) provide access to peripheral regions; (4) provide key cross-border routes to

Scotland and Wales; and (5) include Trans-European Networks. These all relate to geography and politics, not traffic flow.

19   Two caveats must be applied to the suggested pervasiveness of arteriality. First, it applies to any network that is contiguous in the first place; in the case of nations with separate landmasses, where island roads form sub-networks, there is no physical contiguity and therefore arteriality is broken. Second, arteriality applies to networks where road types are categorised independently of form. When a road type is wholly or partly based on form, it would not necessarily fit the pattern of arteriality. This applies in the case of motorways, which may be legally defined by designation, but conditional upon the form being to motorway standard.

20   Morrison (1966: 21).

21   There is an element of self-referentiality about this: roads seem to be defined by how they are connected within the network, yet what they connect to may be limited – or ensured – by their designated role.

22   Of course, these partly relate to wider international networks: Dover and Portsmouth to the Continent; Holyhead to Ireland, and Scrabster – the current termination point of the A9 – with ferry links to Iceland, the Faeroe Islands and Norway.

23   Gibberd (1967: 36).

24   Tripp used the term 'sub-arterial' to indicate routes of an intermediate level below the arterial level. Tripp's sub-arterials formed a 'sub-arterial' network as defined here (Tripp, 1942: 41; 1950: 303, 331). Note that a district level sub-arterial is the equivalent of sub-district level arterial. Incidentally, in *Constitutional Code*, Jeremy Bentham divided districts into subdistricts, bis-subdistricts and tris-subdistricts (Bentham, 1830). Hence we could (hypothetically) create a Benthamite hierarchy featuring tris-subdistrict arterials, or tris-subarterials.

25   Bartlett (2003a).

26   Tripp (1950: 331).

27   Rykwert (1978: 15).

28   These are 'distributors' in the sense that they are vehicular. The waters are muddied by the fact that these also give access to frontages.

4 PATTERN TYPE

Shape has proved one of the most elusive of geometric characteristics to capture in any exact quantitative fashion. Many of the terms in common usage . . . turn out to be arbitrary so that misclassification is common, while some of the more mathematical definitions fail to do justice to our intuitive notions of what constitutes shape.

Haggett and Chorley, *Network Analysis in Geography*[1]

Hamlet: Methinks it is like a weasel.

Shakespeare

The complexities of shape and structure set street pattern apart from many other objects of urban or transport analysis. For example, road width is merely a linear quantity and traffic flow is a simple ratio (vehicles per hour). Even the issue of density boils down to a straightforward ratio, however fiercely the significance of different numerators or denominators may be contested. By contrast, there is no straightforward or standard descriptor that is used to capture street pattern. This fuels the profusion of verbal descriptors encountered in Chapter 2.

Yet, unless we have an adequate description of pattern or structure, it will remain difficult to compare structures across cases – identifying patterns that are 'good' or 'bad' for different purposes – and hence make robust, generalisable recommendations for the design of urban layout.

This chapter explores the nature of pattern through a variety of ways in which *street* pattern may be characterised. The chapter first explores a diverse range of existing characterisations of pattern, before using what has been learned to develop some new qualitative and quantitative descriptors of pattern. These will address several of the issues of pattern description flagged up in Chapter 2, while pointing forward to the resolution of the structure of those patterns in subsequent chapters.

CLASSIFICATION OF PATTERN

Far from being a simple 'neutral' activity, the task of classification is often in practice a highly complex and contested one. Classification – from hierarchies of roads to taxonomies of species – has at times been associated with ambiguity and acrimony, effort and controversy, and 'names and nastiness'.[2]

Within the urban sphere, Julienne Hanson puts it this way:

> Time and time again, authors suggest that all towns are made up of a limited vocabulary of urban forms, yet when called upon to specify the elements of that vocabulary, the temptation to multiply categories seems to be irresistible.[3]

Hanson's exploration of the pitfalls of the territory continues:

> Descriptive typologies are generally speaking either too simple to be useful – radial/orthogonal, street village/green village, and so on, or so detailed as to be idiosyncratic . . . The search for typology is perhaps doomed to failure because, faced with reality, one is faced with a morphological continuum.[4]

Bill Hillier echoes this theme, warning of the possibility of ending up with 'an arbitrary list'.[5] The attempt to label types of settlement by their road pattern has been described as being 'futile' or 'impossible'.[6] It is therefore not without some forewarning that we enter into this territory of arbitrary lists and multiplication of categories, as we attempt to tackle the issue of structural characterisation.

In this section, we will first look at a wide range of types of urban pattern, and then progressively focus on those most usefully distinguishing types of street pattern.

Descriptors of urban pattern

Table 4.1 sets out a selection of pattern descriptions. An immediate concern here is that there is not necessarily any consistency of use. The labels are describing different things – these could be referring to whole settlement patterns, clusters of development or road network patterns, or a

Table 4.1 **Examples of settlement pattern typologies**

Unwin (1920)	*Moholy-Nagy (1968)*
Irregular	1. Geomorphic
Regular	2. Concentric
1. Rectilinear	3. Orthogonal-connective
2. Circular	4. Orthogonal-modular
3. Diagonal	5. Clustered
4. Radiating lines	

Lynch (1981)	*Satoh (1998)*
1. Star (radial)	1. Warped grid
2. Satellite cities	2. Radial
3. Linear city	3. Horseback
4. Rectangular grid city	4. Whirlpool
5. Other grid (parallel, triangular, hexagonal)	5. Unique structures
6. Baroque axial network	
7. The lacework	*Frey (1999)*
8. The 'inward' city (e.g. medieval Islamic)	1. The core city
9. The nested city	2. The star city
10. Current imaginings (megaform, bubble,	3. The satellite city
floating, underground, undersea, outer space)	4. The galaxy of settlements
	5. The linear city
	6. The polycentric net, or regional city

Note: for more examples, see Appendix 4.

combination of these, at different degrees of resolution. The degree of resolution may vary not only across but *within* particular typological sets.[7] The recognition and representation of patterns as 'blobs' or 'structures' are effectively in the eye of the beholder. Perhaps – like the Rorschach ink-blot test, or Hamlet's 'weasel' – we tend to see in patterns whatever we want to see. Indeed, Kevin Lynch himself comments that many of the forms in his catalogue are held as articles of faith[8] – from which one might conclude that their objective existence defies verification.

There is also a confusion of ways in which each label relates to each kind of form (Figure 4.1). In some cases, the same form could be described by different labels. Conversely, a particular label may have different structural connotations, and could be used to describe quite different patterns in different contexts.

The linear city is a case in point. According to Keeble, discussion of the linear idea is 'impeded by difficulty in establishing just what is and what is not a linear town'. Referring to the grid of routes for traffic and

4.1 • Types of settlement pattern. This selection illustrates the complexities and ambiguities of pattern description. The graphics are all taken from Lewis Keeble's *Principles and Practice of Town Planning*; the captions are added interpretations. (a) Different names for the same thing. This pattern is described variously as an 'octopus', 'starfish' or 'umbrella'. (b) The same name given to different things. Two different patterns are given as examples of the 'linear' type. (c) A pattern with no name. Perhaps the left-hand pattern has 'no name' because forms significantly resembling it are rarely, if ever, found in practice. (d) A pattern with a unique name? Is this linear, or L-shaped? In the end, each pattern is unique, and each town has its own more or less unique label: its own name (Burnley).

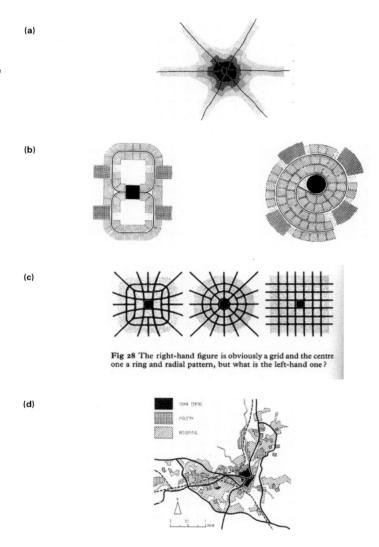

(a)

(b)

(c)

Fig 28 The right-hand figure is obviously a grid and the centre one a ring and radial pattern, but what is the left-hand one?

(d)

pedestrians in the plan for Hook (the unbuilt new town in Hampshire, England), Keeble argues that 'If Hook is a linear town then almost any town must be linear'.[9] It is possible that as soon as a remotely elongated town form emerges, one may be tempted to call it a linear city. However, as the deviance from linearity increases, we are forced to consider inventing new categories to accommodate any emerging shape (Figure 4.1(d)). Moreover, as soon as the gaze is widened to take in neighbouring settlements, a branching or circuit formation might materialise, or perhaps a satellite system, or a galaxy of stars.

Having said that, however, since each urban area is unique, perhaps the diversity of terms in Table 4.1 is too constraining rather than too lax. The suspicion is that there are as few or as many types as there are names that the typologist cares to invent. At one extreme, each settlement has its own unique category (i.e. its own name); at the other, all are lumped into a single category labelled 'unique'.

What kind of pattern

The first thing to be clear on is what kind of pattern we are describing. Kevin Lynch leads by example, by clearly distinguishing those types constituting settlement forms from those constituting network patterns. This is useful in clarifying what kinds of pattern are being considered, helping to allow a consistent basis for distinction. This book follows this approach by focusing on a single attribute: street pattern. Street pattern is not the only way of depicting settlement pattern – but it is of core interest to this book, and the focus from now on.[10]

Street pattern descriptors

A range of street pattern descriptors is presented in Table 4.2. Here, as with overall settlement pattern, there is a great diversity of descriptors. But, these descriptors appear to be pointing to the same kinds of pattern. Certain familiar labels recur, such as 'radial', 'rectangular' and 'linear'. These are sometimes presented as if they are universal or generic, or falling into neat sets of fundamental types. However, not all commentators would agree what such fundamental types might be, and most actual street patterns would not fit neatly in any of these neat tripartite or bipartite sets.

Ray Brindle suggests that there are just two broad types of layout: the grid and the tributary.[11] This distinction relates to some of the debate discussed in Chapter 2, and reflects the existence of a type of formation (tributary, or loop and cul-de-sac) that has only become commonplace in the second half of the twentieth century, and then generally only recognisable at the scale of street pattern rather than overall settlement pattern.

What we find is that – like the street typologies studied in the last chapter – there are several different classification themes used as bases for distinction. Some descriptors are referring to the configuration of streets, others to the shape of the interstices, yet others the alignment of the routes. And these are not necessarily mutually exclusive.

The problem seems to be that, on one hand, there are not enough descriptors to account for the great variety of patterns on the ground, yet on the other hand there often seems to be an overabundance of terms used to signify the same general property. For example, there are nine terms incorporating the word grid (Table 4.2), yet there is no guarantee that each one maps uniquely to a particular pattern type. In practice, many terms may be used interchangeably, even if theoretically they have distinct

Table 4.2 **Examples of street pattern typologies**

Urban design related	**Transport network related**
City design according to artistic principles	*Ministry of War Transport; also Traffic Planning and Engineering*
1. Rectangular	1. Gridiron
2. Radial	2. Linear
3. Triangular	3. Radial
plus 'bastard offspring'	
Town and country planning	*Transport Technology and Network Structure*
1. Gridiron	1. Spinal or tree
2. Hexagonal	2. Grid network
3. Radial	3. Delta network
4. Spider's web	
	Road System Design
Site planning	1. Radial and circumferential
1. Grid	2. Grid
2. Radial (including branching)	3. Hyperbolic grid
3. Linear	
	Transport Network Analysis
Good city form	1. Path
1. Axial network	2. Tree
2. Capillary	3. Cycle
3. Kidney	
4. Radio-concentric	*Traffic Engineering and Management*
5. Rectangular grid	1. Grid
	2. Tributary
AIA guidance	
1. Curvilinear	
2. Diagonal	
3. Discontinuous	
4. Grid with diagonals	
5. Organic	
6. Orthogonal	

Note: for more examples, see Appendix 4.

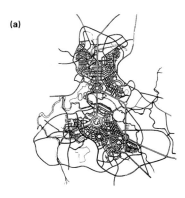

(a)

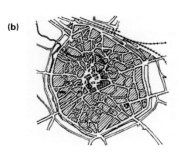

(b)

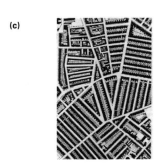

(c)

4.2 • Examples of regular and irregular pattern types. Graphics and labels are Keeble's. (a) 'Artificially created'. (b) 'Extreme formlessness'. (c) 'Chaotic'.

meanings. For example, 'orthogonal', 'rectilinear' and 'gridiron' might mean the same thing to different people, or different things to the same individual. The multiplicity of types, then, is not necessarily doing much descriptive work.

For maximum descriptive work we would wish to encourage standardisation of use, but without reducing diversity of terms. For example, Paul Groth makes the distinction between the generic 'orthogonal street pattern' or 'street grid' and the specific terms 'gridiron' which should properly refer to a grid arranged in long narrow blocks, and 'checkerboard' which should be composed of square blocks.[12] This methodical care is a start towards an efficient 'division of linguistic labour'.[13] We can take further steps to assist in sorting out strategies for classification, which may be illustrated, in the remainder of this section, by referring to distinctive cases from the literature.

Regularity and irregularity

Raymond Unwin and Lewis Keeble both make their first division of pattern into those 'deliberately planned' and those 'unplanned', taking forward the 'planned' branch for further subdivision into recognisable types of regular pattern. Keeble also explicitly identifies the 'amorphous' type of road system, which appears to defy categorisation (Figure 4.2).[14]

The recognition of irregular patterns is also seen in typological sets where there is a series of definite categories followed by a final catch-all 'other' category.[15] These examples draw attention to the possibility of focusing classification on specific regular attributes of pattern.

Hybrids and permutations

Camillo Sitte makes a distinction between pure geometric patterns and their hybrids, or 'bastard offspring'. These different 'offspring' can be seen as hybrids, which are permutations of basic 'pure' types. This offers another possibility for a typological distinction, based on explicit permutations of simpler forms.

One area where this is particularly useful is when combining different structures at different scales. An example is seen in the systematic study of patterns undertaken in the *Mosborough Master Plan*, a consultants' report on a proposed (but unbuilt) new town near Sheffield.[16] Here, an analysis is undertaken of three basic kinds of structure, each considered at the macro and micro scale (Figure 4.3).

Although the Mosborough analysis is sophisticated in differentiating structure at different scales, the elemental types chosen do not seem

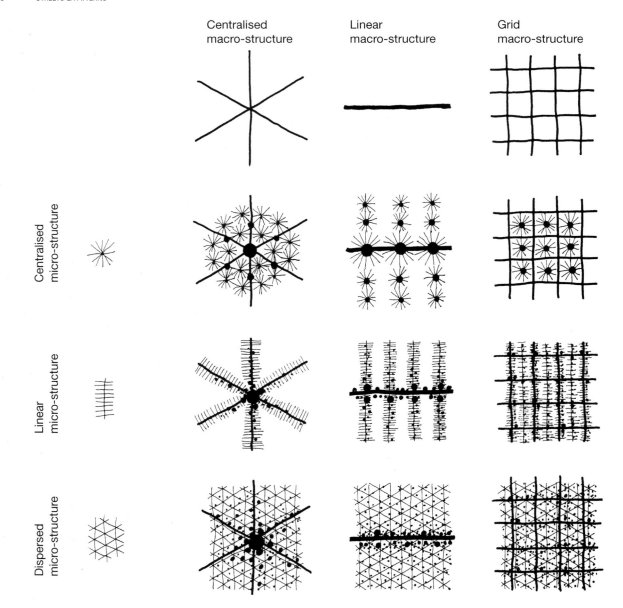

4.3 • *Mosborough Master Plan*: macro and micro scale permutations.

particularly helpful. For example, there is no rectangular grid considered at the micro-level, and no 'tree-like' forms as such (except insofar as the repetitive addition of linear 'twigs' effectively gives rise to trees in the aggregate). Not only do most of the resulting patterns not intuitively look like 'optimal' forms, but most do not even look likely as street patterns in the first place. For a start, neither the centralised (radial) nor dispersed (mesh) forms, as depicted, faithfully resemble typical micro structures – which immediately cuts out two-thirds of the possibilities in Figure 4.3.[17]

The use of hybrids and permutations can certainly assist the generation of possible types of pattern, based on combinations of 'elemental' types. While some simple discrete permutations have so far been demonstrated, there is further scope for a more finely graded impression of the 'morphological continuum'.

The 'morphological continuum'

The act of classification effectively carves a series of discrete types from the 'morphological continuum' of all patterns. In order to arrive at a higher resolution classification, we can consider more than one spectrum of differentiation between types of pattern. The *Mosborough Master Plan* also explores a 'generic range' of 21 network structure types, which are effectively points arranged on a three-way 'spectrum' or continuum, whose extreme vertices are three elemental types: centralised, linear and dispersed. All 21 forms can be represented graphically in relation to each other (Figure 4.4).

While the particular structural types in Figure 4.4 are not necessarily the most useful for present purposes,[18] the *Mosborough Master Plan* is useful in demonstrating a systematic approach to urban structure, where named types may be equated to regions in the morphological continuum. This ultimately points the way to the potential for a quantified typology.

What is needed first, however, is a more useful set of elemental types, and a better description of the continuum, with explicitly calculable positions on it. The latter exercise will be tackled in due course in Chapter 6. To arrive at the former, it is necessary to consider what elemental types there might be.

Elemental types

The geographers Haggett and Chorley use a systematic basis for distinction, to create a structured dendrogram of mutually exclusive types. This leads us to a first appreciation of how possible elemental types might be distinguished. Haggett and Chorley's system is based on the topology of planar

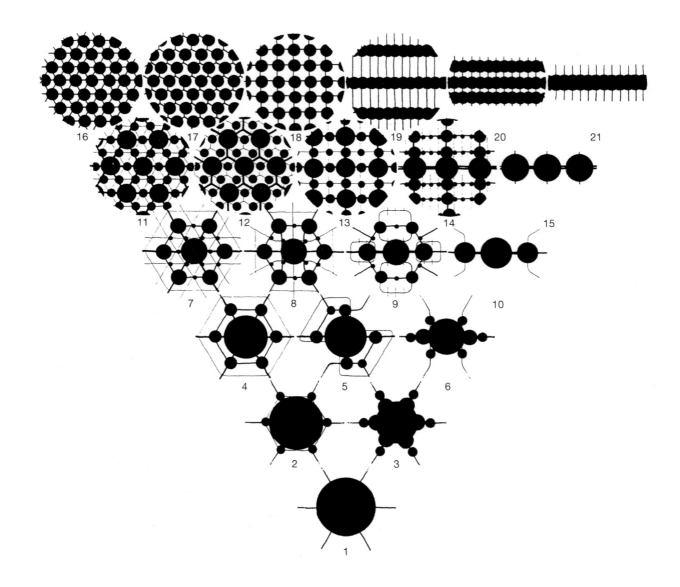

4.4 • The 'morphological continuum' of the *Mosborough Master Plan*. This shows
21 theoretical structures of the 'the generic range' (listed in Appendix 4.1).

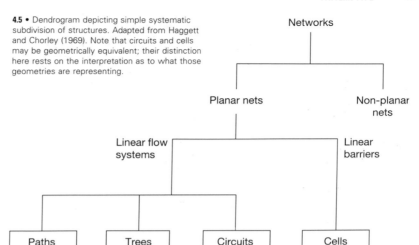

4.5 • Dendrogram depicting simple systematic subdivision of structures. Adapted from Haggett and Chorley (1969). Note that circuits and cells may be geometrically equivalent; their distinction here rests on the interpretation as to what those geometries are representing.

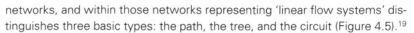

networks, and within those networks representing 'linear flow systems' distinguishes three basic types: the path, the tree, and the circuit (Figure 4.5).[19]

These are the most clear, simple and abstract descriptors, providing clear divisions into typological categories. Yet the question becomes to what extent these are useful, compared to more familiar labels of urban patterns such as 'radial' and 'gridiron' (in effect, echoing the dilemma in the quote at the opening of this chapter).

A conclusion here is that there is no single 'fundamental' set of elemental types. The types or sets of types recognised will depend on the purpose of the classification and its intended application. For example, a transport classification might quite justifiably emphasise route or junction topology, while an urban morphological classification might equally justifiably emphasise the geometry of the blocks formed. In this way, a given pattern could be described respectively as a 'hex-nodal network' or a 'triangular tessellation' (Figure 4.6).

To develop a system of characterisation of street pattern, it will serve to combine what has been learned from analysing the examples from the literature so far with an ultimate purpose relating to design guidance set out in Chapter 2.

(a)

(b)

4.6 • Classification depends on the purpose of its application. (a) The transport modeller might see a 'hex-nodal network' of routes, while (b) a planner might see a 'triangular tessellation' of land parcels.

DEVELOPING TYPOLOGIES OF PATTERN

The purpose of pattern classification, as far as this book is concerned, is to distinguish different kinds of pattern relating to desired formations of

4.7 • ABCD typology as transect. The four types are presented as if extending out from the core of a settlement (left) to the periphery (right). Not all types are necessarily present or in order; but normally, where present, the A-type would be the core and the D-type at the periphery.

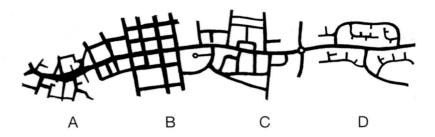

A   B   C   D

urban streets. This section develops a series of qualitative descriptors that culminate in a systematic classification system.

ABCD typology

The typology introduced here has been developed with the intention of reflecting typical street patterns that are encountered in different kinds of urban analysis. The four types are best introduced by considering different patterns featuring at different stages of growth of towns and cities, arranged as if stretching outwards from the historic core of a settlement to its outskirts (Figure 4.7).

The A-type is typical of the core area of old cities, especially walled cities; we may use as a mnemonic for the A-type the term *Altstadt*.[20] The angularity of routes, oriented in a variety of directions, generates a rudimentary radiality, where such a pattern is located at the core of a settlement.

The B-type is typical of planned extensions or newly founded settlements. The prevalence of four-way perpendicular junctions naturally gives rise to bilateral directionality, with the implication of a grid form at the wider scale. The term 'bilateral' may be used as a mnemonic for the B-type.

The C-type is the perhaps the most general type which may be found at various positions in a settlement, but most characteristically astride an arterial route, whether constituting the central armature of a village, a whole settlement or a suburban extension along a radial route (as shown in Figure 4.7). A mnemonic for the C-type could be 'characteristic' or 'conjoint' (terms whose significance is explained in Chapters 6 and 7 respectively).

Finally, the D-type is typical of modern hierarchical layouts, and is often associated with curvilinear layouts of distributor roads, forming looping or branching patterns. Indeed, we may use the mnemonic 'distributory' to characterise the D-type, connoting a combination of 'distributor' and 'tributary' – with a hint of 'disurbanity', perhaps.[21]

(a)

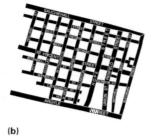

(b)

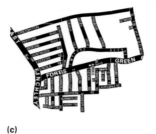

(c)

(d)

4.8 • Examples of ABCD street patterns. (a) A-type, Tunis. Angular and irregular streets of the 'Medina'. (b) B-type, Glasgow. Blythswood, Glasgow's second gridded extension. (c) C-type, East Finchley. This illustrates a typical suburban, indeed a typically urban, arrangement. (d) D-type, Thamesmead. A 'distributory' arrangement, giving a clear impression of a hierarchical structure, with a bristling of culs-de-sac.

Table 4.3 Urban associations of ABCD types

Type	Example pattern	Typical location	Frontages	Transport era
A-type *Altstadt*		Historic core	Built frontages	Era of pedestrian and horseback
B-type Bilateral		Gridiron (central, or extension, or citywide)	Built frontages	Era of horse and carriage
C-type Characteristic/ Conjoint		Anywhere; including individual villages or suburban extensions: often astride arterial routes	Built frontages or buildings set back in space ('pavilions')	Any Era of public transport; car
D-type Distributory		Peripheral development: off-line pods or superblock infill	Buildings set back in space, access only to minor roads	Era of the car

Some cities may have all types present, arranged in the order of centrality shown in Figure 4.7. In some 'planned settlement' cases, there will be no central A-type; in others, A-type and B-type may be both present but separate. In other cases, the B-type would be entirely absent. Where present, the D-type would usually be the most recent, outermost layer. Some examples from real cities are shown in Figure 4.8(a) to (d).

These types are intended to illustrate some aspects of the kinds of pattern we seem to have been trying to distinguish. The first two might be equated with 'preferred' structures, the last with 'discouraged' structure (as viewed by urban designers and planners). Some typical associations are suggested in Table 4.3.

Further nuances and implications of the A, B, C and D-types, and more precise distinctions between them, will be developed in the course of this

BOX 4. COMPOSITION AND CONFIGURATION

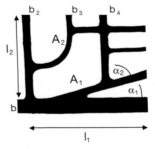

Composition refers to absolute geometric layout, as represented in a scale plan, featuring absolute position, lengths, areas, orientation.

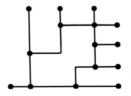

Configuration refers to topology, as represented on an abstract diagram, featuring links and nodes, their ordering (relative position), adjacency and connectivity.

book. Most immediately, they will be used simply as examples to illustrate different properties developed in the next few sections.

Composition and configuration

As a first and fundamental step, we can make a distinction between two types of formation: those relating to absolute physical geometry, as opposed to those referring to abstract topology.[22] These may be referred to respectively as *composition* and *configuration* (Box 4). The terms are set up here so that they may refer either to the product of formation (a composition or configuration) or the process of formation.

The distinction can be readily appreciated as the distinction between the representation of the London Underground network as a geographical map and as a diagram (Figure 4.9).[23]

The distinction between composition and configuration can be made specifically and systematically. This means that we can make a distinction between compositional properties and configurational properties of patterns (Table 4.4).

Composition and configuration can be used to interpret some of the labels encountered earlier. We can recognise the labels 'rectilinear' and 'orthogonal' as compositional, and the label 'cellular' as configurational. Therefore the term 'grid' – which connotes rectilinear, orthogonal and cellular properties – can be seen as a composite, combining compositional and configurational overtones.

4.9 • Representations of the London Underground network. (a) Geographical map (composition). (b) Network diagram (configuration).

(a)

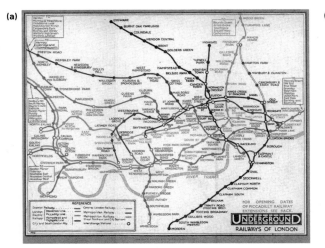

(b)

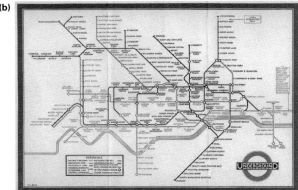

Table 4.4 **Associations between composition and configuration (see also Box 4)**

	Composition	**Configuration**
Association	Geometry	Topology
Dimension	Fully two-dimensional	Lying between one and two dimensions
Properties	Length Area Angle/orientation	Adjacency Continuity Connectivity
Examples of overall shapes or structures	Square Oblong Quadrilateral	Circuit (cell) Tree
Properties of elements	Rectilinear Orthogonal Wide or narrow Straight or curved	With three-way nodes (T-junctions) With four-way nodes (X-junctions) With pendant nodes (culs-de-sac)
Values	Real numbers, including fractions	Rational numbers, typically integers
Examples	10.5 m long 7.3 m wide 62° angle	Links = 72 Nodes = 49

The ABCD typology can also be interpreted in terms of composition and configuration (Figure 4.10). In terms of composition, we can distinguish between the narrow crooked streets of the A-type, the straight orthogonal streets of the B-type and the sprawling curvilinear patterns of the D-type. Alternatively, in terms of configuration, we could draw a distinction between the connective properties of the B-type versus the tributary properties of the D-type.

Going back to Chapter 2, then, we can make a distinction between descriptors of pattern that were used in 'preferred' and 'discouraged' exemplars: we can distinguish between those intending to express geometric composition – rectangular blocks versus straggling curvilinear networks – and those intending to express topological properties of configuration – the use of grid-like networks (of whatever absolute shape) versus tree-like networks (of whatever absolute shape).

This specific terminology can allow a subtle distinction between the properties *permeability* and *connectivity* – terms sometimes used interchangeably in practice (Figure 4.11). We can use permeability as a

4.10 • Compositional and configurational properties of ABCD types.

Composition

Configuration

A-type

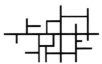

Irregular, fine scale angular, streets mostly short or crooked, varying in width, going in all directions.

Mixture of configurational properties (T- and X-junctions, some culs-de-sac; moderate connectivity.

B-type

Regular, orthogonal, rectilinear, streets of consistent width, going in two directions.

Mainly grid with crossroads (high) connectivity). Continuity of cross routes.

C-type

Mixture of regularity and irregularity, streets typically of consistent width; curved or rectilinear formations, meeting at right angles.

Mixture of configurational properties (T- and X-junctions, some culs-de-sac; moderate connectivity).

D-type

Based on consistent road geometry. Curvilinear or rectilinear formations, mostly meeting at right angles.

Loop roads with many branching routes in tree-like configurations (mainly T-junctions, mainy culs-de-sac; low connectivity).

(a)

(b)

(c)

4.11 • Permeability and connectivity. Layout (a) has greater permeability than (b), but both have the same connectivity (c).

compositional property, referring to the extent to which a two-dimensional plan area is 'permeated' by accessible space – this relates to distance (circumlocution) and area (available for circulation). Connectivity may then be reserved for use as a configurational property, referring to the degree to which different links or routes connect up in a network.

Overall, it will be possible to use the distinction between composition and configuration in subsequent explorations of structure from now on. The immediate question here is: how can we use this distinction between composition and configuration to help arrange types of pattern in a general system of classification?

(a)

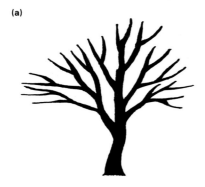

(b)

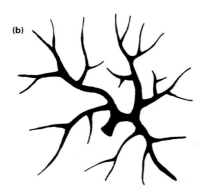

4.12 • Tree patterns. This shows two different 'compositions' with the same 'configuration': (a) could represent the 'tree-like' layout of modern road networks, while (b) could be the radial pattern for a whole settlement.

An integrated taxonomy

We can set up an integrated 'taxonomy' of patterns, combining consideration of possible elemental types (as discussed earlier) with the distinction between composition and configuration.

For a start, we see that the radial form is, topologically, a special kind of tree structure. That is, while it appears as a distinct form, as an absolute composition, with a familiar 'hub and spoke' arrangement, when analysed configurationally, it reduces to a tree (Figure 4.12). The linear form could also be seen as a special kind of tree – a 'spinal' structure that happens to have no branches.[24]

In doing this we have already linked three of the main types together in a systematic way (linear, radial and tree). We can add in a fourth – cellular – and then create a fifth category to represent 'other' cases: irregular forms or hybrids (Figure 4.13).

What we find is that, rather than a simple list of types, we have a structured set of types. We can regard this as a *taxonomy*, from which any particular *typology* is but a selection.[25] The taxonomy is taken to mean a systematic structure of relatedness; any discrete typology is just one particular slice through this. This explains why we could decide on, for example, a division of two types (e.g. pure versus hybrid; grid versus tree) or three types (linear, radial, grid), etc. It is a matter of how far down the diagram we make the cut, to get the desired level of resolution.

In effect, the taxonomy in Figure 4.13 reflects three tendencies from the literature:

1. typologies which express a tripartite set of grid, radial and linear;
2. the bipolar distinction between grid and tree; and
3. the use of an 'other' category to mop up irregular cases.

In doing so, this accommodates four particularly popular cases: these are the grid, radial and linear forms, which are well established as settlement patterns (Tables 4.1 and 4.2), together with an emerging fourth category, relating to tree-like or tributary layouts. Any other kinds of pattern would be tidied into the 'hybrid' category.

The five-way classification suggested in Figure 4.13 can be used to help sort out the diverse set of typological labels encountered previously. One possible interpretation is shown in Table 4.5, which sorts all labels into one of five categories.[26]

By elaboration of Figure 4.13, it is possible to create a very detailed taxonomy of patterns, to any desired degree of precision or elaboration (Figure 4.14).

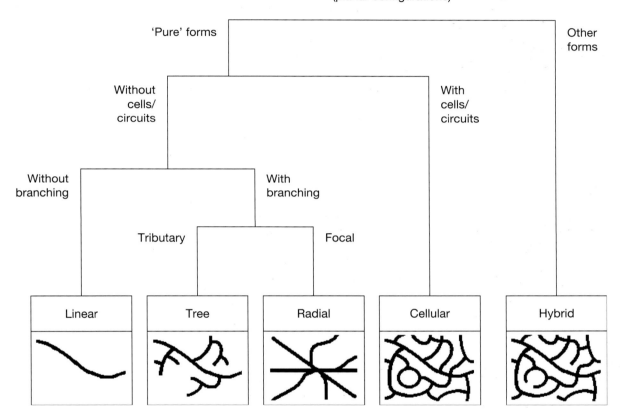

4.13 • Integrated taxonomy of patterns. This taxonomy both distinguishes and unites the main general pattern types encountered in the literature. This 'taxonomic structure' can be 'sliced' at different levels to create different typologies for different degrees of resolution.

Using this systematic kind of taxonomic structure (Figures 4.13, 4.14) we have developed a system of variable resolution: we can either use the broader, blunter end of the spectrum (distinguishing, say, three or four most basic types) or a much finer distinction. The whole system can retain a systematic integrity, yet in practical application it can be flexible through selective use of the most useful types for particular purposes.

This taxonomy can be seen to be structured by recognising pure (elemental or homogenous) types at each level of resolution. From this starting point, we may deal with heterogeneous layouts in at least two different ways. We may create permutations of basic types, to create

Table 4.5 **Descriptors of street pattern arranged in five categories**

Linear forms	Tributary and 'hierarchical'	Radial	Grid-like	Other forms
Linear	Branch-and-twig	Asterisk	Axial grid	Amorphous
Serial	Branching pattern	Cartwheel	Checkerboard	Axial network
Serpentine	Cul-de-sac network	Concentric	Deformed grid	Capillary
Single strand, double	Hierarchical	Octopus	Directional grid	Curvilinear
strand etc.	Lollipops on a stick	Ortho-radial	Fragmented parallel	Diagonal
	Loop and cul-de-sac	Radial	Grid	Discontinuous
	Loops and lollipops	Radial-concentric	Gridiron	Dispersed
	Tree-like	Radial star	Grid with diagonals	Hexagonal
	Tributary	Radioconcentric	Lazy grid	Interrupted parallel
		Ring and radial	Loose grid	Irregular
		Spider's web	Modular grid	Kidney
		Starfish	Orthogonal	Net-like
		Umbrella	Quincunx	Organic
			Rectangular	Tangential
			Rectilinear	Topographical-informal
			Tartan grid	Unique
			Warped grid	Warped parallel
				Web pattern

Note: for sources and fuller catalogue see Appendix 4.2.

hybrids; or we can create a continuous spectrum or continuum interpolating between two (or more) basic types.

Structures at different scales

Having arrived at a possible set of elemental types, we can combine these at different scales to create further, hybrid types. Most simply – and recalling one of the approaches of the *Mosborough Master Plan* – we can combine macro scale and micro scale. For example, Figure 4.15 shows permutations of four macro and two micro structures.[27]

Being slightly more heterogeneous, these start to look like accounting for more real cases than the elemental types they are derived from. The top row all look like modern layouts of one type or another – of the kind often depicted as 'discouraged' by neo-traditionalists. The lower row suggests that Soria y Mata's *Ciudad Lineal* is linear at the macro scale but a grid at the micro scale (linear/grid); a New Urbanist style grid appended to a tributary arterial road system (tributary/grid); a traditional city (radial/grid) and a typical planned grid form (grid/grid).[28]

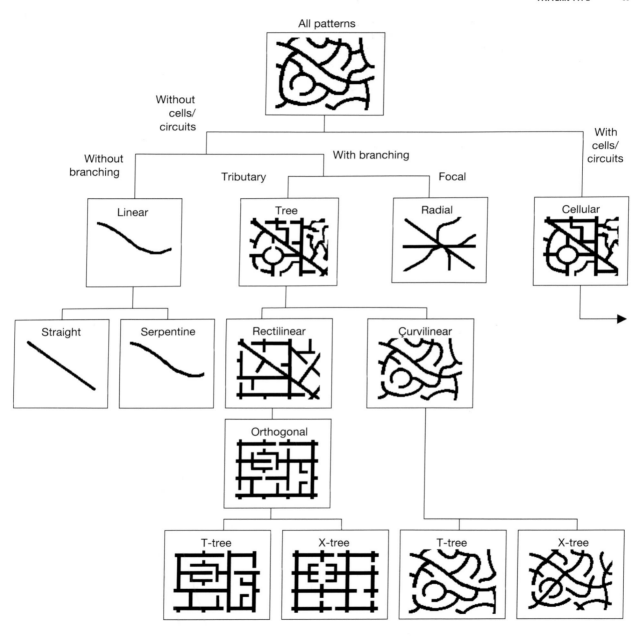

All patterns

Without cells/circuits

With cells/circuits

Without branching

With branching

Tributary

Focal

Linear

Tree

Radial

Cellular

Straight

Serpentine

Rectilinear

Curvilinear

Orthogonal

T-tree

X-tree

T-tree

X-tree

4.14 • Elaborated taxonomy of patterns.

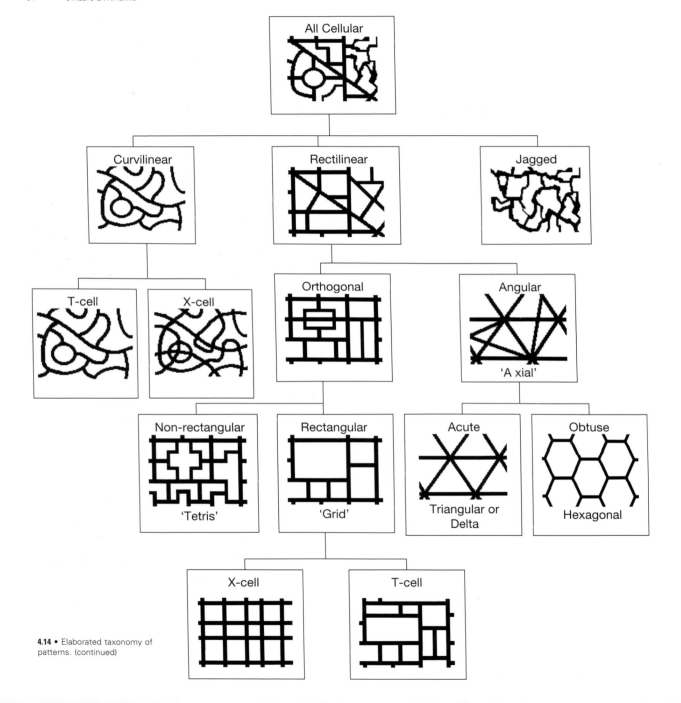

4.14 • Elaborated taxonomy of patterns. (continued)

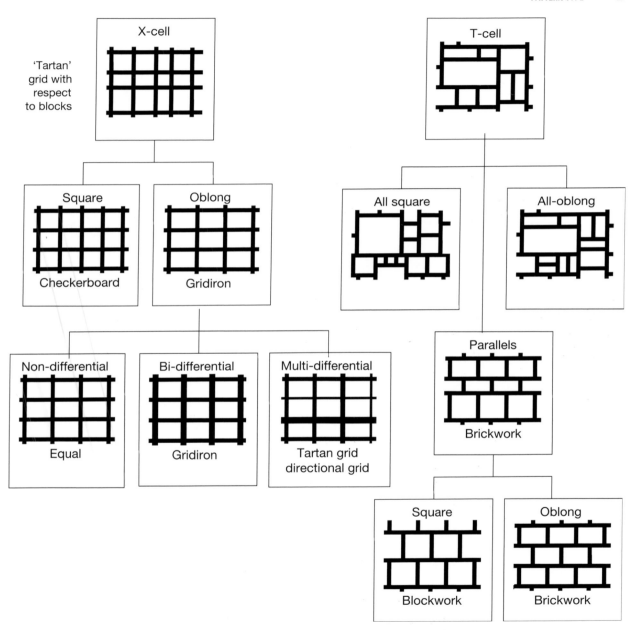

4.14 • Elaborated taxonomy of patterns. (continued)

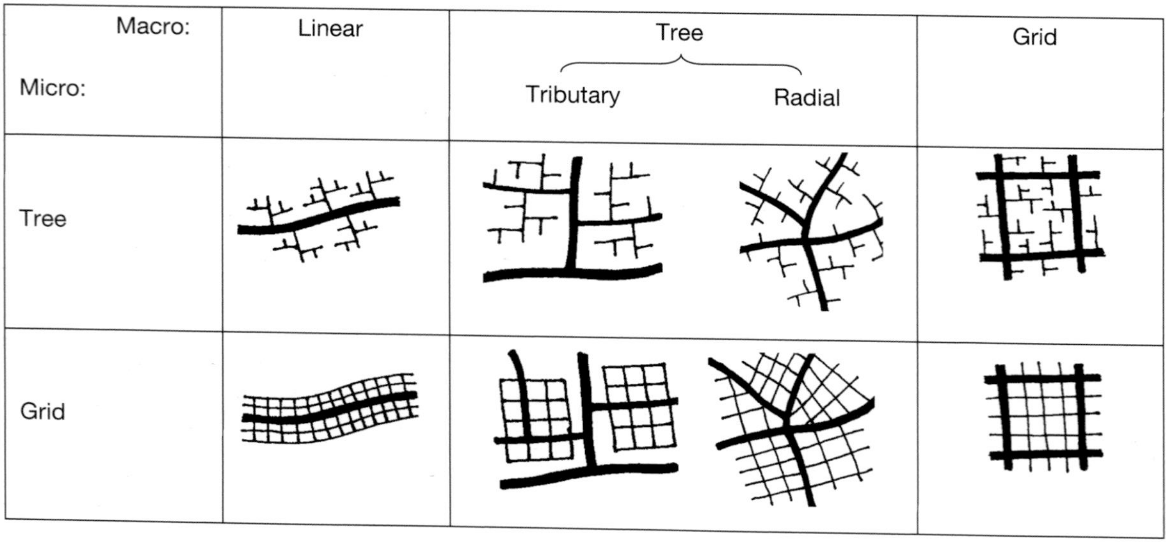

Macro: Micro:	Linear	Tree		Grid
		Tributary	Radial	
Tree				
Grid				

4.15 • Hybrid patterns as permutations of macro and micro scale structures. This echoes the macro/micro permutation exercise of the *Mosborough Master Plan* (Figure 4.3) but uses structures that are felt to be more useful in representing actual types of street pattern.

We could further divide into many different permutations of types, based on different attributes – for example, any combinations of cellular and tree at different levels of scale. As with the homogeneous cases, any degree of resolution is possible in principle; what is important is what is useful in practice.

T- and X-junctions

Another way of creating composite types is to combine different kinds of (non-mutually exclusive) 'elemental' types. In the 'design debate' over urban road layout, one possible useful typology based on permutations is to distinguish between networks with junctions of different type, such as T-junctions, crossroads, and so on. This can be a useful proxy for distinguishing, for example, grid layouts from others.[29]

We can combine the consideration of T- and X-junctions with two of the 'fundamental types' associated with micro structure – cells and trees – to create four basic configurational types. These are rather simple, but can be useful in some circumstances to quickly indicate a particular feature or distinguish between different kinds of tree and grid configuration (Figure 4.16).

We can immediately recognise some correspondence between D-type and T-tree, and correspondence between B-type and X-cell. These, in a sense, represent pure or extreme cases. In contrast, the A-type and C-type

4.16 • Four simple configurational types. Note that the examples shown happen to be rectilinear compositions, but the types themselves are not defined by composition and could equally have been depicted as curvilinear or irregular compositions.

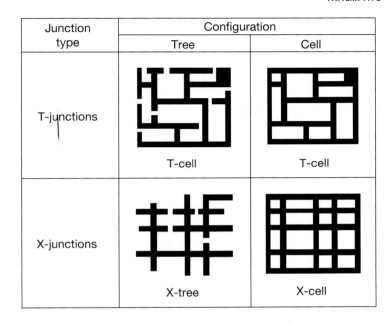

Junction type	Configuration	
	Tree	Cell
T-junctions	T-cell	T-cell
X-junctions	X-tree	X-cell

are both hybrid cases. Their irregularity partly reflects their unplannedness (a topic that shall be returned to in Chapter 6).

QUANTIFYING PATTERN

All grids were *not* created equal.

Paul Groth[30]

We have already seen that distinguishing patterns typically involves discerning regularity in their components parts – for example, a rectangular grid is a pattern made up (in principle, entirely) of rectangular blocks. The recognition of the whole arises from the recognition of the parts. Similarly, the recognition of networks distinguished by possessing T-junctions or X-junctions is based on recognising the properties of constituent parts, in this case, junctions.

Capturing the character of real street patterns, especially, implies the ability to handle heterogeneity. This could imply the proportions of different components present (e.g. proportion of triangular blocks to rectangular blocks, or proportion of T-junctions to X-intersections). Indeed, the very recognition of those elemental components implies quantitatively defined entities: the distinction between triangle and rectangle, or T and X, being essentially based on the numbers 3 and 4.

This section attempts to gain a finer-resolution appreciation of the morphological continuum, by demonstrating some simple quantitative parameters and presentational devices that may be used to analyse and characterise street patterns. The parameters are chosen to home in on features – blocks, crossroads and culs-de-sac – directly associated with 'conventional suburban' and 'neo-traditional' layouts, and hence the 'preferred' and 'discouraged' patterns of the design debate.

Test configurations

Four configurations are used to demonstrate different aspects of quantification. These configurations, shown in Figure 4.17, are based on the earlier ABCD layouts. The quantifications are illustrative of values for A, B C and D layouts, but are not definitive of them.

T ratio and X ratio

First, we can generate a spectrum of configurational types, graduated from those purely composed of T-junctions to those wholly composed of X-junctions. We can define the *T ratio* as the ratio of T-junctions to the total number of junctions, and the *X ratio* as the ratio of X-junctions to the total number of junctions. Clearly, in networks comprising only T-junctions and X-junctions, the sum of the T ratio and the X ratio will equal one. In almost any real street layout, there will be a mixture of T- and X-junctions and the corresponding ratios will lie somewhere between zero and one. Examples are given in Table 4.6.

Cell ratio and cul ratio

Next, we can define the *cul ratio* as the ratio of culs-de-sac to the total number of culs-de-sac plus cells; and the *cell ratio* is the ratio of cells to the total number of culs-de-sac plus cells. The cul ratio and cell ratio sum to one. Clearly, in a pure 'tree' layout containing only branching culs-de-sac, there will be no cells; the cul ratio will be one and the cell ratio zero. Conversely, in a purely cellular layout, such as pure grid, there will no culs-de-sac; in this case, the cul ratio will be zero and the cell ratio will be one. In almost any real street layout, there will be a mixture of the two. Examples are given in Table 4.7.

Combined plot

Next, we can plot T ratio–X ratio against cell ratio–cul ratio, to generate a two-dimensional space (Figure 4.18).

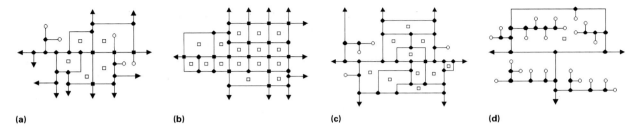

(a)   **(b)**   **(c)**   **(d)**

4.17 • Test configurations. These correspond to the ABCD layouts given in Figure 4.10. For quantified parameters see Tables 4.6–4.8.

Table 4.6 T-ratio and X-ratio for test configurations in Figure 4.17

Example configuration	A	B	C	D
No. of three-way junctions (●)	16	13	27	24
No. of four-way junctions (■)	4	14	1	0
Total no. of junction nodes	20	27	28	24
T-ratio	0.8	0.48	0.96	1.0
X-ratio	0.2	0.62	0.04	0.0

Table 4.7 Cell and cul ratios for test configurations in Figure 4.17

Example configuration	A	B	C	D
No. of cells (□)	5	16	10	1
No. of culs-de-sac (○)	5	0	4	21
Total	10	16	14	22
Cell ratio	0.5	1.0	0.71	0.05
Cul ratio	0.5	0.0	0.29	0.95

Table 4.8 Nodegram parameters for test configurations in Figure 4.17 (in %)

Example configuration	A	B	C	D
Culs-de-sac (○)	20	0	13	47
T-junctions (●)	64	48	84	53
X-junctions (■)	16	52	3	0

4.18 • T and X ratios plotted against cul and cell ratios. The plot shows the positions of example configurations A, B, C and D shown in Figure 4.17.

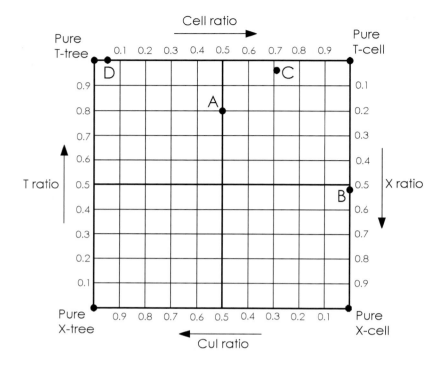

This degree of quantification helps describe how 'griddy' or 'tree-like' the street network configurations are, relative to the four 'pure' cases given earlier in Figure 4.16 – that now form the vertices of Figure 4.18. We can note that configuration A lies midway between being a pure T-tree and a pure T-cell; configuration C is mostly a T-cell; configuration B is mostly X-grid and D is mostly T-tree.[31]

The nodegram

A final suggested analysis is to consider the relationship between T-junctions, X-junctions and culs-de-sac (Table 4.8). These may be plotted in a triangular diagram, which we can call the *nodegram* – so-called since it distinguishes the proportions of different types of nodes (Figure 4.19).[32]

Grid-like layouts lie over to the right, while the tributary and tree-like networks are over to the left. On the left diagonal bound are networks with no four-way junctions (typical of modern suburban layouts), while the right diagonal bound represents networks with no culs-de-sac. We can trace the post-war shift from network types on the right-hand side to those on the

4.19 • The nodegram. Each point represents a network, according to its proportion of T-junctions, X-junctions and culs-de-sac, thereby giving a quantified graphical impression of the 'morphological continuum'.

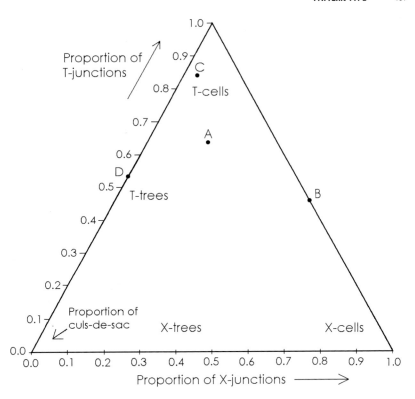

left-hand side – the vogue for the use of culs-de-sac and the decline in crossroads – followed by contemporary aspirations towards a shift back to the right. The nodegram can therefore reflect the broad fluctuations in the favourability of different kinds of street pattern over the years.

CONCLUSIONS

This chapter has demonstrated a number of ways of characterising street pattern, through a variety of properties, typologies and presentational devices. An emergent finding is that there is no single best typology: what kind of typology is best to use in practice will depend crucially on the purpose of that typology – for example, if it is intended as a comprehensive catalogue of any theoretically possible patterns, or a simpler, more selective set of types for practical application to real street patterns.

The characterisations of street pattern in this chapter can be seen to clarify some issues of pattern raised in Chapter 2. The distinctions between composition and configuration, and the characterisations of configurations based on trees versus cells, and T-junctions versus X-junctions, could help to resolve some of the issues pertaining to pattern specification raised in Chapter 2. That is, the various characterisations proposed here could help advocates of properties such as clarity, coherence and connectivity to express those properties in distinct compositional or configurational terms. The graphic presentations allow the demonstration of areas – however precisely or fuzzily identified – in which 'preferred' or 'discouraged' patterns might lie. At the very least, the analysis demonstrates that there is a diversity of such patterns available for working with – not simply one kind of 'tree' and one kind of 'grid'.

From the analysis of this chapter, we can also see that patterns are not just monolithic objects, but their character is strongly influenced by their constituent parts. It is therefore useful to consider what the key constituent parts are to study, in order to influence onward design.

The key constituent parts are in a sense 'active ingredients'. The London Underground diagrams (Figure 4.9) tell us something about the 'active ingredients' of networks. For the London Underground user, it is not the absolute geometry of curvature of the lines, or the shape of the interstices between lines that is important: what is important is the way the lines give access to different stations, and connect up with other lines. In this case, configuration is more significant than composition.

This chapter has demonstrated some simple quantifications of constituent properties of configuration. In addressing the constituent elements of networks such as nodes and circuits, the analysis of this chapter has touched on a more general theoretical tradition of network representation and analysis. It will be useful to take a closer look at these network analysis methods, to pave the way towards a more detailed understanding of structure. This structure is, to a significant extent, related to how component routes connect up to form a whole structure. Routes and route structures are the primary subject of the next two chapters, which address the quantification of structural properties of connectivity and heterogeneity.

NOTES

1   Haggett and Chorley (1969: 57). Lord and Wilson (1984) also address the mathematical description of shape and form.
2   Brindle (1996); Dawkins (1991: 275), after Gould.
3   Hanson (1989: 81).
4   Hanson (1989: 81).
5   Hillier (1987).

6   Dupree (1987: 23); Dickinson (1961: 333).

7   For example, a 'polycentric' form may be depicted as an articulated structure, with the appearance of flexibility and subtlety, whereas a 'compact city' form may sometimes be depicted as a monolithic 'blob', and therefore characterised (caricatured) as being rigid and crude.

8   Lynch (1981: 453).

9   Keeble (1969: 110, 112).

10 Clearly, street pattern is just one of a range of ways in which cities may be categorised or 'typed'. See, for example, King's presentation of a systematic list of over 20 ways of 'typing' cities (1994: 140).

11 Brindle (1996: 52, 97).

12 Groth (1981).

13 Hacking (1983).

14 Unwin (1920: 17); Keeble (1969: 100).

15 Sitte ([1889] 1945: 59); DoE/DoT (1992: 8); Satoh (1998).

16 Clifford Culpin and Partners (1969).

17 For example, the 'centralised micro-structure' is a twelve-pointed star – a very unlikely kind of street intersection to be used as a unit of urban structure. The 'dispersed micro-structure' shows a triangular net – this implies a succession of six-pointed stars on a repetitive basis, which is again unlikely to prevail to any significant extent in practice. Even the so-called 'linear micro-structure' appears to imply an unrecognisably repetitive use of culs-de-sac.

18 The fundamental significance of the three elemental types is open to question. Perhaps surprisingly, the simple rectangular grid is not considered an elemental type, but as a combination of proportions of the centralised, linear and dispersed forms.

19 Haggett and Chorley (1969). This subdivision of types is also echoed by transport analysts Bell and Iida (1997).

20 Larkham and Jones (1991: 14); Morris (1994: 229).

21 We could use either 'distributary' or 'distributory'. The adjective 'distributory' is used by Buchanan, although not specifically denoting a particular configuration.

22 Topology relates to non-metric information: connectivity, orientation, adjacency and containment (Laurini and Thompson, 1992: 41); or proximity, separation, succession, continuity and closure, but not permanent distances, angles and areas, see Norberg-Schulz (1975: 430).

23 For the history of the London Underground map/diagram, see Garland (1994).

24 Lynch considers the branching and the radial to be associated (1962). Morlok (1967) considers both tree and linear to be 'spinal'.

25 The rationale for creating a hierarchically ordered taxonomy (dendrogram) is to make the most useful groupings and points of distinction that can capture the greatest amount of differentiation in the fewest moves. Which subdivisions and order of subdivisions are chosen will depend on at least three factors: the

ultimate purpose and intended use of the classification; the occurrence of common or typical patterns; and the parsimony of the theoretical structure.

26 Strictly speaking, the categories in Table 4.5 are based on connotation (e.g. grid-like) rather than pure configuration (e.g. cellular with no pendant branches). This demonstrates that the theoretical taxonomy of Figure 4.13 can accommodate the patterns encountered in practice. As it happens, Table 4.5 gives a reasonable balance in category size, indicating a reasonable reconciliation of the plurality of patterns with a practical number of labels.

27 The 'tributary' tree and the cellular grid are both useful at any scale, whereas the linear and radial forms are most useful at the macro scale only. That is, real settlement layouts tend to show a characteristic radial, linear or grid pattern for their macro-structure, with their micro-structure being grid or tree-like. This is because a radial macro pattern tends to resolve itself at the micro scale into either a grid-like mesh or a tree form, while the linear form at the micro scale is a trivial case of a single-link network.

28 Soria y Mata (1892).

29 Such methods have been used, for example, by Handy (1992), Cervero (1996) and Southworth and Ben-Joseph (1997).

30 Groth (1981: 68).

31 Note that a configuration representing the B-type could have been drawn as a more regular grid with a much higher proportion of X-junctions; however, the B-type layout as drawn demonstrates, in a sense, how low the actual proportion of X-junctions can be for a grid still to look like a grid.

32 This type of triaxial diagram is conventionally used in soil mechanics to represent proportions of sands, silts and clays in samples of soil (Terzaghi and Peck, 1948; Oglesby and Hicks, 1982).

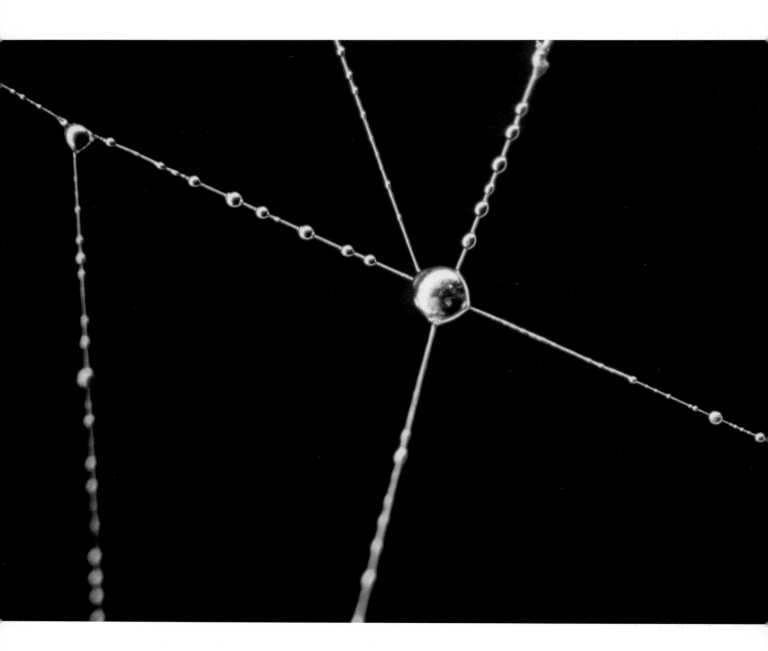

5.0 • Spider's web node

5 ROUTE STRUCTURE

The graph eliminates the flesh and blood, as represented by the sinuosities and the flows . . . for what is left is the skeleton. As in any skeleton, there are links joined at specific places . . . By reducing the complex transportation network to its fundamental elements of nodes and links, it is possible to evaluate alternative structures.

Lowe and Moryadas, *The Geography of Movement*[1]

In a general sense, the term structure alludes to the relationship of parts to each other and to the whole.[2] This means that structure has a subtle duality of interpretation. From the point of view of an individual element, structure implies exterior relationships – to things outside, to a larger unity. From the point of view of the whole, structure alludes to parts within, and differentiation. In a sense, then, structure is a two-way street.

Whatever else we say about urban patterns, we can recognise that a street pattern comprises elemental parts – streets. These relate fundamentally to paths of movement: if there is no movement, there is no street. The character of a whole street pattern will relate to the characteristics of those parts, and the way they fit together. This is a fundamental aspect of this chapter – and the rest of the book.

There is a variety of traditions for analysing urban patterns, from urban morphology to fractals and cellular automata.[3] This chapter is concerned with the structural aspects of street patterns; to gain an understanding of these, the chapter first investigates two existing methods of quantitative analysis – conventional transport network analysis and space syntax. The chapter then develops and demonstrates a new alternative – route structure analysis – that may be used to represent, analyse and characterise streets and street patterns. Route structure analysis will be applied to generate new expressions of route type as well as being used to differentiate types of network, based on their structure of routes.

NETWORK REPRESENTATION AND ANALYSIS

Graph theory is a branch of mathematics that provides a means of analysing the structure of relationships between elements. A graph is a set of discrete points joined by lines: these may be referred to respectively as vertices and edges. In a graph, it is the topological arrangement between elements that is important, rather than the absolute geometry or scale of the elements represented (Figure 5.1).

Graph theory has had a wide range of applications, including electrical circuits, engineering structure, linguistic structures, anthropology, sociology, management, transport geography and built form. This section reviews two kinds of analysis based on graph theory: conventional transport network analysis, and space syntax, a method of analysing urban spatial structure.[4]

Conventional transport network analysis

When a transport network is represented conventionally as a graph, the links in the network become edges in the graph, and the nodes (e.g. junctions, or cities) become vertices in the graph (Figure 5.1(d)).[5] It is then possible to use various graph-theoretical indicators to analyse network structure and capture properties such as connectivity.

In general, graph theoretic analysis may be said to use vertices to represent the primary elements, and edges to represent the relationships between those elements. In the first three cases in Figure 5.1, the vertices clearly represent the primary elements: continental landmasses, people and rooms. The edges represent relationships between these: they are effectively secondary or contingent. For example, inter-professional relationships do not exist without professions. This approach effectively suits situations where we wish to focus on nodes, and distinguish a hierarchy of nodes.

In the case of transportation networks (Figure 5.1(d)), the primary elements could be the nodes (cities) which are joined by lines of movement; or the primary elements could be lines of movement, joining at nodes (junctions). Yet either way, both are represented by a graph in which the nodal points are vertices and the lines of movement are edges.

This form of representation suits the analysis of airline networks, or rail or road networks regarded at a low resolution, where nodes are significant points of terminus or interchange (Figure 5.2(a)). It also suits small-scale pedestrian paths through space, where the paths are articulated into

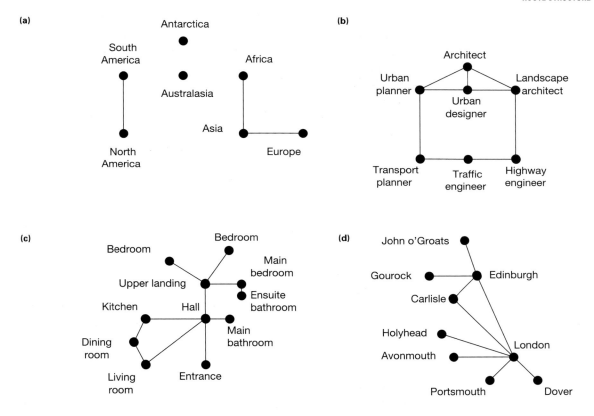

(a)

Antarctica

South
America

Africa

Australasia

Asia

North
America   Europe

(b)

Architect

Urban
planner   Landscape
architect

Urban
designer

Transport
planner   Traffic
engineer   Highway
engineer

(c)

Bedroom

Bedroom

Main
bedroom

Upper landing

Ensuite
bathroom

Kitchen   Hall

Main
bathroom

Dining
room

Living
room   Entrance

(d)

John o'Groats

Gourock   Edinburgh

Carlisle

Holyhead   London

Avonmouth

Portsmouth   Dover

5.1 • Graph representations. (a) Landmasses.
(b) People. (c) Rooms. (d) Networks.

separate trajectories, from point to point (Figure 5.2(c)). In these cases, the nodes are the points of focus, and the lines of movement – which may not correspond to distinct pieces of infrastructure – are only important insofar as they represent relationships between the nodes.

However, this convention is less directly effective for networks in which the routes themselves are the main focus of attention. For example, in street networks, it is often the status of different types of route that is the principal concern; junctions and intersections are effectively by-products of routes meeting or crossing. In street networks, significantly, the lines of movement have continuity through nodes, and the differential continuity creates a structure of through streets and side streets. When a street network is represented directly as a graph (Figure 5.2(b)), the representation does not intrinsically distinguish this structure. Continuity of routes may be inferred, but is not built into the representation.

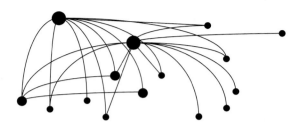

(a)

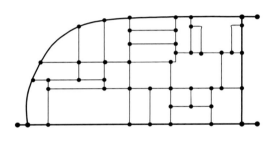

(b)

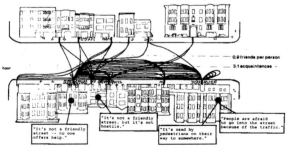

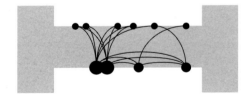

(c)

5.2 • Networks of circulation at different scales.
(a) The hub-and-spoke pattern of an airline
network: a 'hierarchy of nodes'. (b) A street
network. Routes are continuous through nodes,
creating a 'hierarchy of routes'. (c) Network of
pedestrian paths. A 'hierarchy of nodes' again.

5.3 • Two street networks compared.
Each network has 23 links and 18 nodes.
(a) Traditional 'focal web'. (b) Suburban 'layered
loops'. (c) Network graph of (a). (d) Network
graph of (b).

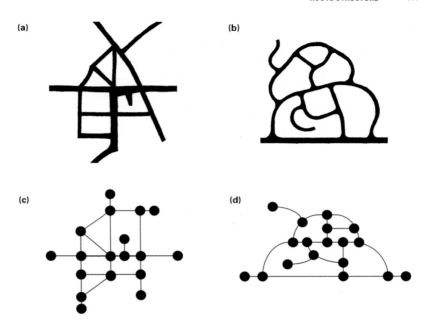

(a)

(b)

(c)

(d)

(a)

(b)

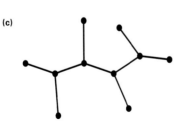

(c)

5.4 • Two street layouts with the same graph
structure. (a) 'High street'. (b) 'Tributary'.
(c) Same graph for both.

This means that conventional graph-theoretic representation does not necessarily distinguish between the kinds of structure that are of interest to urban designers and planners in debates about the form of urban layout (Figure 5.3).

Although the layouts in Figure 5.3(a) and (b) would appear to represent quite different kinds of layout in urban spatial terms, their network configurations expressed as graphs have the same number of links and nodes. Therefore, graph-theoretical indicators cannot necessarily distinguish the particular kinds of structure or hierarchy that these two layouts possess. Indeed, two quite different kinds of urban layout could have exactly the same topology as represented in conventional graph-theoretical terms (Figure 5.4).

This suggests the need to consider alternative forms of analysis, that can appropriately represent the structure of urban street networks, by putting the lines of movement centre stage.

Space syntax

Space syntax is a method of configurational analysis developed by Bill Hillier and associates, which has been applied to the structure of space in buildings

5.5 • Spatial structure as captured by a system of axial lines. (a) Plan of streetspace. (b) Axial lines superimposed.

(a) **(b)**

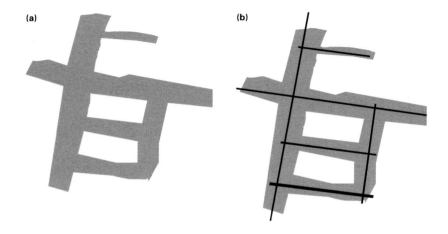

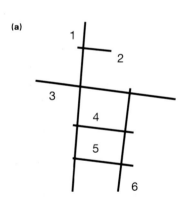

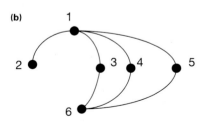

5.6 • Conversion of axial map into a graph. (a) Axial map. (b) Corresponding graph.

and the structure of urban space.[6] Space syntax effectively recognises that the 'link' elements in a layout may have significant spatial presence. For example, within a building, a corridor has a definite spatial extent (that is definable in the same way as the spatial extent of the rooms), rather than being just a connection between spaces (e.g. like a doorway or threshold between rooms). In a modernist urban structure, land use zones and roads may be represented separately as nodes and links, but in a traditional urban street network, the streets themselves are significant spatial entities.

Space syntax analysis is based on the configuration of 'axial lines of sight', where the axial lines reflect the geometry of bounded space (Figure 5.5).

The basic method of analysis boils down to identifying axial lines (which have some correspondence to lines of movement, or physical routes) and transforming these lines into the *vertices* of a graph, while the axial intersections become the *edges*. This transformation creates a graph structure 'underlying' the network structure. The resulting graph may be analysed using conventional graph-theoretic measures – but where the primary elements in the graph (i.e. vertices) represent lines of movement (Figure 5.6).

Since axial lines can continue through intersections, each line has a value of connectivity that relates to the number of intersections along its length. This contrasts with the conventional direct application of graph theory to transport networks, where links terminate at nodes (junctions).

In addition to concepts of connectivity, space syntax also makes use of the concept of *depth*, which is a measure of network 'distance' – steps of adjacency – between network components. The depth of any axial line relative to any other can be calculated, and hence an average depth can be calculated for the whole network. In Figure 5.6, for example, line 6 is the 'deepest' with respect to line 1, and vice versa. The way in which depth is distributed about major streets, which tend to be constituted by the most 'integrated' lines, gives an impression of a 'hierarchy', or distinction between major and minor routes, which may equate with intensity of use.[7]

Space syntax has provided some important insights into the structure of urban street networks. For example, Hillier and associates have contrasted the structural properties of successful traditional settlements with dysfunctional quasi-traditional housing estates, demonstrating how their success or failure is significantly related to their layout structure, rather than their architectural style. This has lessons for neo-traditional urbanism, since it implies the importance of a clear grasp of the spatial structure of development, and not just the form of the buildings.[8]

The focus on linear elements sets space syntax apart from the conventional graph-theoretical treatment of networks discussed earlier. It captures properties of urban street networks that other methods based on links and nodes do not. If we look again at the two small network examples, we see that space syntax successfully distinguishes these as distinct structures (Figure 5.7).

Note, however, that while Figure 5.7(e) reveals the central 'high street' as the least deep line, in Figure 5.7(f) the least deep (most integrated) line is one of the side roads. This may or may not be significant – depending on whether the axial map is going to be used as the basis of predicting movement, as well as describing spatial structure.

Clearly, the structural depiction of any layout will depend on the objective of the depiction, and on the 'object' chosen for selection in the first place – where the boundaries of the plan are drawn, and which spaces within it are selected for representation. In this respect, space syntax is no more subjective than conventional transport network analysis, whose connectivity values will depend on whether the network representation includes, for example, all minor roads and pedestrian links and passageways. Any network representation could be considered subjective; the key point is whether a given representation actually captures what it sets out to capture.

The effectiveness of space syntax for representing movement structure will depend on how strongly axial lines of sight correspond with lines of movement. In the bounded space of a traditional street grid, these typically have a good fit. But in a modern open plan layout, the correspondence is not necessarily reliable. Movement – especially vehicular movement –

5.7 • Two street layouts differentiated by space syntax. (a) High street. (b) Modern tributary. (c) Axial map (6 lines). (d) Axial map (9 lines). (e) Graph (6 vertices). (f) Graph (9 vertices).

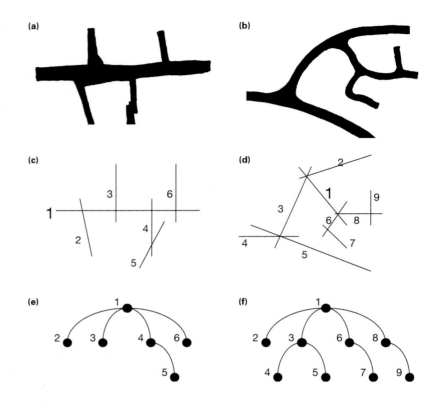

may be more related to the continuity of roads and paths as routes, than on their intervisibility across space.

This opens up the question of what might be the most appropriate elemental units for representing the 'active ingredients' of movement structure.[9] In discussing the workings of space syntax, Bill Hillier draws attention to the importance of the connective topology of street grids, stressing that 'connectivities . . . and their topological arrangement into a network by the geometry of the system, are by far the most important formal attributes of the system from the point of view of movement'; and 'Deviation . . . from strict rectilinearity will make no difference provided the connective topology of an orthogonal grid is realised.'[10] This seems to suggest that it is the abstract connectivity of a system that is important (configuration), rather than the absolute disposition of space (composition); and it implies that continuity of through routes is more important than their strict linearity of alignment.

This appeal to connectivity and continuity seems to point essentially to the importance of lines of movement – but does not seem inevitably to point to 'axial lines of sight', a unit of intervisibility which builds in deviations from rectilinearity in absolute space. In other words, while the axial line is useful for some purposes, it is not the *only* unit on which to base measures of connectivity or continuity of lines of movement. This opens up the horizon to consider an alternative, an analysis based on *routes* of movement.

ROUTE STRUCTURE

Route structure analysis is based on the contention that the structure of a network is a product of the way that the routes connect up with each other. This means that the character of the whole is influenced by the character of the parts and the way they fit together, collectively. Conversely, the character of the parts may be defined by how they relate to each other and to the whole.

The basic element of route structure is the *route*, where a route is a linear element which may be continuous through junctions with other routes. Routes are different from *links*, which span only from one node to the next. To the extent that routes may be more or less continuous – some shorter, others longer – then different kinds of route will be differentiated, and recognition of *route type* becomes possible.

This section sets out some definitions and conventions for route structures, and how these may be used to represent street networks.

The formation of routes from links

A *route* may be considered as a linear aggregation of links, just as a link is a linear aggregation of points. Figure 5.8 shows a street layout – (a), represented conventionally as a graph comprising twelve links – (b), which is subsequently converted into a *route structure* comprising six routes – (c).

The points at which links are joined together to form routes may be referred to as *joints*. We can establish a convention that each joint has one *through route* through it, formed by conjoining two links. Therefore, at each joint the number of links will exceed the number of routes by one; and for the whole network, the number of links will exceed the number of routes by the number of joints. This gives us a fundamental relationship between routes, links and joints (Box 5).

For example, in Figure 5.8, there are twelve links and six nodes where links meet, which will form joints. Hence we obtain six routes.

(a)

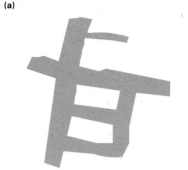

(b)

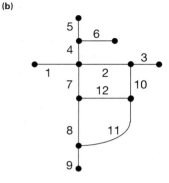

(c)

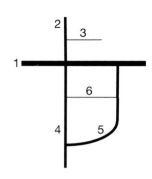

5.8 • Layout plan, network graph and route structure. (a) Layout plan. (b) Graph of 12 links. (c) Route structure comprising 6 routes.

BOX 5. ROUTES AND JOINTS

1. A route comprises a link or a linear aggregation of conjoined links.
2. A joint is a node with one, and only one, conjoined route passing through it.

Each joint in a structure *reduces by one* the number of routes relative to the number of links. Hence: Routes = Links – Joints. See Appendix 5 for more elaboration on these conventions.

Alternative representations

The joining up of links to form routes implies a choice as to which links become through routes. This choice will affect the structural character of the resulting representation. There is no single 'correct' route structural representation of a given graph of nodes and links, nor automatic correspondence between the set of nodes and links and the set of routes formed from it. The fact that the graph representation in Figure 5.3(c) could represent either a 'high street' (Figure 5.3(a)) or a tributary (Figure 5.3(b)) demonstrates that the route structural interpretation must add something (or retain something from the original plan) not present in the bare graph.

This may appear to introduce a degree of indeterminacy into the proceedings. However, this is no different from the degree of indeterminacy in selecting which links are included in the network in the first place: which parts of a street plan are recognised as the object of analysis, and where the boundaries of the network are drawn. This situation applies equally to conventional transport network analysis and to space syntax. As with these other methods, the specification of elements for analysis relies on contextual interpretation. In each case, a judgement is necessary to allow significant characteristics of the actual site context to be taken into account, for the particular purposes of the analysis. This is explained by Buckwalter:

> Network models consist of abstractions designed to encompass
> the *significant aspects* of real world features while omitting details.
> The usefulness of network analysis results from reducing the
> complexity of real systems, but it depends on *judgement* about
> significance because this controls the relevance of the feature
> abstractions. Nevertheless, geographers have produced little literature
> on the judgement decisions of converting features into model
> abstractions. Instead, the emphasis has been on mathematical
> concepts of topology and network structure. Perhaps this is not
> surprising because feature abstraction is a *subjective* process.
> [emphases added][11]

In other words, topology and network structure can be cleanly and objectively analysed, only once they have been abstracted subjectively from the possibly messy reality on the ground.

The judgement on 'feature abstraction' will be concerned with the relationship between what is being represented and the key determinants of operation at that scale. Consideration of Figures 5.9 and 5.10 suggests that there is not a one-to-one relationship between a physical situation and its abstract representation.

Figure 5.10 focuses on the crossroads – the street pattern context. Of the different representations, none is 'right' or 'wrong' of itself. Some may be more useful than others, for different purposes. Clearly, only (a) directly represents the shape and area of the streetspace. The space syntax representation (b) captures the straight-through orientation of the lines of sight, but does not 'see' the junction as such. The conventional graph representation (d) loses the angular orientation of the junction arms, but records the presence of the junction – although not the junction priority, which would have to be coded into the description of the node. Finally, the route structure

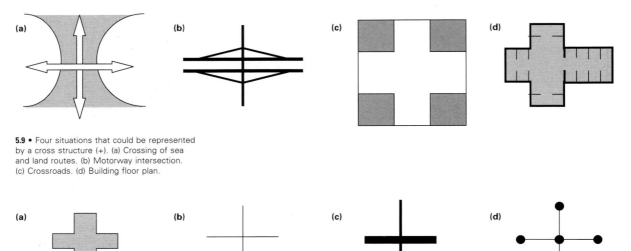

5.9 • Four situations that could be represented by a cross structure (+). (a) Crossing of sea and land routes. (b) Motorway intersection. (c) Crossroads. (d) Building floor plan.

5.10 • Four ways of representing a crossroads. (a) One area (dodecagon). (b) Two axial lines. (c) Three routes. (d) Four links.

representation (c) represents the junction as comprising one through route and two side routes. This captures the sense of continuity, hierarchy and structure present at this location – this is what route structure representation does.

Contextual interpretation

The choice of inclusion of links, and aggregation of those links into routes, will influence how meaningful are the results of the abstract analysis of the resulting route structure.

In route structure analysis, the aggregation of links into routes is supposed to represent the most continuous paths of movement through a junction. A suggestion for determining appropriate patterns of aggregation that would give rise to meaningful route structures is as follows.

1. Where there is a designated route classification known, this classification can be used to form routes. Hence, at any junction, a single through route may be selected from two links with the same route designation (e.g. 'A' road number).
2. Where the route structure is not resolved by (1), then actual junction priority may be used, where known. That is, at any junction where a single through route has priority, that route is allocated as 'the' through route.
3. Where the route structure is not resolved by (1) or (2), then continuity of physical alignment may be used to select the through route. This tactic may

5.11 • Two street layouts differentiated by route structure analysis. (a) High street. (b) Tributary. (c) Route structure representation (5 routes, 4 joints). (d) Route structure representation (5 routes, 4 joints). (e) Graph (5 vertices, 4 edges). (f) Graph (5 vertices, 4 edges).

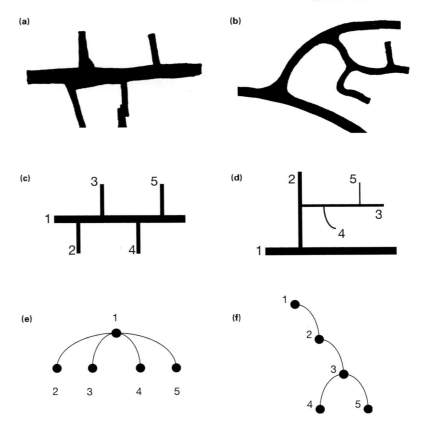

be useful where working (only) from a plan rather than site experience. Other possible means of determining the through route would be continuity of street name, or traffic flow patterns, where known.

Figure 5.11 demonstrates the earlier pair of layouts, this time analysed using route structure analysis. Here, the underlying graphs (i.e. (e) and (f)) *are* different. Whichever way round (e) and (f) might be contorted, it is clear that their configurations are not the same. It is this differentiation, arising out of the recognition of continuous routes, that allows route structure to be resolved, and hence analysed.

Effectively, the key issue is whether the set of graph configurations here (Figure 5.11(e) and (f)) provides a better representation of the arrangement of streets than the graphs obtained using conventional transport network analysis (Figure 5.3(c)) or space syntax (Figure 5.7(e) and (f)).

On this matter, we may note that the graph structures of the route structure representation clearly show the contrast between Figure 5.11(e) which expresses the 'focal' nature of the main street – connecting to all other streets – while Figure 5.11(f) expresses the somewhat isolating effect of the layers of hierarchy, with the final culs-de-sac at some remove from the main road. This therefore gives a good representation of the intuitively held understanding of significant features of street patterns, not only their connectivity, but their continuity of routes and their hierarchy of depth.

ROUTE STRUCTURE PROPERTIES

Route structure analysis is built on three basic route properties: continuity, connectivity and depth. These three properties are now defined and then their application is demonstrated.

Continuity, connectivity and depth

Continuity is taken as the number of links that a route is made up of, or the length of a route measured in links (l). The label 'continuity' reflects how many junctions a route is continuous through.

Connectivity is taken as the number of routes with which a given route connects (c). Connectivity reflects both the number and nodality of joints along a route.

Figure 5.12 demonstrates the distinction between continuity and connectivity. Route 1.1 is said to be more *continuous* than route 1.2.1 – even though the former might end in a cul-de-sac – since it is continuous through a junction, and comprises two links, (i.e. l = 2). Route 1.1 is also more *connective* than route 1.2.1 because the former connects with three routes in total (c = 3), while the latter connects only to two (c = 2). Meanwhile, route 1.2 is the most connective route (c = 4).

Depth measures how distant a route is from a particular 'datum', measured in number of steps of adjacency (d). The more steps distant a route is from the datum, the 'deeper' it is; the fewer steps distant, the 'shallower'.

The convention used here will be that the datum route will have a depth of 1, and routes connecting directly to the datum will have a depth of 2, and so on. Routes may be numerically labelled according to their branching. Hence, the route labelled '2' in Figure 5.8(c) becomes route '1.1' in Figure 5.12, and route '3' becomes '1.1.1'. In this way, length of the label reflects the depth of the route.

The pattern of depth of routes in a network will be affected by the choice of *datum*. In principle, a datum could be

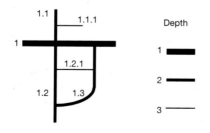

5.12 • Example illustrating continuity, connectivity and depth of routes.

1.   the national route network (e.g. the 'A' road network);
2.   the exterior to a sub-network;
3.   the network of routes used by public transport; or
4.   any selected route (the 'datum route').

In this book, the fourth convention will be adopted, that is, to measure depth from a single datum route, selected by judgement, such that the datum reflects outward strategic linkage to the wider network (e.g. regional or national linkage). The selection of the datum is no more or less arbitrary than the selection of network to be analysed in the first place – given that most urban networks are selective sub-networks of national or continental networks. The important point is to be consistent in choosing the datum when comparing across networks.

Illustrations of the basic route-structural properties

Route structure analysis can now be demonstrated via application to an actual street network. The example chosen is Bayswater, a nineteenth-century suburb of inner London, equating with a 'traditional' urban layout, a kind of irregular grid. The main through route is Bayswater Road – an extension of Oxford Street, the A40, that goes not only to Oxford but ultimately to Fishguard on the west coast of Wales.

The Bayswater network is shown as a street plan (Figure 5.13(a)), from which a conventional network graph of nodes and links is abstracted (Figure 5.13(b)). In total, there are 73 links and 49 nodes. Of the 49 nodes, 46 are junctions proper – represented as joints – while the remaining 3 nodes represent external connections.

The 73 links and 46 junctions can be formed into a number of possible permutations of routes, each a potential route structure representation. In fact, there are over two hundred thousand million *million million* possibilities (283 614 019 828 880 035 069 728 to be precise – see Appendix 6.2) each representing a possible permutation of junction priority, or a possible route structure representation. Nevertheless, we know – from Box 5 – that whatever pattern is selected, the number of routes formed will be 73 – 46 = 27.

In choosing a route-structural representation of the Bayswater network, we can be guided by the official route classification and actual junction priority, to form a selected route structure (Figure 5.13(c)). The bottom route (Bayswater Road) is taken as the 'datum' (labelled route 1; depth 1). The depth of all other routes is measured from this datum route. The resulting values of continuity, connectivity and depth are given in Table 5.1.

(a)

(b)

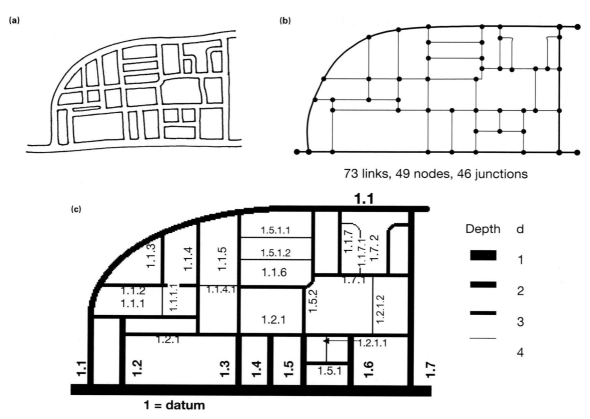

73 links, 49 nodes, 46 junctions

(c)

1.1

1 = datum

27 routes, 46 joints; maximum depth 4

5.13 • Representations of the Bayswater
network. (a) Street plan representation.
(b) Graph representation (links and nodes).
(c) Route structure representation.

Already, we can see that route structure analysis says something about
the network through its structure of individual routes. (Clearly, graph-
theoretic measures could not express route properties, since they possess
no routes, only links.) We can see a general distribution of a small number
of long, connective routes and a larger number of shorter routes. Note that
the deepest routes are short: all routes at depth 4 are one link long. Yet
even short, deep routes can be *relatively* connective (e.g. Dawson Place
East, route 1.1.4.1); while routes adjoining the datum – having low absolute
depth – can yet be *relatively* deep (e.g. Palace Court, route 1.4).

This route structure analysis also tell us something about the character
of the network as a whole. The network character is of significance to the
following chapter, and the reader primarily interested in network type might

Table 5.1 Bayswater network: continuity, connectivity and depth

Route name	Route	Continuity[a]: l	Connectivity: c	Depth: d	Route type[b]
Bayswater Road	1	8	7	1	a
Pembridge Rd/Westbourne Gr.	1.1	9	9	2	b
Pembridge Gardens	1.2	2	3	2	c
Ossington Street	1.3	1	3	2	d
Palace Court	1.4	1	2	2	e
St Petersburg Place	1.5	2	4	2	f
Bark Place	1.6	2	3	2	c
Queensway	1.7	4	5	2	g
Pembridge Square	1.1.1	3	4	3	h
Dawson Place (West)	1.1.2	2	5	3	i
Pembridge Place (North)	1.1.3	1	3	3	j
Chepstow Place	1.1.4	3	5	3	k
Hereford Road	1.1.5	4	7	3	l
Garaway Road/Princes Sq (Sth)	1.1.6	5	7	3	m
Kensington Gardens Sq (West)	1.1.7	2	3	3	n
Moscow Road	1.2.1	8	11	3	o
Orme Lane	1.5.1	2	3	3	n
Ilchester Gardens	1.5.2	1	3	3	j
Porchester	1.7.1	5	6	3	p
Redan Place	1.7.2	1	2	3	q
Pembridge Place (South)	1.1.1.1	1	3	4	r
Dawson Place (East)	1.1.4.1	1	4	4	s
Leinster Square	1.1.5.1	1	2	4	t
Princes Square (North)	1.1.5.2	1	2	4	t
Kensington Gardens Sq (East)	1.1.7.1	1	2	4	t
St Petersburg Mews	1.2.1.1	1	2	4	t
Salem Road	1.2.1.2	1	2	4	t
Network total		73	112	79	20 types

Notes

(a) The sum of continuities equals the number of links (73).

(b) This identifies routes by their specific combination of continuity, connectivity and depth. This network has 20 such route types (a–t).

advance directly to Chapter 6 at this point. Otherwise, it will be fruitful to proceed to demonstrate what these route-structural properties tell us about the character of the individual routes.

ROUTE TYPE

Route structure analysis can be used to define different types of route, based on their combination of continuity, connectivity and depth. In terms

Table 5.2 **Suggested route types based on structural role**

Route type		Structural description	Typical street network role
Stem		Intermediate junctions are three-way	Varied, including conventional distributory networks. (Also boundary routes to griddy networks.)
Spine		Intermediate junctions are four-way	Traditional connective grid networks. A spine is often the main road, locally or otherwise
Corridor		Both ends are pendant (usually both are externally connecting)	Typically the datum or main through route of a network
Cantilever		One end is a three-way junction, the other is free	Typical of suburban 'cul-de-sac' networks
Collector		All junctions are three-way	Typical of networks of suburban distributors connected by priority junctions
Connector		All junctions are four-way	Typical of traditional grid networks
Cross-connector		A short, deep connecting street which, due to its depth and relative discontinuity, would have a high value of relative connectivity	Found in interior of grid networks

of Chapter 3, this is classification by *relation*. The particular sense of route type addressed here refers to the 'structural role' played by a route in the network – for example, the distinction of 'spine route' or a 'side road' – or a 'connector street'.

It is possible to suggest a series of types of route that might be recognised according to their structural role. Table 5.2 explains some possible definitions for different kinds of route defined according to their structural role. The question arises as to how these might be expressed quantitatively, or related to each other systematically.

The final column in Table 5.1 showed that in the Bayswater network there are 20 distinct types of route identifiable or, rather, 20 unique combinations of continuity, connectivity and depth. At present these are simply expressed as numerical combinations. But we can gain a better impression of the meaning of these types by means of a graphical presentation.

To do this, we can usefully employ a graphical device to represent the continuum of possible route types, so that route types that are structurally alike will appear close together, while those less alike will appear further apart. In this way we should be able to distinguish systematically the degree to which one route type is more or less like a 'spine route' or a 'side route'. The use of graphic depiction allows a readily appreciable impression of type to be gained, based on quantified parameters, without precise numbers or proportions needing to be explicitly held in mind.

The routegram

It is possible to create a new triangular diagram to demonstrate the character of route types, by plotting the relative proportions of the values of continuity, connectivity and depth for each route. This diagram can be called the *routegram*: each plotted point on the routegram represents a route (Figure 5.14). A full explanation of the routegram and its parameters is given in Appendix 5.

Figure 5.17 shows the position of Bayswater Road, which demonstrates that the route forming Bayswater Road is relatively continuous – continuous through several junctions – and also relatively connective, although slightly less so (i.e. slightly over to the left rather than the right). Relatively speaking

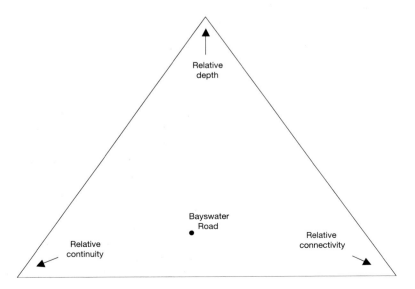

5.14 • The routegram. Each plotted point on the routegram represents a route, whose position is specified by the relative proportional values of continuity, connectivity and depth. The triangular logic of the routegram echoes that of the nodegram (Figure 4.19). See Appendix 5 for formal definition of properties.

5.15 • The routegram for the whole Bayswater network. This plots all the route types featured in Table 5.1, representing the route structure shown in Figure 5.13 (c). There are 20 individual route types (labelled 'a' to 't' in Table 5.1) – representing 20 distinct permutations of continuity, connectivity and depth – hence 20 plotted points on the routegram.

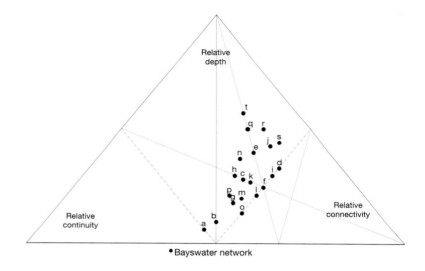

• Bayswater network

it is not 'deep' (i.e. close to the bottom of the plot). This set of characteristics is in accord with a road that is a major through road with several side roads.

The routegram may be used to compare the structural role of different routes in a network, or different routes across networks, or to compare the complete set of routes in a network with those in another network. These aspects will be demonstrated in the remainder of this chapter.

The routegram for a whole network

The procedure carried out for Bayswater Road can be carried out for all 27 routes in the Bayswater network. We can then plot the positions for all of the different types of route in the network on a routegram, to show the overall distribution of routes in the whole network. The distribution of routes for the Bayswater network is shown in Figure 5.15.

From Figure 5.15 we can see that type 'a' (corresponding to Bayswater Road, route 1), is relatively both the most 'continuous' route (i.e. highest value of relative continuity), as well as being the least deep route. A series of routes types vie for being the most 'relatively connective', among them is type 'o' (corresponding to Moscow Road, route 1.2.1). In such a way, the routegram can be used to map out the different combinations of route type in a given network.

Before proceeding to formally identify what these types might be, let us consider a contrasting type of network, which might offer different kinds of route, therefore adding to the total spread of types recognisable.

5.16 • Routegram for Thamesmead v. Bayswater.

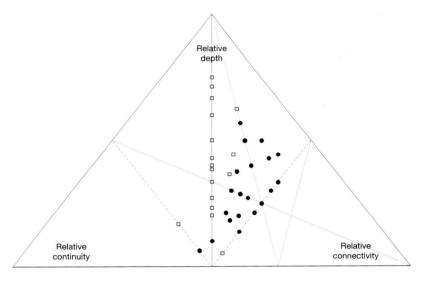

□ Thamesmead network   ● Bayswater network   ■ Coincident

Using the routegram to compare networks

The presence and variety of different route types in a network can tell a lot about the character of that network. Hence, as well as identifying route types, the routegram can also be used to compare networks. For this purpose we can analyse the route structure of Thamesmead, a highly tributary portion of the new town (earlier identified as a classic D-type layout). Figure 5.16 shows the distribution of routes for Thamesmead on the same plot as Bayswater.

Figure 5.16 clearly shows that the Bayswater network is more connective than that of Thamesmead, since the scatter of routes for Bayswater lies to the lower right, towards high relative connectivity. It is also apparent that the 'traditional' Bayswater network has, relatively speaking, a wider scatter of routes than the 'tributary' Thamesmead network. This reflects the greater relative diversity of route types in the traditional case, and the narrower range available in the modern 'engineered' layout. In fact, it can be seen that in the Thamesmead case, the plotted position of almost every route lines up in formation on the central vertical line – this is typical of a network with many branching culs-de-sac.[12]

The routegram can therefore be used to compare networks as well as comparing individual routes within a network, or across networks. Further

5.17 • Route structure representing a 'connector' network. This is adapted from Calthorpe's diagram (Figure 2.4). The equivalent streets labelled 'connector streets' in Figure 2.4 are 'c', 'd,', 'g' and 'l'.

means of characterising and comparing whole networks are elaborated in Chapter 6. Before doing this, however, we can consolidate what we have learned about the structural role of routes, focusing on the issue of route type.

Using the routegram to distinguish route type

The routegram has been used to demonstrate the complete scatter of routes in a network. Each position on the routegram may be associated to some extent with a kind of route type. We can therefore use the routegram to identify route types based on their structural role in the network; that is, based on the relative combinations of continuity, connectivity and depth.

As an example, we can take a network based on Calthorpe's connector streets (Figure 2.4) and analyse this in route structural terms (Figure 5.17), plotting the resulting routes on the routegram (Figure 5.18).

From this, we can see where the types of route identifiable as 'connector streets' lie. We can now 'point to' the region generally occupied by connector streets, and hence can check explicitly whether a proposed route could be regarded as a connector street.

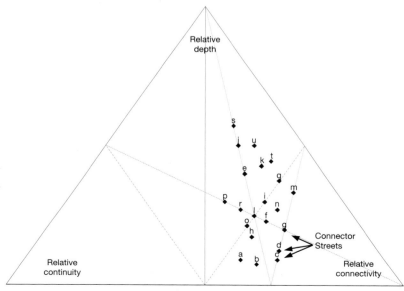

5.18 • Routegram for 'connector' network. This shows the route structural properties of routes from Figure 5.17 plotted on the routegram.

Indeed, we can be more specific, since positions on the routegram can all be explicitly quantified. We can create a general working definition of a *connective street* as one embodying a route with high relative connectivity. We can also separately give the *connector* a more specific definition based on having four-way intersections at either end and at all intermediate junctions.

Here we are using the term 'connector' to refer to a route type defined purely by its structural role (relation) as defined by its combination of route-structural properties. Clearly this is independent of the form or use of such a street. A 'connector' could therefore be a 'connector street', if it took the form of a street, but could also be a 'connector road', or 'connector boulevard', if its physical characteristics so dictated.

The routegram as a map of route types

We can do similar exercises with various permutations of route type in different kinds of network, and plot out a theoretical solution space of all types of route. From this, we can mark out areas and lines on the route-gram (Figure 5.19) that correspond to different route types, for example, the types suggested earlier in Table 5.2.

Figure 5.19 demonstrates several route types suggested earlier in Table 5.2. These refer to several commonly recognisable types, which seem to offer the most useful applications in accounting for route types that are the

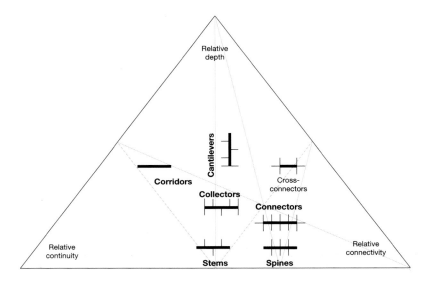

5.19 • Route types defined on the routegram. A more systematic exploration of the 'solution space' of route types on the routegram is given in Appendix 5.

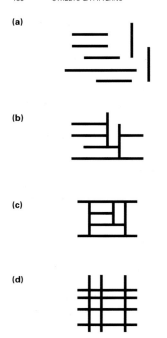

(a)

(b)

(c)

(d)

5.20 • Network types defined by route type. (a) All-corridor (not a network). (b) All-cantilever network. (c) All-collector network. (d) All-connector network.

subject of practical interest. A more detailed presentation of the 'solution space' of the routegram is given in Appendix 5.

The connector and cross-connector streets are those with the highest relative connectivity. These give the typology its greatest 'breadth', yet these are precisely the types most likely to be discouraged in conventional engineering practice. This is because main roads with many side roads are discouraged, as are any roads with crossroads.

The route types may also be equated with network types (Figure 5.20). This demonstrates how the character of the network is directly related to the character of the constituent routes, and vice versa. This reflects the two-way nature of structure alluded to at the opening of the chapter.

CONCLUSIONS

This chapter demonstrates that links and nodes are not the only ways of representing networks. It suggests that structural interpretation is not just a matter of analysing abstract topologies, but needs to take account of how those topologies relate to what is being represented. Different forms of analysis may be suitable for treatment of different scales of resolution or different modes of movement. This opens the way for those wishing to analyse urban systems – whether engineers or urban designers – to do so without necessarily having always to start from the conception of the system of streetspace as a 'transport network'.

Accordingly, a method has been developed that conceptualises streets as *routes* that form components of urban structure. Route structure analysis recognises structure in terms of how parts relate to wholes; in this regard route structure analysis directly builds in the relationship between minor and major routes as constituted by the continuity of routes through junctions. Route structure analysis therefore provides a means of analysing street networks that is alternative to either conventional transport network analysis or to space syntax – although the development of route structure analysis has learned from useful features of both. Broadly speaking, one could say that space syntax is particularly useful for bounded spaces and streets, route structure analysis for street and road layouts, and conventional transport analysis for road, rail, air and other transport networks.

Since routes can be directly derived from links, route structure analysis can directly plug into conventional transport-related practices. Moreover, the fundamental elements of route structure analysis – routes – are obvious elements by which networks are normally designed. That is, designers tend to consciously construct a network by adding discrete route sections (roads, paths, etc.) to an existing network structure.

Route structure analysis also provides a means of differentiating route type – defined by relation – where route type is defined by combinations of a route's relative connectivity, continuity and depth. This allows, for example, the quantification of definition of types such as 'connector route'. The routegram allows a 'solution space' of all possible route types to be generated, and different generic types of route, based on structural or configurational role, become identifiable (Figure 5.19, Table 5.2).

Route structure analysis may also be used to distinguish *networks* based on their relative distribution of route types on the routegram. The next chapter now demonstrates how route structure analysis can further be used to characterise a diversity of patterns, and cement the link between the parts and whole of a structure – and hence directly relate 'streets' and 'patterns'.

NOTES

1   Lowe and Moryadas (1975: 81).
2   Kansky uses the term 'structure' generally to refer to 'the set of relations between building blocks both in respect to each other and to the transportation network as an organised whole' (1963: 1).
3   Other methods of analysis of urban pattern include urban morphology (see, for example, Conzen, 1969; Whitehand, 1981; Moudon, 1997); fractal analysis (Batty and Longley, 1994); cellular automata (Batty, 1997) and traffic pattern analyses (for example, Vaughan, 1987; Taylor, 2000).
4   Thompson (1948: 989, after James Clerk Maxwell); Berge (1958); Haggett and Chorley (1969: 7); March and Steadman (1971); Krüger (1979); Hillier and Hanson (1984); Broadbent (1988).
5   See, for example, Kansky (1963); Morlok (1967: 41); Sheffi (1985: 10); Dupuy and Stransky (1996); Bell and Iida (1997: 3; 17); Rietveld (1997: 1); Banks (1998: 163); Buckwalter (2001: 126); Vickerman (2001: 48). Graph theoretical indicators include alpha index, beta index, gamma index and accessibility index (Kansky, 1963).
6   Hillier and Hanson (1984); Hillier (1996).
7   See also Jiang *et al.* (1999) on a formalised discussion on space syntax, axial lines and integration.
8   Hillier *et al.* (1983). Space syntax has also been used to predict movement (see for example, Hillier *et al.*, 1993; Penn *et al.*, 1998).
9   See also discussion on elements of morphological analysis by Batty (1999).
10 Hillier (1999: 190; 186).
11 Buckwalter (2001: 127).
12 Thamesmead has almost three times as many routes (68) as Bayswater (27), so its limited range of types (19) is all the more significant. And although Thamesmead musters a modest 'breadth' of scatter, with a handful of points lying off the central vertical, actually over 90% of the routes are represented by those points lying on the vertical.

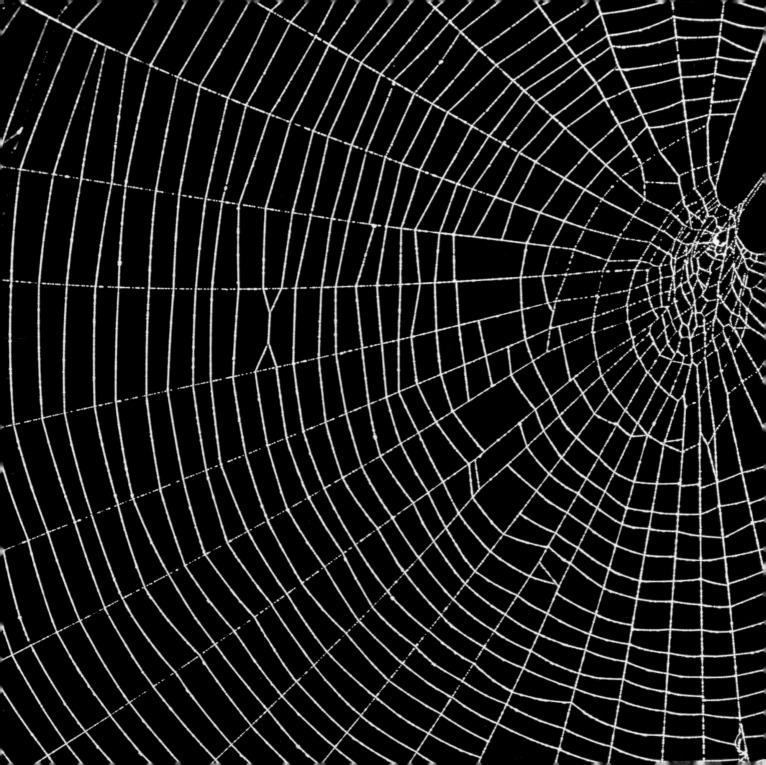

6 CONNECTIVITY AND COMPLEXITY

The characteristic structure of traditional street patterns has not tradition-ally been subject to systematic scrutiny as a basis for design. For a start, it has habitually been written off as being fundamentally 'unstructured' or 'amorphous', in association with its being 'unplanned'. Moreover, in the era of Modernism, traditional street patterns were regarded as dysfunctional, to be swept away, and so little attention was paid to how they might be formed. Yet today, neo-traditionalists would wish to replicate the currently back-in-favour qualities of traditional patterns – if only these qualities could be adequately captured. As far as the design debate is concerned, then, the primary question is 'what is desirable structure?' – or, more specifically, 'what is the structure of those patterns considered desirable?'

Already it has been pointed out that, structurally, neo-traditional devel-opments do not necessarily emulate the structure of traditional street patterns. If these traditional settlements are to be held up as exemplars, their structure deserves more scrutiny. Perhaps they are more 'structured' than we have supposed. The suspicion is that they do possess structure, albeit structure of a complex nature, that is not readily apparent on super-ficial inspection.

We have already seen a multitude of types of descriptor of street pat-tern, principally in Chapter 4, where a taxonomic approach has been used to give systematic qualitative classification of different patterns. However, this tended to focus on recognisable 'pure' forms such as grids and trees, whereas the majority of real street patterns – especially traditional ones – are more irregular. These irregular patterns tend to find themselves lumped together in some 'other' category, in which a disparate range of patterns may have less in common with each other than they have with some of the more regular categories. Therefore, so far, the consideration of pattern has not distinguished the kind of connectivity and complexity that are hallmarks of street patterns in general, and neo-traditional patterns in particular.

In the last chapter, we have seen how the structure of a network reflects the kinds of routes that make up that network. Chapter 5 showed that it is possible to recognise different kinds of route – such as the 'connector' – according to route structural properties. This chapter now looks at whole networks, and seeks ways of using route structural properties to characterise network structure in a way that can help identify and distinguish 'preferred' and 'discouraged' patterns. In this chapter, then, the 'design debate' will be informed not so much by scrutiny of the debate (as in Chapter 2), but by a detailed investigation of the 'nature of structure' itself.

EXAMPLE NETWORKS

This chapter focuses on the study of 60 example networks, which are analysed in terms of their route structure. The example networks include not only a range of actual street patterns, but some prototype and demonstrative patterns. These serve the various purposes of calibration and explanation as well as empirical comparison. The three categories of network analysed are shown in Table 6.1.

The distinctions between the actual and more theoretical structures are not incidental. Part of the exploration will be to find out how the properties of actual street networks may differ from those that were never built, or from those structures which are not otherwise seen as street network structures.

Table 6.1 **Categories of example networks analysed**

Network category	Description of category	Figure ref.	Number
Actual	As-built networks, including historic as well as contemporary examples	6.1	36
Prototype	Settlement prototypes, or plans for parts of settlements	6.2	4
Demonstrative	Networks used to demonstrate representative types, or individual structural characteristics	6.3	20
Total			60

Actual street patterns

The 'actual' street patterns are drawn from 21 cities and towns in the UK and 15 elsewhere. The selection is eclectic – even somewhat idiosyncratic – but this is for a reason: the aim here is not to compile a representative sample of urban patterns, but to demonstrate that any diverse kind of pattern should be capable of analysis and interpretation in route-structural terms.

Some of these examples have been selected from different parts of the same city (distinguishing traditional inner areas versus modern suburban areas). Some networks are more 'planned' than others. Apart from these distinctions, the detailed contextual circumstances of particular examples are not of primary concern here. The aim here is not so much to study or explain the nature of particular sites from their structural properties, but to establish what the structural properties can distinguish in a variety of network cases.

Figure 6.1 is organised loosely by network type, ranging from inner city grids to peripheral tributaries.

Prototype street patterns

The four cases in the 'prototype' category are 'pure' designs. In two cases, these designs have remained unbuilt (North Bucks New City and Hilberseimer's *New City*); in the other two cases; versions of these plans appeared on the ground (Craig Plan, Edinburgh; *Ciudad Lineal*, Madrid). The idea here is to demonstrate the idealised structures to give an impression of the 'pure' forms of the drawing board, before these collide with the reality of application to real sites (Figure 6.2).

The excerpt from North Bucks New City (a) is a development 'pod' for the unbuilt new town proposed for a site near present-day Milton Keynes. The Craig Plan (b) is an example of a 'hierarchical' grid of traditional streets (Figure 2.13). The excerpt from Hilberseimer's *New City* (c) could be described as an H-shaped excerpt of an X-fractal. *Ciudad Lineal* is an example of what might be termed a pioneer form of Transit Oriented Development, designed along the backbone of a tramway spine (d). Its creator, Arturo Soria y Mata, claimed it to be a 'higher' or 'vertebrate form' in contrast to the more organic, 'vegetable' form of the garden city.[1]

Demonstrative street patterns

The 'demonstrative' networks include examples from the literature – which may be based on actual cases – and networks devised within the research process to demonstrate specific structural properties of significance. Some of these have already been presented for demonstration purposes earlier in the book. These can help to 'calibrate' the analysis, relating the actual street patterns to typical types (Figure 6.3).

The basis for analysis

The overall range of 60 networks was chosen to depict a variety of types of structure, and is not supposed to be a statistically representative 'sample' of urban networks in general. Particular attention was paid to selecting certain kinds of 'traditional', inner urban layout, which are rich in route diversity and structural complexity – these are particularly significant to the analysis in the second half of the chapter. Therefore, examples of these are well represented numerically. By contrast, pure grids and tributaries are simpler to grasp and distinguish, and fewer examples seemed necessary

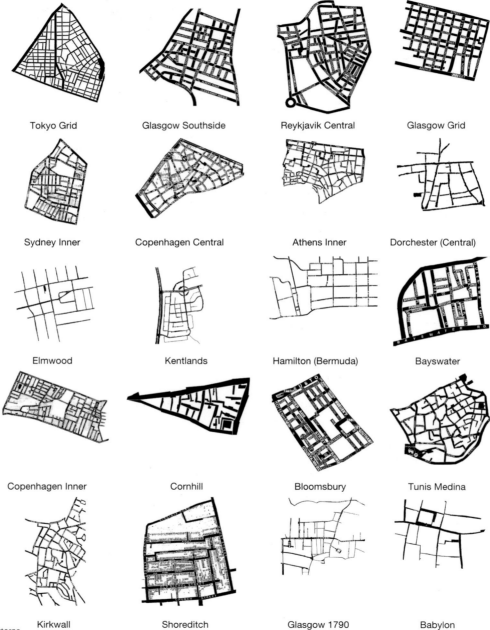

Tokyo Grid   Glasgow Southside   Reykjavik Central   Glasgow Grid

Sydney Inner   Copenhagen Central   Athens Inner   Dorchester (Central)

Elmwood   Kentlands   Hamilton (Bermuda)   Bayswater

Copenhagen Inner   Cornhill   Bloomsbury   Tunis Medina

Kirkwall   Shoreditch   Glasgow 1790   Babylon

6.1 • Street patterns.

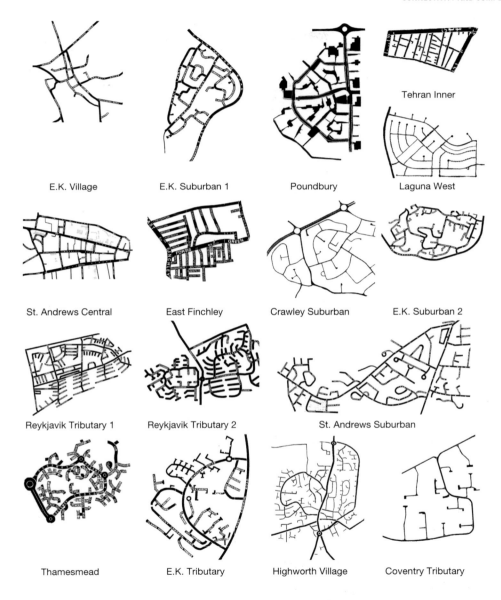

E.K. Village   E.K. Suburban 1   Poundbury   Tehran Inner

Laguna West

St. Andrews Central   East Finchley   Crawley Suburban   E.K. Suburban 2

Reykjavik Tributary 1   Reykjavik Tributary 2   St. Andrews Suburban

Thamesmead   E.K. Tributary   Highworth Village   Coventry Tributary

6.1 • Street patterns. (Continued)

(a)

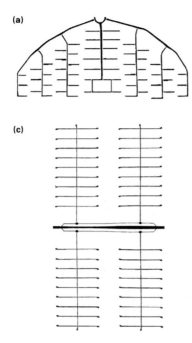

(b)

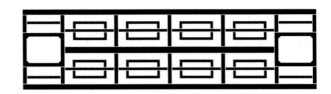

(c)

(d)

6.2 • Prototype street patterns. (a) North Bucks New City. (b) Craig Plan. (c) Hilberseimer. (d) *Ciudad Lineal.*

to characterise these types. Background details of the example networks are given in Appendix 6.1.

This chapter contains two principal analyses. The first concerns the properties of relative continuity, relative connectivity and relative depth, applied at the network level and is referred to for the sake of simplicity as 'connectivity analysis', to distinguish this kind of analysis from the 'complexity analysis' to be undertaken subsequently.

CONNECTIVITY ANALYSIS

This section analyses whole networks (represented as route structures) in terms of their relative continuity, connectivity and depth. This is referred to for simplicity as 'connectivity analysis'. In a sense, continuity and depth are also to do with connectivity: continuity relates to the internal connecting up of links that form each route, while depth relates to the relative connective position of a route in the widest possible network context.

In the last chapter we have already seen how it is possible to compare different networks using the routegram – as with the examples of Bayswater and Thamesmead (Figure 5.16). This is useful for comparing a couple of cases in detail, almost on a route-by-route basis. But we can also generate measures that allow comparison of larger numbers of networks, considered as whole (aggregate) entities.

This section demonstrates a series of graphic presentations based on route-structural parameters derived from the initial route-structural properties of continuity, connectivity and depth, but formulated at the network level. The graphical presentations show the positions of networks in the 'morphological continuum', allowing *network types* to be identified.

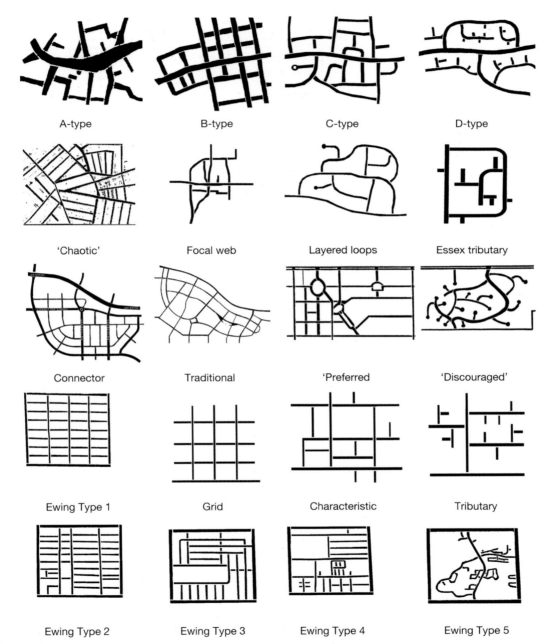

A-type

B-type

C-type

D-type

'Chaotic'

Focal web

Layered loops

Essex tributary

Connector

Traditional

'Preferred

'Discouraged'

Ewing Type 1

Grid

Characteristic

Tributary

Ewing Type 2

Ewing Type 3

Ewing Type 4

Ewing Type 5

6.3 • Demonstrative street patterns.

To do this, we first work out the set of route-structural properties applicable at the network level, and then present these graphically on a triangular diagram, the 'netgram'.

Network properties of continuity, connectivity and depth

The process that we applied to routes to generate the routegram (Chapter 5) can be replicated for whole networks to create a 'netgram'. That is, we can generate values of continuity, connectivity and depth for a whole network, based on the total summation of each of those properties over all routes. By this process, we obtain three numbers:

1.   the sum of continuity values for all routes in the network;
2.   the sum of connectivity values; and
3.   the sum of depth values.

The relative weighting or proportion of *these* three numbers (relative to *their* sum) gives rise to three ratios: relative continuity, relative connectivity and relative depth, at the network level. A formal expression of these relationships is given in Appendix 6.2.

As an example, in the Bayswater network presented previously, we see from Table 5.1 that the sum of individual route continuities is 73; the sum of route connectivities is 112 and the sum of route depths is 79. The respective ratios of relative continuity, relative connectivity and relative depth are 0.28, 0.43 and 0.3 respectively. Therefore, the position of the Bayswater network is closer to the bottom left-hand vertex than to either of the other vertices. This all indicates that, relatively speaking, the Bayswater network is 'relatively more connective' than it is 'relatively deep' or 'relatively continuous'. This would confirm our intuition that this grid-like network is relatively 'connective' or 'inter-connected', as networks go.

The netgram

Having obtained this set of proportions, these can be plotted on a triangular diagram, to demonstrate the relative character of a network (Figure 6.4). The triaxial logic of this diagram, which we can call the *netgram*, echoes that of the routegram (Figure 5.16). Just as each plotted point on the routegram represents a route, each point on the netgram represents a network – or more strictly speaking, a network's route structure.

The position on the netgram is effectively a weighted average of all the points on the equivalent routegram. Therefore, there is a clear relationship between the routegram and the netgram (Figure 6.5). As routes

6.4 • The netgram. Each position on the netgram represents a combination of relative continuity, relative connectivity and relative depth, for a whole network. Here, the values are respectively 0.28, 0.43 and 0.3, for the Bayswater network.

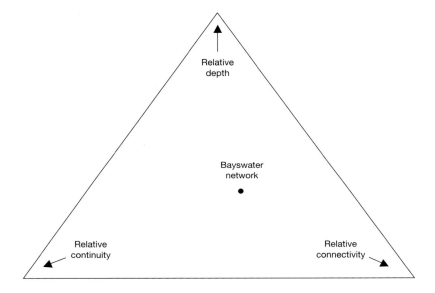

are added to (or subtracted from) a network, points will appear on (or disappear from) the routegram, and the position of the resultant network on the netgram will tend to shift slightly.

The netgram may now be used to compare different networks and recognise network types based on their relative connectivity.

Sixty route structures compared

Table 6.2 shows the range of 60 actual, prototype and demonstrative route structures listed in their order of relative connectivity. Demonstrative networks are listed in a separate column since these help to 'calibrate' the table. There is an approximate correspondence between relative connectivity and the placing of networks in Figure 6.1.[2] Figure 6.6 then plots these 60 route structures on the netgram.

6.5 • Bayswater structure represented on routegram and netgram. (a) Routegram (Figure 5.15). (b) Netgram (Figure 6.4).

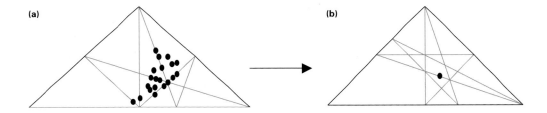

(a)   (b)

Table 6.2 **Relative connectivity values for example networks**

Informal description	Demonstrative networks	Relative connectivity	Actual or *prototype network	Relative connectivity
Regular and connective grids	Ewing-1	0.50	*Ciudad Lineal	0.52
	Focal web	0.50	Glasgow Grid	0.50
	B-type	0.49	Tokyo Grid	0.48
	Ewing-2	0.47	Reykjavik Central	0.47
			Glasgow Southside	0.47
	Traditional	0.47	*Craig Plan	0.47
	Grid	0.46	Athens Inner	0.46
	Connector	0.46	Copenhagen Central	0.46
	Preferred	0.446	Dorchester Central	0.45
	Ewing-3	0.44	Sydney Inner	0.445
			Kentlands	0.44
			Hamilton	0.43
			Elmwood	0.43
			Bayswater	0.42
	Chaotic	0.42	Tunis Medina	0.42
			Bloomsbury	0.42
			Copenhagen Inner	0.42
Traditional grid-like structures			Cornhill	0.42
			Glasgow 1790	0.415
	Ewing-4	0.41	Shoreditch	0.41
			Kirkwall	0.41
	Characteristic	0.40	Babylon	0.39
			E.K. Village	0.39
Suburban 'grids' and cellular	A-type	0.39	St Andrews Central	0.39
	C-type	0.385	East Finchley	0.38
			Laguna West	0.38
			Tehran Inner	0.38
			Poundbury	0.37
	Layered loops	0.36		
			*Hilberseimer	0.36
Suburban	Ewing-5	0.35	E.K. Suburban 1	0.35
			Reykjavik Tributary 1	0.34
			Crawley Suburban	0.32
Suburban with significant tributary components			Reykjavik Tributary 2	0.315
			E.K. Suburban 2	0.31
			St Andrews Suburban	0.31
			Coventry Tributary	0.31
			Highworth Village	0.31
	Essex Trib.	0.275	*North Bucks New City	0.30
Tributaries and pure trees	Discouraged	0.275	E.K. Tributary	0.28
	D-type	0.265		
	Tributary	0.25	Thamesmead	0.26

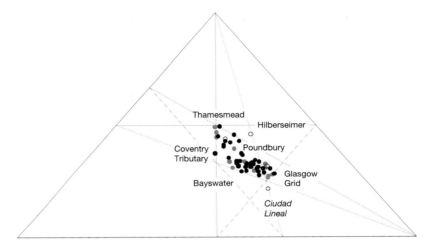

6.6 • Full netgram demonstration showing full set of real, prototype and demonstrative networks. Most cases fall within the central 'diamond'. Two notable outliers are Hilberseimer and *Ciudad Lineal* – significantly, these are prototypes rather than actual street patterns.

From Figure 6.6, we can discern a differentiation of recognisable 'network types'. Generally speaking, the modern suburban layouts are towards the top and left (indicating relative depth and lack of connectivity), while the traditional layouts are towards the bottom and right (indicating relative connectivity and lack of depth). There is some variation in continuity, although this is narrower than the variation in the other two parameters. In practice, it will often be possible to base distinction only on the comparison of relative connectivity and relative depth, giving a spectrum from (high relative connectivity, low relative depth) to (low relative connectivity, high relative depth). In fact, it will often be convenient to simply rank networks by relative connectivity alone (as in Table 6.2).

We could graduate this spectrum into four convenient divisions (from top left to bottom right), for example:

- *tributary* – implies deep branching, with systematic use of culs-de-sac and/or layered loop roads. These have been commonly used in the UK since the 1960s, for example in new towns and outer suburbs, and are typical of 'hierarchical' road systems;
- *semi-tributary* – refers to the kind of pattern typically found in older suburban neighbourhoods, with some degree of layering and some use of culs-de-sac, but with less hierarchical distinction (allowing more direct connections between minor access roads and major roads). In the example networks here, these are typically mainly configured with T-junctions;

- *semi-griddy* – refers to typical grid-like layouts with a variety of T- and X-junctions, typically found in the inner areas of traditional settlements;
- *griddy* – implies a relatively high proportion of X-junctions, typical of regular 'planned' layouts such as the original planned extensions to traditional settlements, or to new settlements laid out on a grid pattern from the outset.

Typical sectors in which these types would fall are suggested in Figure 6.7. By such divisions, we create (at least) four intermediate classes between the polarised extrema of ultra deep tributaries and ultra connective grids.

Overall, the spectrum of possible patterns has been divided up in a way that is transparent and objective. The characterisations of network type relate to the kinds of concerns expressed in Chapter 2: relating to different kinds of connectedness, grids and tributaries.

Having calibrated the netgram with a series of real networks of recognisable and established structure, it is then possible to assess the classification, or structural similarity, of networks with respect to the six categories identified in Figure 6.7.

Historically, we might note a very broad chronological development from semi-griddy to griddy to semi-tributary to tributary (cf. A, B, C, D types),

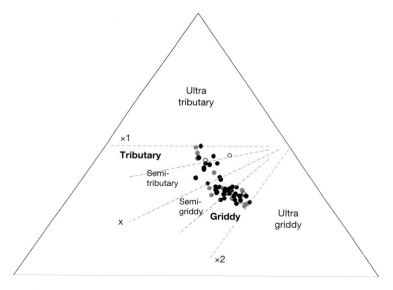

6.7 • Classification by connectivity: the tributary–griddy spectrum. The most basic distinction bisects the netgram between tributary and griddy structures (line x). A second division brackets moderate cases (lying between x1 and x2). Finally, the central range can be further bisected to give 'semi-tributary' and 'semi-griddy' cases.

although, of course, there are many counter-trends and variations within this development. We can see that Calthorpe's 'connector street' network is seen to lie close to the 'traditional' and 'preferred' exemplars. The netgram plot can therefore show what a 'connective' network is, and where it lies in relation to other network types.

We can also see that Poundbury lies close to the 'semi-griddy' layouts, but falls (just) within the 'semi-tributary' category; clearly, it is more connective than the modernist tributary category, but is less connective than the 'semi-griddy' type. Indeed, it is noticeably less connective than traditional grids such as that of central Dorchester.[3]

The results demonstrate how there may be greater differences in structure within settlements than between settlements. For example, the central Reykjavik network resembles more closely that of central Athens than it does those route structures of the suburbs of Reykjavik (this is also seen clearly in Table 6.2).

We may also see where proposed or imaginary cities such as the *Ciudad Lineal* and Hilberseimer's *New City* would fit on to the netgram. As it turns out, these particular cases have positions that lie outside the area occupied by the real cases: they are therefore more extreme in terms of combinations of continuity, connectivity and depth. An exploration of 'netspace' – or the solution space of the netgram – for a range of theoretical structures is presented in Appendix 6.4.

Finally, we can note where street patterns characteristically lie – in the central zone. In this central zone, street patterns are not so much 'tree-shaped' or 'grid-shaped' as they are 'street-pattern-shaped', with a characteristic combination of continuity, connectivity and depth.

In conclusion, this analysis has demonstrated a possible way of relating network structures to their positions in netspace (the continuum of possible network structures); we can see how different 'types' can be systematically mapped, and their relative likeness compared. In this way, we are able to go beyond stereotypical patterns and characterise any network structure – however extreme or irregular – based on their proportions of continuity, connectivity and depth.

COMPLEXITY ANALYSIS

There is more to 'preferred' networks than being 'griddy'. Often, the kind of street pattern desired by urban designers and planners is not necessarily a formal gridiron, but a more irregular (though still grid-like) pattern, often associated with traditional networks. Although there are many kinds of theoretical structure that fill out the theoretical solution space of the netgram, many of those tend to be extremely regular structures that do not look like typical street patterns (Appendix 6.4). Actual street patterns tend to fall within a limited area of the netgram. The characteristic 'street pattern shape' is one of heterogeneity.

The second half of this chapter concerns an analysis of the differentiation, regularity and complexity of network structures – referred to, for convenience, as 'complexity analysis' to differentiate it from the analyses of the preceding section. This analysis also demonstrates how properties of the *route* types present influence the character of the whole network, although in a slightly different way: it is concerned with the amount of differentiation among types of route – whatever their individual constituent properties such as connectivity. In a sense, the issue of complexity opens up a new dimension for identifying different types of pattern, which is the subject of the remainder of this chapter.

Recognising heterogeneity

It was noted earlier, in Chapter 5, that each route in a network can be regarded as a specific type, based on its combination of the properties continuity, connectivity and depth. For example, in the case of Bayswater, we saw that there were 20 such route types (Table 5.1, Figure 5.15).

Now, as well as telling us something about the relative connectivity of the network, the spread of the scatter in a sense tells us something else about the character of the network. The more different types of route a network has – relative to the total number of routes – the more irregular and complex it tends to be. This may possibly be equated with the 'plannedness' of a layout. For example, the Bayswater layout, which was built up in a relatively piecemeal fashion, with various lanes and mews off side streets, had a diverse array of route types – 20 distinct types out of a total of 27. In contrast, we saw that the Thamesmead case – a planned development – had far fewer types relative to the total number. In a network of 68 routes, there were only 19 distinct types. Thamesmead therefore has much less variety, and more regularity, than the traditional example of Bayswater.

Regularity and irregularity

We can capture properties of heterogeneity by considering three small demonstrative networks (Figure 6.8). Layout (b) in Figure 6.8 is intended to represent the typical 'irregular' shape that networks tend to take on when not deliberately configured as a particular pattern, such as a tree or a grid. Layout (b) lies somewhere in between (a) and (c) in terms of

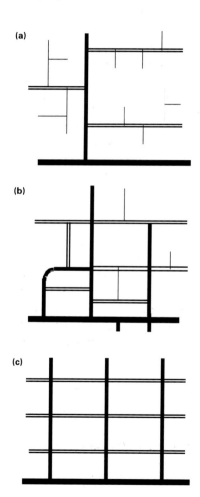

(a)

(b)

(c)

6.8 • Three network types demonstrating differentiation of route type. (a) Tributary. (b) Mixed. (c) Grid.

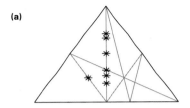

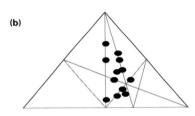

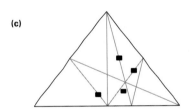

6.9 • Routegrams for three representative types of network. The 'mixed' case has three times as many types of route as the grid. (a) Tributary. (b) Mixed. (c) Grid.

connectivity, but it appears to have a degree of irregularity or complexity that sets it apart from either of the other two. It is the task of this section to demonstrate quantitative measures of this kind of heterogeneity.

The distributions of route types for these three layouts are first plotted on routegrams, to give an impression of their distribution of differentiation (Figure 6.9). Figure 6.9 shows the difference between the networks in terms of diversity of route type. The 'mixed' layout (b) has twelve distinct route types, whereas the grid (c) only has four (where a distinct route type is taken as a unique combination of continuity, connectivity and depth). In this case, all three networks have the same total number of routes (16). In order to compare networks of different sizes, we can divide the number of distinct route types by the total number of routes, to obtain a property that we can call *irregularity*. The irregularity of the tributary layout (a) is 7/16 = 0.44; that of the 'mixed' case (b) is 0.75, and that of the grid (c) is 0.25.

We can also define *regularity* as the complement of irregularity, such that irregularity and regularity sum to one. In the above examples, then, the tributary layout (a) has a regularity of (1 – 0.44) = 0.36. The grid layout (c) is the most regular with a regularity value of 0.75, while layout (b) has the lowest value of regularity, 0.25.

Recursivity and complexity

We can also identify two further properties that help to distinguish different kinds of heterogeneity, by considering the three structures shown in Figure 6.10. Layout (a) shows a 'comb' structure, which is clearly regular, in having a series of identical cantilevers off a collector stem. Layout (c) shows an irregular structure, which is indeed singularly irregular, in that all 11 routes are of a distinct type. But what of layout (b)? Layout (b) is 'irregular' in the sense of having all routes of a distinct type (since each route

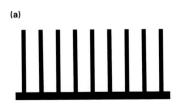

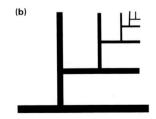

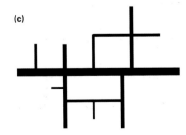

6.10 • Networks embodying three differentiation properties. (a) Regular. (b) Recursive. (c) Complex.

has a different depth); yet it is also has a kind of regularity due to the recursive, fractal-like branching, where the same basic topological form is repeated at different depths (cantilevers off cantilevers off cantilevers). To distinguish these three kinds of structure, we can identify two further – and final – route structural properties.

Recursivity can be defined by the number of *depths* divided by the number of routes (where the number of depths is simply equivalent to the maximum depth). The property of recursivity clearly distinguishes layout (b) from the other two: layout (b) has maximum recursivity of 1, whereas layouts (a) and (c) have recursivity values of 0.2 and 0.36 respectively.

Complexity can be defined as the number of distinct types of route present over and above the number of distinct types generated by difference in depth alone – that is, the number of distinct types present less the value of maximum depth – all divided by the total number of routes. The property of complexity clearly distinguishes layout (c) from the other two: layout (c) has a complexity value of (11 – 4)/11 = 0.64, whereas both layouts (a) and (b) have a complexity of zero.

Given the way that these properties are defined, for any structure, regularity, recursivity and complexity sum to one (Appendix 6.2). From this troika of properties we can create a new graphical presentation of heterogeneity.

The hetgram
Just as it was possible to construct the netgram as a triangular plot from three relative properties summing to one, it is also possible to construct a triangular plot from three of the differentiation properties, namely, complexity, regularity and recursivity.

We can call the resulting plot the *hetgram*, since it addresses the issue of heterogeneity, assisting the recognition of networks according to the differentiation of route types. The hetgram has a triaxial logic similar to that of the netgram, except that the axis properties are different (Figure 6.11). Some orientation to Figure 6.11 is provided by plotting the three layouts from each of Figures 6.8 and 6.10.

Sixty networks compared using the hetgram
Having set up the hetgram, we can now demonstrate its use to present 60 example networks. First, Table 6.3 lists relative complexity values for the 40 'actual' and 'prototype' cases (demonstrative cases are omitted for clarity). All 60 example cases are then plotted on the hetgram (Figure 6.12).

As with the earlier netgram results, the hetgram shows a band of results representing where street pattern structures typically lie. This time,

6.11 • The hetgram. This plots the positions of regularity, recursivity and complexity. The plotted cases here suggest that the mixed street pattern structure is not simply an intermediate type between the grid and the tributary, but a distinct kind of type in its own right.

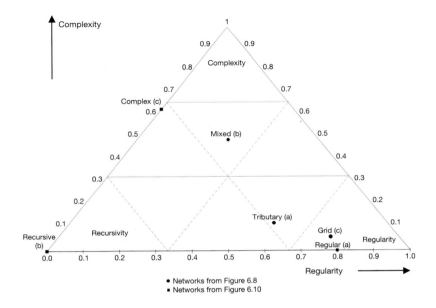

● Networks from Figure 6.8
■ Networks from Figure 6.10

the spectrum is from complex to regular. All the most complex layouts (in the upper left part of the Table 6.3), are the characteristic traditional, 'unplanned' layouts uppermost in Figure 6.12. Below these come suburban layouts of various sorts, followed by increasingly regular tributary and grid networks. Significantly, it can be seen that the prototype layouts lie lowest of all: these have the pristine symmetry of the drawing board. For all that Soria y Mata considered that *Ciudad Lineal* was a higher, vertebrate form, here, it is interpreted as one of the simplest possible specimens.

Complex, characteristic structures are found in traditional street layouts, from Babylon to Bayswater. Indeed, Bayswater turns out to be the most complex of all examples studied. This reflects the mixture of planned and unplanned sections of layout, with a variety of long and short streets at different depths.

We can note that the Glasgow Grid layout – the central part of the city centre – has a very low complexity value. This would be expected of a *planned* grid. In contrast, the grid of Glasgow Southside – which is almost as connective as the Glasgow Grid – is much more complex. This greater

Table 6.3 **Complexity values for 40 networks (actual and prototype)**

1	Bayswater	0.59	21	East Finchley	0.33
2	Shoreditch	0.52	22	Reykjavik Central	0.33
3	Dorchester Central	0.52	23	Tehran Inner	0.33
4	Kentlands	0.47	24	St Andrews Central	0.30
5	Kirkwall	0.45	25	Poundbury	0.30
6	E.K. Village	0.44	26	E.K. Suburban 2	0.29
7	Babylon	0.44	27	E.K. Suburban 1	0.27
8	Bloomsbury	0.43	28	St Andrews Suburban	0.26
9	Cornhill	0.43	29	Reykjavik Tributary 1	0.24
10	Crawley Suburban	0.43	30	Thamesmead	0.21
11	Hamilton	0.43	31	Tokyo Grid	0.20
12	Laguna West	0.42	32	Highworth Village	0.19
13	Glasgow Southside	0.40	33	Glasgow Grid	0.18
14	Tunis Medina	0.39	34	E.K. Tributary	0.16
15	Glasgow 1790	0.39	35	Reykjavik Tributary 2	0.15
16	Elmwood	0.38	36	Craig Plan*	0.13
17	Athens Inner	0.38	37	Coventry Tributary	0.11
18	Copenhagen Central	0.37	38	North Bucks New City*	0.07
19	Sydney Inner	0.36	39	*Ciudad Lineal**	0.00
20	Copenhagen Inner	0.34	40	Hilberseimer*	0.00

* Prototype cases

degree of complexity would be typical for unplanned layouts, where there was no artificially low value of complexity (or artificially high degree of regularity).

We can contrast both of the Glasgow grids with the Edinburgh case, the prototype Craig Plan. This is also regular and connective, but not as regular or connective as the Glasgow Grid. The Craig Plan, in fact, was a deliberately 'complex' layout, with a hierarchically stratified system of streets and mews lanes, deliberately devised to express and reinforce the intended social hierarchy (Figure 2.13). This plan may be contrasted with the more simple, open, 'democratic, mercantile and mobile' gridiron of Glasgow, of a similar period.[4]

A more modern example of a hierarchical layout is seen in the case of the Thamesmead network, whose extremely tributary nature is clearly apparent from a visual inspection of its plan layout. As seen before, this tributary nature is associated with low relative connectivity. We now see how it is also associated with the low complexity typical of planned layouts.

Structures with multiple repetitions of the same type of route, and often exhibiting some form of symmetry, occur near or on the base line

6.12 • Hetgram plot of all 60 example networks. The more complex, typically unplanned layouts lie to the upper centre, the more regular, typically planned layouts, lie to the lower right.

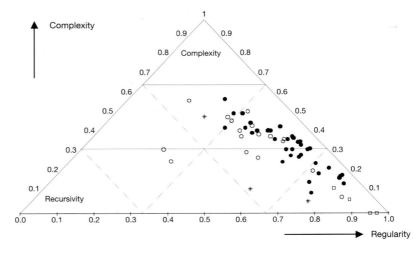

• actual street network   □ prototype   ○ demonstrative   ✳ networks from Figure 6.8

(where complexity is zero). This means that both regular grids and 'regular' tributaries will occupy the same region of the diagram. This is clearly the case for *Ciudad Lineal* (regular grid) and Hilberseimer (regular tributary).

The prototype layouts have some of the most extreme values observed. The tendency to extremity is also partly boosted by the size of these networks, which are able to rack up high values of regularity, connectivity, and so on. For example, both Hilberseimer's *New City* and Soria y Mata's *Ciudad Lineal* have high values of regularity.

Overall, the hetgram is useful in distinguishing regular from irregular networks in a quantitative way, and in a broad sense identifying 'more planned' and 'less planned' networks. This echoes the first basic distinction between planned (or regular) and unplanned (or irregular) layouts noted in Chapter 4. The present analysis allows a quantitative appreciation of this distinction.

CHARACTERISTIC STRUCTURE

We can now put together two of the key parameters from this chapter, relative connectivity and complexity, to identify a particular kind of street pattern structure that can be referred to as *characteristic structure*.

6.13 • Complexity versus relative connectivity. The three 'representative' cases are the tributary, 'mixed' and grid layouts illustrated in Figure 6.8(a), (b) and (c) respectively. The apparent inverted 'V' shape of this diagram reinforces the interpretation of 'characteristic' structure as a distinct type, and not merely an intermediate position between the pure grid and the pure tributary.

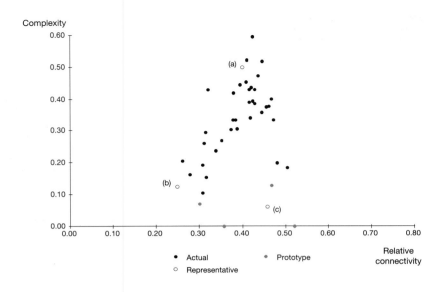

Connectivity and complexity

The properties of relative connectivity and complexity can be plotted on the same diagram – this time, a simple Cartesian plot (Figure 6.13). Figure 6.13 suggests the recognition of three extrema: the bottom left has regular unconnective layouts (tributaries), the bottom right has regular connective layouts (grids) while the top central part has irregular layouts of intermediate connectivity. This triangular distribution implies three distinct types of structure.

Figure 6.14 is an overlay of the three structures represented earlier in Figure 6.8 on Figure 6.13. This suggests that the middle type – earlier described as 'mixed', of intermediate connectivity between the tributary and grids patterns – is actually a distinct kind of pattern in its own right.

In other words, the middle type is not just some intermediate case between grids and tributaries, but has distinct properties of complexity (and irregularity) that set it apart from the other two types. This clearly suggests that the characteristic irregular, traditional pattern occupies a region of distinct structural consistency, and is not necessarily an 'amorphous' form at all. Indeed, it is possible to recognise this distinct type of structure as *characteristic structure*.

The term 'characteristic' embodies two senses of meaning. First, it implies the possession of distinctive *character*. Here, this means structures that have a quintessential 'street pattern shape'. We can usually recognise

6.14 • Characteristic structure as combination of high complexity and mid-range relative connectivity. (a) Tributary. (b) Characteristic. (c) Grid.

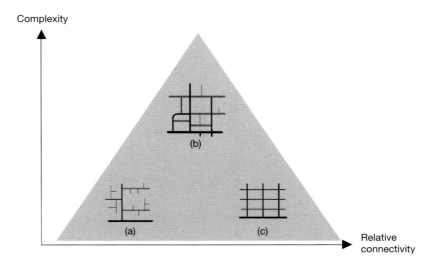

an image of a street pattern when we see one: an abstract image of a street pattern – no matter how tree-like, or skeletal – is likely to be recognisable as a street pattern, whereas an image of a real tree or skeleton is unlikely to be mistaken for a real street pattern. Those patterns that look like nothing other than street patterns (rather than metallic grids or astronomical stars or botanical trees) occupy the upper part of the plot.

The second connotation of 'characteristic' is that of *likelihood*; and refers to the sense that a certain kind of characteristic structure is somehow 'likely' to exist as a street pattern. This second sense – of likelihood – is concerned with processes of growth and evolutionary morphology, and lies outside the scope of this book.[5] It will suffice to note here that, effectively, the extremes of connectivity correspond with the most ordered or contrived patterns, requiring the greatest design intent or effort to form them, whereas the 'natural' or unplanned patterns – those left to their own devices, as it were – form the mid range of connectivity. Put another way, it seems that it requires careful planning or ordering to achieve the balance required to avoid a natural differentiation of routes. This reflects the existence of 'likely' patterns.

The characteristic structure tends to have a bundle of associated characteristics (Box 6).

Overall, the complexity–relative connectivity plot (Figures 6.13, 6.14) can be used to characterise patterns, and can graphically encapsulate both

---

BOX 6. CHARACTERISTIC STRUCTURE

The 'characteristic' street pattern structure is the almost definitive 'street pattern shape'.

Characteristic structure has a relatively high degree of complexity and a medium to high level of connectivity.

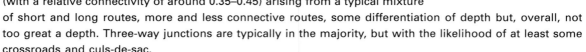

Characteristic structure has a medium or 'semi-griddy' level of connectivity (with a relative connectivity of around 0.35–0.45) arising from a typical mixture of short and long routes, more and less connective routes, some differentiation of depth but, overall, not too great a depth. Three-way junctions are typically in the majority, but with the likelihood of at least some crossroads and culs-de-sac.

Characteristic structure is typified by a relatively high degree of irregularity and complexity (complexity typically in the range 0.35–0.6).

---

the distinction between 'more planned' and 'less planned' layouts, and 'more grid-like' and 'more tributary' forms.

We could use such a diagram to assess where advocated or proposed layouts would fit. For example, we can note that Poundbury – the neo-traditional enclave on the edge of Dorchester – shows a fairly 'regular' pattern with moderate connectivity; this was, after all, a master planned neighbourhood, designed with connectivity in mind.

We can also contrast the example of Poundbury with the central grid of Dorchester. Although the aim of Poundbury was to some extent to emulate the character and street pattern of traditional settlements, and to relate to the historic core of the town, the Poundbury layout here is seen to be lower in both connectivity and complexity than Dorchester. However, Poundbury does have values of connectivity and complexity higher than typical conventional suburban cases (e.g. St Andrews Suburban, Crawley Suburban).

CONCLUSIONS

This chapter has shown three basic demonstrations. The first has used 'connectivity analysis' to characterise network patterns expressed as route structures. It has used the graphic device of the netgram to distinguish and graduate a spectrum of connectivity from 'griddy' to 'tributary' structures. This echoes the approach of the *Mosborough Master Plan* (Chapter 4), but here the basic properties of the forms are systematically defined, and can be plotted on the basis of explicitly quantified values. This allows the quantification of properties of 'preferred' ('connective' or 'griddy') networks (Chapter 2).

The second demonstration has used 'complexity analysis' to characterise network patterns based on their differentiation of route structure. The graphic device of the hetgram has been used to distinguish and graduate a spectrum of complexity from 'characteristic', typically unplanned networks to more regular, typically planned layouts.

Both of these analyses home in on – and provide quantification for – the properties of traditional street patterns, whose structures neo-traditional planners might wish to emulate.

These are united with the third and final demonstration of 'characteristic' structure, which combines a relatively high degree of complexity and a medium to high level of relative connectivity.

The analysis suggests the recognition of particular kinds of structure – identified as characteristic structure – which equates with typical traditional street pattern structure. Figure 6.13 demonstrates that a whole host of traditional street patterns from Bayswater to Babylon possess this identifiable kind of characteristic structure – this combination of connectivity and complexity – that sets them apart from either pure geometric grids or pure trees. This means that instead of placing this structure into some 'hybrid' or 'other' category – a rag-bag with a disparate array of weird and wonderful patterns that would never see the light of day as street patterns – we can recognise the characteristic structure as the quintessential 'street-pattern-shape'.

In other words, when urban designers call for 'more connective' layouts, or for 'less standardised traditional-like' layouts, they may well be pointing to a kind of structure that in fact is not some elusive amorphous entity, but a very specific type of structure, whose properties can be pinned down – to a specific combination of complexity and relative connectivity. This means that, where appropriate, 'preferred' layouts can be expressed in terms of specific route-structural properties, rather than having to rely on elusive terms like 'inter-connected' or having to resort to depicting a stereotypical pattern on plan.

As noted at the end of Chapter 4, patterns are not monolithic, but are articulated assemblies of elements. Taken together, this chapter and Chapter 5 have demonstrated a direct (and quantifiable) connection between the character of the routes and the whole route structure. Connector streets reside in connector networks (grids); culs-de-sac fit together to make 'cul-de-sac networks' (trees). Street patterns, then, can be seen significantly as products of their constituent elements – streets.

However, there are still some major issues of structure to resolve. It has been argued earlier that streets, as such, do not necessarily comfortably fit within hierarchies – at least, within conventional road hierarchies. To complete the investigation of the 'nature of structure', it will be necessary to establish more clearly how different kinds of streets might fit within different kinds of hierarchies. To do this involves a closer look at the issue of hierarchy, and how hierarchical structure relates to different kinds of street and different kinds of pattern. This synthesis is the subject of the next chapter.

NOTES

1   Tunnard (1970: 65).
2   Exceptions are the Hilberseimer and Reykjavik Tributary networks which, despite being tree-like – and hence appearing low in Figure 6.1(b) – have higher values of relative connectivity, due to their high proportion of four-way junctions (cf. X-tree, Chapter 4). X-tree layouts are uncommon in UK practice, in which context this subtle distinction is effectively immaterial.
3   The relative connectivity of Poundbury is 0.37, just less than its relative depth of 0.38. The corresponding values for Dorchester Central are 0.45 and 0.31 respectively.
4   Gordon (1984); McKean (1996); Walker (1996: 63).
5   This is being explored by Marshall (*Cities Design and Evolution*).

7 THE CONSTITUTION OF STRUCTURE

It is therefore necessary to introduce the idea of a 'hierarchy' of distributors, whereby important distributors feed down through distributors of lesser category to the minor roads which give access to the buildings. The system may be likened to the trunk, limbs, branches, and finally the twigs (corresponding to the access roads) of a tree.

Traffic in Towns [1]

A tree is a useful object of contemplation when considering issues of structure and hierarchy, since it is both a familiar and intuitively understood object, and yet it also has a manifold complexity that reveals itself under closer examination.

Consideration of the structure of a tree can help to answer questions that relate rather directly to specific aspects of structure and hierarchy, as applied to streets and patterns. What exactly do we mean by hierarchy – which is more than just 'classification' or 'typology', but implies order and structure? What is hierarchical structure? What is a tree-like hierarchy? Can we use understanding of hierarchical structure to distinguish the structure of conventional road hierarchy, and what makes this 'bad' hierarchy, and explore other possible kinds of structure, that might equate with 'good' hierarchy?

While Christopher Alexander classically argued that 'a city is not a tree',[2] in relation to city structuring in general, Colin Buchanan explicitly likened road network structure to the structure of a tree, as in the opening quotation to this chapter. This chapter 'deconstructs' the issue of structure and hierarchy through use of an extended tree analogy. This leads to the suggestion that the system formed by types and their hierarchical relationships is a distinct kind of structural system – or *constitution* – that lies beyond composition and configuration. This conceptualisation ties together the main structural concepts of the book into a single system.

The chapter provides new, constitutional interpretations of route type and network structure, to add to those developed previously on the basis of configuration or composition. These interpretations help to explain the 'structure of car orientation' and the 'structure of disurban creation' which lie at the heart of the challenge of streets and patterns.

HIERARCHICAL STRUCTURE

Hierarchy implies more than just a spectrum from 'major' to 'minor' (Figure 7.1). As we saw earlier, in Chapter 3, hierarchy tends to bundle together a variety of elements or dimensions, some of which will have definite structural relations implied. For example, arterial roads and local roads are differentiated because arterial routes all connect up in a single national system, whereas local roads form a more fragmented set of sub-networks. In this section we can explore the nature of hierarchy in more detail, to unpick different aspects of hierarchical structuring.

Structural conditions

The quotation at the opening of this chapter relates the structure of the road network to the structure of a tree. This stimulates the question: in what sense – or senses – is the structure of the road network like the structure of a tree (Figure 7.2)? Although at first sight it is a simple analogy, it is open to more complex interpretation, and potentially harbours no less than six different connotations of tree structure.

These six connotations equate to different aspects of the meaning of 'hierarchy' that we can refer to as 'structural conditions'. These structural conditions are worth exploring in detail, as they help to articulate fundamental aspects of structure that will be referred to throughout the rest of the book. These are interpreted with respect to the tree analogy in Figure 7.3.

The first structural condition is the *differentiation of components*: each component is a different type of thing – these could be 'things' as disparate as trees and roads themselves.

The second condition is the *ordered ranking of elements*, for example, a ranking from wide boulevard to narrow lane.

The third condition is the *necessary connections* between different types of element. In the case of a tree, 'necessary connections' means, for example, that a branch cannot 'float alone' in a matrix of twigs: it must

(a)

(b)

(c)

(d)

7.1 • Aspects of hierarchy. (a) Stacking of similar items. (b) Ordering by size, and spatial nesting. (c) Distinction by position, order and colour. (d) Structure of self-similar elements.

(a)

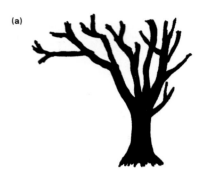

(b)

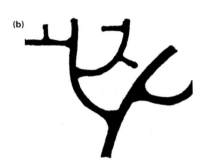

7.2 • The analogy between a tree and road network structure. How many connotations are implied?

at least connect to another branch, or to a limb or the trunk. For the road network, this means that principal routes should all connect up, to form a single contiguous network. This equates with the property of *arteriality* (Box 3). It reinforces the establishment of differentiation and ordering (conditions 1 and 2); indeed, it may suggest them in the first place.

The fourth condition is the *allowable connections* between different types of element. As applied to roads, this condition may be referred to as *access constraint*. It suggests that a residential road should not connect directly to a motorway, except via intermediate distributors.

We can pause in our progress through the tree analogy, to consider where we have got to so far. Already we have four separately identifiable conditions of hierarchy (although they seem to be linked in some ways). These four kinds of conditions can be seen manifested in actual street typologies used in practice. Some examples are given in Table 7.1. In the examples in Table 7.1 – and road networks in general – the structural conditions are normally cumulative: those lower in the table are assumed to incorporate the structural conditions higher in the table. The full set of four conditions represents what conventional road hierarchy is about.

From these first four structural conditions, we have a fairly comprehensive sense of hierarchy – but not as yet any suggestion of the actual configuration of routes. In other words, although these four conditions are embodied in the structure of a tree or a road network, we have yet to make any specification for the 'tree' structure of mathematical abstraction (a branching structure with no circuits). As far as the road network is concerned, although a 'hierarchical' network may have access constraint, there is not yet a suggestion that minor roads might not form a complete

Table 7.1 **Four kinds of road hierarchy relating to the first four structural conditions in Figure 7.3**

Structural condition (Figure 7.3)	Example of typology/hierarchy
1. Differentiation	Streets and squares; Poundbury (Figure 2.9)
2. Ordered ranking	Typologies based on street width (form), traffic flow (use), etc.
3. Necessary connections	Designation by arteriality – as with national inter-urban networks (Figure 3.15)
4. Allowable connections	Access constraint built into modern road layouts; conventional urban road hierarchy

Note: In road networks, the structural conditions are normally cumulative: those below are assumed to incorporate those above.

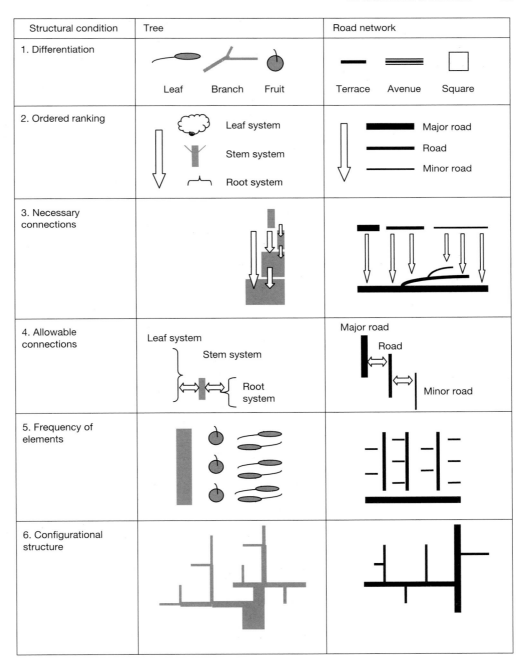

Structural condition	Tree	Road network
1. Differentiation	Leaf Branch Fruit	Terrace Avenue Square
2. Ordered ranking	Leaf system / Stem system / Root system	Major road / Road / Minor road
3. Necessary connections		
4. Allowable connections	Leaf system / Stem system / Root system	Major road / Road / Minor road
5. Frequency of elements		
6. Configurational structure		

7.3 • The tree analogy: six connotations relating to structural conditions.

connective network at its own level, or that there need be a single cul-de-sac.

Picking up on the tree analogy again (Figure 7.3): a fifth structural condition is the *frequency distribution* of the different elements, in inverse proportion to their rank order – there is one trunk, a few main limbs, many branches and a multitude of twigs. Although this distribution may be associated with 'branching structure', it could still refer to non-physical organisation, such as a 'pyramidal' distribution of employees in a company – or a tree possessing tens of fruits and hundreds of leaves. At this stage, the analogy implies that there would be a few main roads, several intermediate roads and many minor roads. As yet, there is still no definite implication of configuration.

The sixth and final condition is that of the *structural configuration* of the elements. This is the sense that the tree forms a 'tree-like' system of branching, where each path eventually ends as a twig. Now, finally, we have the implication for layout: the discontinuity of the minor routes in the network, epitomised by the full stop of the cul-de-sac. Here, finally, the road network becomes, mathematically, a 'tree'.

We can rest here in the tree analogy, metaphorically, and look back at the view. We have covered the first four structural conditions, which seem to equate more or less with issues of hierarchy. The last two bring us closer to the conception of a mathematical tree, relating to configuration. A network could be represented with a set of elements which had definite number (condition 5) and configuration (condition 6), but no explicit hierarchical ordering. Indeed, this is the case for a typical graph-theoretical arrangement of elements, as in conventional transport network analysis. For example, Figure 7.4 shows a network which has a definite number of links in a definite configuration; but there is no indication of arteriality or access constraint or ordering, since each link is hierarchically undifferentiated.

From this point, we can see where the rest of the tree analogy would take us – without necessarily going there in detail. Having arrived at the configuration of a tree, we can see further connotations of the tree analogy that relate to composition. These would relate to the orientation of elements, the size of elements and the shape of elements. Beyond the sixth condition – which is configurational – road networks start diverging from trees in shape, size and so on, and any analogy becomes less useful.

Conclusions on the nature of structure

We have already seen several different ways of interpreting a tree's structure – there are at least six tree-like connotations of structure: conditions

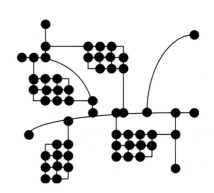

7.4 • A network of links without hierarchical differentiation.

by which the structure of a street pattern could match the structure of a tree.[3] Only one of these equates with the classical mathematical condition of a tree as a branching structure. In other words, there is more than one way for a structure to be 'tree-like'.

In particular, the first four conditions seem to relate to street type and hierarchy, whereas the subsequent two relate to configuration. The hierarchical aspect of tree structure seems to be distinct from the configuration, just as in a building structure there may be a 'hierarchy' of different structural members (e.g. main columns, cross-beams and brackets) but this does not necessarily imply a 'tree shape' (e.g. an all-cantilever structure).

This distinction echoes the way that the configuration of a tree structure (or a traffic light sculpture, Figure 7.1(c)) is quite distinct from its composition (the size and shape of the component parts). Indeed, we can recognise the system of hierarchical differentiation as a *separate* kind of structure from configurational structure, that we can refer to as *constitutional* structure.

COMPOSITION, CONFIGURATION AND CONSTITUTION

The concept of constitution has just been suggested, to add to those of composition and configuration. This section draws all three together in an integrated framework that helps crystallise the meaning of constitution.

Structural assemblies

At the start of Chapter 5, it was suggested that 'structure' is something that relates parts to each other and to the whole. Now, when referring specifically to '*a*' structure, we tend to be alluding specifically to the whole assembly, rather than the parts.

A street hierarchy is an assembly of street types – a set of relationships between parts – just as a network is an assembly of links or routes. In other words, 'a' hierarchy is not just an abstract 'system' of relationships, or a vague 'means' of organising types, or a general 'kind of organisation'. A hierarchy is itself a specific kind of structure.

The relationship between street types *within* a hierarchy is analogous to the relationship between streets *within* a street network (or routes within a route structure). In other words, a hierarchy is a 'structure of types' in the way that a network is a 'structure of routes'. Just as a network of routes expresses and contains within it all the connections between individual routes, a hierarchy expresses and contains within it all the connections (or relationships) between individual types.

BOX 7. COMPOSITION, CONFIGURATION AND CONSTITUTION

A constitution is a system of types and relationships (c). It is like an abstraction from a configuration (b) – or a second-order abstraction from composition (a).

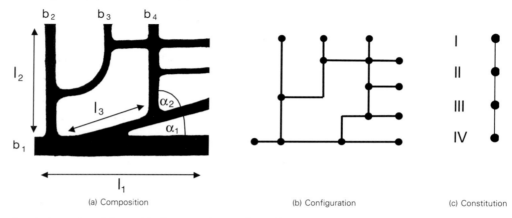

(a) Composition   (b) Configuration   (c) Constitution

Constitution is based on hierarchical properties such as tier and type, which may be expressed as ordinal numbers – here denoted by Roman numerals. Compare with Box 4.

We can reinforce these parallel relationships by referring to systems of hierarchy and type as systems of *constitution*. We can regard constitution as an abstraction from configuration, just as it was possible to regard configuration as an abstraction from composition. Similarly, a hierarchy can be seen as a structural abstraction from a network, just as a network can be seen as a structural abstraction from a two-dimensional layout of streetspace (Box 7).

It is possible to explicitly relate the properties of composition, configuration and constitution to the earlier tree analogy, by equating different properties or structural conditions with different aspects of structure. It is suggested that necessary and allowable connections are constitutional properties, while the number and placing of those elements relate to configuration (Table 7.2). Table 7.3 summarises the properties and associations of composition, configuration and constitution.

Conceptual distinctions

A hierarchy can be recognised as a *particular kind* of constitution, usually associated with an asymmetrical ranking of a particular sort, such as a

Table 7.2 Properties and associations of composition, configuration and constitution

	Composition	Configuration	Constitution
Association	Geometry	Topology	Hierarchy
Types	Rectangular, circular, triangular, etc.	Grid or mesh Tree-like	'Hierarchical', 'non-hierarchical', etc.
Properties of elements	Area Length Width Angle/orientation	Continuity Connectivity	Type Rank Arteriality Access constraint
Values	Real numbers	Integers and ratios	Ordinal numbers
Examples	37 m long 62.2° angle	Links = 72 Nodes = 49	Tier = I, II, III Type II.5, etc.

Table 7.3 Aspects of structure related to the tree analogy connotations (Figure 7.3)

Constitution	Configuration	Composition
1. Differentiation 2. Ordered ranking 3. Necessary connections 4. Allowable connections	5. Frequency of elements 6. Configurational structure	7. Size of elements 8. Shape of elements 9. Orientation of elements

pyramid formation, or tree structure with branches and sub-branches. However, a constitution could be a more general system of relationships, implying neither stratification nor asymmetry.

This parallels the distinction between the specific term 'network' and the more general term 'configuration'. A network is a particular kind of configuration – one which implies a certain degree of linearity and connectivity, like a net or mesh. A cluster of buildings or pattern of paving slabs – or a bank of traffic signals – could also be termed 'configurations' but would not normally be regarded as 'networks'.

Progressive abstractions of structure
As configuration is like a first-order abstraction of composition, then constitution is like a second-order abstraction of composition (or first-order abstraction of configuration).

When we convert a planar layout of roads from a composition to a skeletal network configuration, we convert from a metric amount of road-space (length and width, measured in real numbers' worth of metres) to a set of links, each of a nominal length or 'unit length' (and no breadth).[4] For example, a two-dimensional town plan that resolves itself into a structure of main streets and side streets is crystallised as a *configuration*, generating information about the quantities of discrete streets (routes), which have integer quantities of continuity (their 'length' measured in links), connectivity and depth.

Then when we convert from a configuration to a constitution, we convert from a definite topology of main streets and side streets to a single hierarchical structure that only recognises the existence of 'main street' and 'side street'. The quantitative information is stripped off: the number of main streets and the number of side streets is reduced to nominal, or unit values, and type reduced to ordinal values.

7.5 • Composition, configuration and constitution: assemblies and elements.

	Assembly	Elements
Composition	Whole space (area) 	Individual space (area)
Configuration (1st order abstraction)	Network or route structure 	Route Stem cul-de-sac
Constitution (2nd order abstraction)	Hierarchy I II III 	Route type I II III

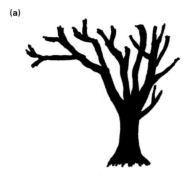

(a)

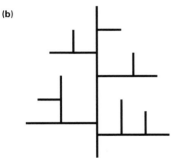

(b)

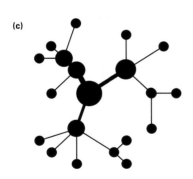

(c)

7.6 • Three ways in which the trunk is the highest ranking element of a tree. (a) Composition. The trunk is the largest element (greatest girth). (b) Configuration. The trunk connects to most elements (highest continuity and connectivity). (c) Constitution. The trunk is the single central element through which everything else connects.

In other words, going from composition to configuration, we 'lose' things like metric length, width and angle of orientation; but gain resolution of routes with properties such as continuity and connectivity. Then, going from configuration to constitution, we 'lose' things like the actual number and arrangement of routes in the network, but gain resolution of type or tier. Going in the other direction, from constitution to configuration to composition, the gain and loss are the other way around.

Elements and assemblies

Composition, configuration and constitution each have correspondence with particular types of assemblies (wholes) and elements (parts). Figure 7.5 demonstrates these graphically. This diagram can be regarded as a conceptual 'key' to the understanding of structural relationships, as employed in the rest of this chapter.

We now look in turn at types of constitutional element (constitutionally defined street type) and assembly (types of constitutional structure).

CONSTITUTIONALLY DEFINED STREET TYPE

The definition of 'arterial' route or street proposed in Chapter 3 is a constitutional definition. A constitutionally defined street or route type is one defined only in constitutional terms – relating to other types within a network – rather than referring to aspects of configuration (e.g. spine road) or composition (e.g. straight road). We can understand the distinction by considering a further tree analogy, to do with trunks and twigs.

Trunks and twigs

Let us consider the possible ways in which a trunk could be the highest ranking element in a tree structure (Figure 7.6). Although size, continuity and connectivity could all equate with the trunk being the highest ranking element of tree structure, they do not essentially define the pre-eminence of the trunk. Size, continuity and connectivity could all differentiate the status of limbs relative to branches, and branches relative to twigs. Effectively these are the same kinds of stem-like elements, but at a different scale.

At each scale, the elements are similar – all elements are 'cantilevers' and 'stems' (as defined in Chapter 5). In particular, each branch has exactly the same configuration as each limb (each has a continuity of 4 and a connectivity of 4). Therefore limbs and branches are not essentially distinguished by configuration, but must be distinguished by something else. What differentiates these absolutely is their *depth* – which defines them in relation to the whole (Figure 7.7).

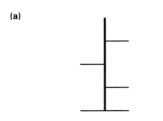

(a)

(b)

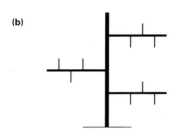

(c)

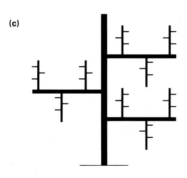

7.7 • Distinction of elements in a self-similar system. To the extent that a tree structure is self-similar, elements at different scales cannot necessarily be distinguished by configuration alone. (a) Trunk and limbs. (b) Trunk, limbs and branches. (c) Trunk, limbs, branches and twigs.

This equates with arteriality. A trunk may be defined as 'the main stem' of a tree. Here, the word 'stem' is configurational; but 'the main' is constitutional, and based on arteriality. This is effectively the basis of trunk road designation: a 'trunk road' is therefore, in principle, a constitutional definition of road type. Hence, we can have route types defined by constitution just as we can have route types based on configuration or composition (Figure 7.8).

We can, of course, superimpose the 'multiple personalities' of constitution, configuration and configuration in a single street type. For example, an Arterial Connector Boulevard would have the form of a boulevard, configured as a connector (all four-way intersections) and constituting part of the arterial (strategic) network.

Relation to conventional hierarchy

Many kinds of route type applied in conventional hierarchy are effectively constitutional – rather than configurational or compositional. As it happens, Buchanan explicitly rejected the notion of road types based on composition and configuration, such as 'ring roads', 'tangential roads' and 'spine roads' which would presuppose the final layout of a road with respect to overall network structure:

> It is not being inferred here that a ring road is in no circumstances likely to form part of an urban network. The objection that is taken is against the slavish adoption of the ring as a standardised pattern . . . The pattern may eventually comprise a ring, but it must be allowed to 'work itself out'.[5]

Instead, Buchanan opted for route types that were almost purely constitutional – the route types could almost be defined independently of configuration, function or use, but purely in the sense of which route type must (or must not) connect to which other type. Indeed, the arterial, subarterial and local route types discussed in Chapter 3 (Figure 3.22) are defined and related to each other constitutionally.

In fact, rather than having any sort of fixed association with a particular kind of layout or network configuration, constitutionally defined street types do have an association with particular kinds of constitutional structure. In other words, constitutional types like arterials belong in constitutions possessing arteriality, in the way that connectors belong in networks possessing connectivity.

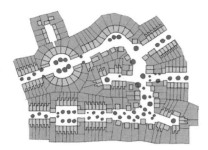

Street

Lane

Square

Crescent

Boulevard

(a)

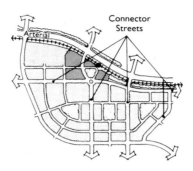

Through route

Cul-de-sac

Spine

Connector

Collector

(b)

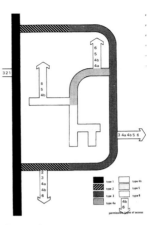

Arterial

Sub-arterial

Local

Trunk

Type II.5

(c)

7.8 • Compositional, configurational and constitutional street types. (a) Defined by composition. (b) Defined by configuration. (c) Defined by constitution.

TYPES OF CONSTITUTIONAL STRUCTURE

We are accustomed to associating hierarchy with 'hierarchical' layouts, possessing a particular kind of constitution, namely, a stratified system of distributors and access roads, where the major routes may only connect to minor roads via intermediate roads. However, we have also seen how there may be other, looser kinds of hierarchy, such as those advocated by some urban designers, where there are still recognisable types, but the connections between them are not so strictly controlled (Chapter 2). This investigation is concerned with demonstrating how these different possible kinds of hierarchy or constitution may be expressed as explicit permutations of arteriality and access constraint.

Arteriality and access constraint

Arteriality equates with the third structural condition of the tree analogy, namely 'necessary connections'. This is a form of strategic contiguity: the condition by which all the strategic (arterial) routes form a single contiguous network (Box 3). Arteriality is a feature of road systems in general (traditional and modern, urban and inter-urban).

(a)

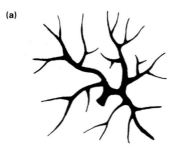

(b)

(c)

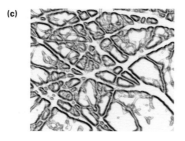

7.9 • Tree patterns and constitutions. (a) A tree has in-built arteriality and access constraint. (b) Removal of access constraint – but retention of arteriality. (c) Hence the conjoint structure of traditional street patterns.

Access constraint is a condition typical of 'modern', 'planned' or 'hierarchical' layouts, whereby each road type is controlled in terms of which other types it may connect to. This equates with the fourth structural condition, namely 'allowable connections'. While access constraint is typically built into modern road layouts, it has often been retrofitted to traditional street grids, where main streets have side streets closed off, to improve traffic circulation and safety on the main routes.

The term access constraint is used specifically in connection with road network structure. Additionally, the term *stratification* can be used as a more general version of access constraint, just as 'strategic contiguity' is used as a more general version of arteriality. Stratification can be applied in other contexts, such as geological strata, or institutional hierarchies, where the term 'access constraint' is not so appropriate.[6]

Together, arteriality and access constraint form a pair of properties that can distinguish different types of constitutional structure.

Types of constitutional structure

From the combination of the two fundamental properties of arteriality and access constraint, we can generate four permutations of *constitutional type* (Table 7.4).

The most 'hierarchical' constitutional structure would combine both arteriality and access constraint. This case can be termed *dendritic*, which is 'tree-like' in that it embodies all of the first four structural conditions of the tree analogy (Figure 7.3). In other words, just as a 'tree configuration' is as tree-like as a configuration can get (i.e. as far as the sixth condition), the dendritic constitution is about as tree-like as a constitution can get (i.e. as far as the fourth condition). The dendritic constitution could therefore be described as the 'tree-like' hierarchy associated with conventional road hierarchy and modern distributory urban layouts (e.g. Thamesmead, Figure 4.8(d)).

Now if we imagine the image of a set of tree branches and allow them to interfere and intersect in a single plane, this creates a pattern that loses the access constraint, but retains arteriality, to form a conjoint structure (Figure 7.9).

The *conjoint* case implies 'all joined up', and makes use of the first three structural conditions of the tree analogy (Figure 7.3). It is typical of inter-urban networks (Figure 3.15), and is also typical of traditional settlements where major streets have joined up to form through routes, forming a 'natural hierarchy'. This is seen in the case of the Bayswater network (Figure 5.13) with its strategic continuous roads and short, deep minor

Table 7.4 **Types of constitutional structure**

Type (label plus icon)	Structural conditions	Example layout
Dendritic	Arteriality plus access constraint	
Conjoint	Arteriality without access constraint	
Mosaic	Neither arteriality nor access constraint	
Serial	Access constraint without arteriality	

streets. The conjoint case is also typical of many engineering structures, where minor members connect progressively – or directly – to major members.

If we then lose the arteriality condition, we get the simplest arrangement where different street types are discernible: it has neither artificial constraint on access, nor the degree of organisation required to ensure arteriality. The term *mosaic* is used for this case to imply qualitative differentiation (distinct 'bits and pieces'), but distributed with no particular order ('here and there').

The mosaic case encompasses the first two discernible senses of hierarchy in the tree analogy (structural conditions one and two). While elements might be capable of ordering (such as street types of different width), there

(a)

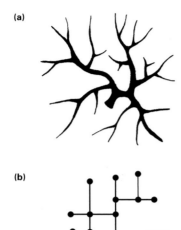

(b)

(c)

7.10 • Examples of type of pattern or structure. This echoes Figure 7.8 – but for assemblies rather than elements. (a) Radial composition. (b) Tree configuration. (c) Dendritic constitution.

is no definite spatial or structural ordering according to types defined in this way (there is nothing to prevent or require connection between, say, a street and a square). This could represent an urban designer's 'preferred' type of hierarchy, such as the case of Poundbury (Figure 2.9).

Finally, in the *serial* case, there is access constraint between 'major' and 'minor' types, requiring transition via an intermediate level, but the 'major' types do not connect up contiguously. This could represent cases where a 'hierarchical' system was incompletely implemented (e.g. fragments of urban motorway). The serial case could also represent any case where there is a spectrum of types whose extremities are incompatible (e.g. vehicular road, all purpose street, pedestrian path) but where there is no arteriality (spatial nesting) necessarily directed towards either end of the spectrum.

Table 7.4 effectively demonstrates an additional – constitutional – typological set to those types previously recognised in Chapters 4 and 6, based on composition or configuration (Figure 7.10).

The concept of constitution has therefore given us another way of defining network type. For example, Poundbury can be seen as a mosaic type, Bayswater as a conjoint type and Thamesmead as a dendritic type. In other words, although strictly these labels refer to constitutions, they could be used to apply to any set of configurations with those constitutions, just as 'grid' or 'tree' could be used to describe a composition with those configurations.

Similarly, the ABCD types introduced in Chapter 4 could be reinterpreted in constitutional terms. Figure 7.11 shows the relationship between composition, configuration and constitution relative to the ABCD types introduced in Chapter 4.

Desired structures

Constitutional structure allows us to make some new interpretations of desired properties that could contribute to the design debate.

Coherence

Any street pattern with a consistent constitution (e.g. conjoint all over) could be interpreted as a 'coherent pattern'. This constitutional interpretation of coherence could allow tree-like layouts with consistently dendritic structure to be considered coherent as well as traditional layouts with a consistent conjoint or mosaic constitution. In this sense, Poundbury, Bayswater and Thamesmead are all 'coherent'. A network that was not coherent could be imagined by considering a hybrid of these distinct types.[7]

	Composition	Configuration	Constitution
A-type *Altstadt*			
B-type Bilateral			
C-type Conjoint or Characteristic			
D-type Distributory			

7.11 • ABCD and the three Cs.

Legibility

It is suggested that arteriality is the 'active ingredient' of hierarchy that contributes to legibility. One can clearly determine one's way about a layout if it possesses arteriality (strategic contiguity), since as long as one heads towards the higher status route, one knows where one is with respect to the whole. In this sense, legibility applies to conjoint and dendritic constitutions, but not to mosaic or serial cases. In this interpretation of legibility, the Thamesmead road network would be considered more 'legible' than the Poundbury case: the structure of the former is more easily grasped, and progressive movement through the hierarchy is possible.

Clear typology

This suggests, simply, the existence of clearly recognisable types. (This accords with the first structural condition of the tree analogy.) Such types would be particularly apparent where these were expressly designed as particular types in the first place – which would be typical for 'planned' layouts – as in the case of Poundbury (Figure 2.9).

Clear hierarchy

This suggests any case in which recognisable route types are both clearly ordered and connect to each other in consistent ways. Hence, any constitution with both a clear typology *and* clear explicit rules for arteriality or access constraint could be equated with a 'clear hierarchy'. Such constitutions have a clear rank order related to spatial layout.

'Less rigid' hierarchy

This might be a hierarchy which relaxes either the access constraint or the arteriality condition: in short, anything other than a dendritic constitution.

'Good' hierarchy

The type of hierarchy often deemed desirable by urban planners and designers seems to allow explicit differentiation of route type, but not necessarily arteriality or access constraint. This encompasses a range that includes both the Poundbury case (mosaic constitution) and also the Craig Plan (dendritic constitution). To cover all these kinds of cases, we could interpret an urban designer's 'good hierarchy' as one in which streets play a satisfactory structural role in route hierarchy (where streets are functional as streets, not just 'access roads').

Inter-connected networks

The conjoint constitution could be seen as the structure most predisposed to offer inter-connectivity, since it assures a certain connectivity through arteriality, while not constraining connections through access constraint. Conversely, the serial constitution is the least inter-connected, since it constrains access without assuring arteriality.

The foregoing suggested associations – conclusions from the nature of structure for the design debate – are summarised in Table 7.5.

Table 7.5 Interpretation of desired properties related to constitutional structure

Constitution		Coherent pattern	Legibility	Clear typology	Clear hierarchy	Less rigid hierarchy
Mosaic		👍	☒	👍	☒	👍
Conjoint		👍	👍	👍	👍	👍
Dendritic		👍	👍	👍	👍	☒
Serial		👍	☒	👍	👍	👍

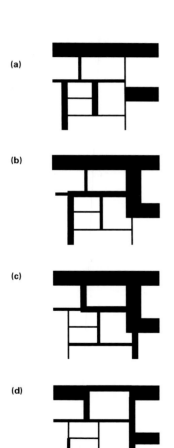

(a)

(b)

(c)

(d)

7.12 • The independence of constitution and configuration. Four different constitutions are illustrated using the same configuration. (a) Mosaic. (b) Conjoint. (c) Dendritic. (d) Serial.

Constitution and configuration

Although tree-like configurations and tree-like hierarchies may often be associated (and often confused, Chapter 2), constitution is conceptually independent of configuration. This can be demonstrated by using a single configuration to illustrate each of the four distinct kinds of constitution (Figure 7.12).

This means that a given configuration could have its routes classified according to a wide variety of constitutions. This reflects the ability of road classification to turn any jumbled mass of urban streetspace on the town plan into a discrete set of coloured lines on the road atlas. Conversely, this flexibility also means that constitution can be used to proactively *generate* a wide variety of configurations (as will be seen in Chapter 9).

The independent nature of constitution also means that, although the dendritic constitution is most immediately recognised as the structure of modern 'distributory' road layouts (Figure 7.13(a)), it does not inevitably lead to them, but might be applied to form grids or other patterns. This is seen in the classic case of the Craig Plan, which despite being a pedestrian-friendly 'urbanistic grid', employs a dendritic constitution (Figure 7.13(b)). In such a kind of 'hierarchical network', the minor routes need not necessarily be any more discontinuous than those higher in the hierarchy.

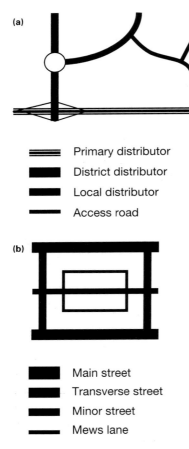

(a)

━━━ Primary distributor
▬▬▬ District distributor
▬▬ Local distributor
── Access road

(b)

▬▬ Main street
▬▬ Transverse street
▬▬ Minor street
── Mews lane

7.13 • Dendritic classics. (a) Classic modern tributary. (b) Classic grid (Craig Plan).

The urban (or disurban) effects of the dendritic constitution are therefore not simply due to the abstract constitution itself, but are significantly due to what types occur where in the structure – in particular,

1. where routes for different modes of movement occur, and
2. where 'streets' fit relative to 'roads'.

The structural concepts of the first half of the chapter can now be applied in the rest of the chapter to explain issues of concern to the design debate.

THE STRUCTURE OF CAR ORIENTATION

The structure of car orientation refers to the way in which the routes and networks used by different modes of movement are related and structured in such a way as to favour cars (and other forms of private motor travel) relative to the combined system of public transport plus non-motorised access. This section focuses primarily on the constitutional aspects that make up the 'the structure of car orientation'.

Arteriality

We saw in Chapter 3 that arteriality is a conventional feature of road networks in general. Arteriality also seems to make sense for public transport in particular. The strategic contiguity afforded by arteriality is positively beneficial for a public transport system, since it ensures that any service connects with the wider network, ultimately upwards to the national level. Ideally, once connected at the highest level, one continues at that level uninterrupted, until descending again towards the destination.

It would also be useful if routes for pedestrians and other access modes also connect 'upwards' to the public transport system. That said, the pedestrian system itself does not necessarily require a hierarchical ranking based on arteriality – in the sense that it is not essential that all of the most 'major' pedestrian streets all connect up contiguously.

Access constraint

Access constraint is perhaps the most familiar structural feature of conventional road hierarchy's dendritic constitution. Access constraint is a desired property for roads in general, since it minimises conflicts, boosting both safety and efficiency. For the car and general traffic, access constraint is desirable, in as far as it means that routes with high-speed traffic have a minimisation or removal of junctions with low-speed roads. A stratified hierarchy is no problem for the private vehicle, since each change in 'level' may require little more than a change of gear (Figure 7.14(a)).

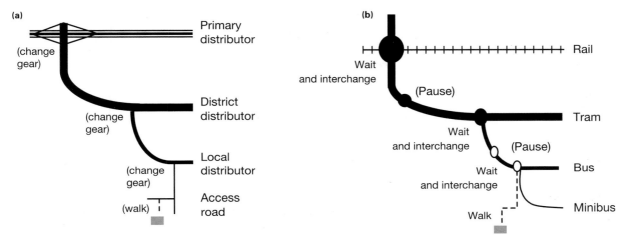

7.14 • Stratified hierarchies contrasted. (a) Private transport. (b) Public transport.

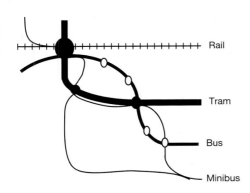

7.15 • Example network configuration with conjoint constitution, recommended for public transport. This is strategically contiguous (the most strategic systems are contiguous) but not stratified (any level can connect to any level).

However, access constraint is not generally beneficial for a public transport system. While the more strategic routes and services may have fewer points of access, at those access points themselves (e.g. stations) all levels of the hierarchy should be able to converge and interchange. A stratified hierarchy would, in general, be disadvantageous to a public transport system where tiers are based on different mode, since each change in tier implies a change of mode (Figure 7.14(b)). Access constraint would also be a barrier to users wishing to access the public transport – if minor pedestrian streets were barred from connecting to major transit streets.

Similarly, access constraint for a pedestrian route hierarchy would seem counter-productive, since access constraint implies lack of connectivity and directness, and greater distance. Any minor pedestrian route should be allowed to connect to any major pedestrian route.

Preferred constitutions

Overall, the preferred constitution for public transport is the conjoint constitution: arteriality without access constraint. This means the most direct access to the highest level, and continuity at that high level once there. All major routes must connect up to form a single high-level network; but there is no bar on the most local feeder services connecting to the most strategic (Figure 7.15).

Ideally, the pedestrian system will 'plug into' the public transport hierarchy, thereby forming a combined conjoint constitution; but the pedestrian route system itself need not be 'hierarchical', and can function without arteriality or access constraint, namely, a mosaic constitution.

The preferred road system in general is conventionally regarded as being the dendritic constitution: a combination of arteriality and access constraint. However, strictly speaking, arteriality here is applying to strategic routes, designated in such a way as to form an arterial pattern. This does not necessarily mean that all route sections of high speed, flow or capacity are contiguously connected. Within urban areas, it is more typical for high-speed or high-capacity sections to form a more fragmented pattern, with underpasses, relief roads, short sections of urban motorways, and so on. These may each have appropriate access constraint locally, thereby forming a *serial* organisation.

The dendritic structure of car orientation

One of the problems of the conventional hierarchy is in cases where it equates the pedestrian with occupying the lowest rung in the vehicular hierarchy. This pegs the pedestrian network to the stratified hierarchy of vehicular movement, rather than ensuring integration with the public transport system. Indeed, in some hierarchies there may even be a gap in the ranking between routes used by pedestrians and routes used by public transport.

This is seen where bus stops on distributor roads are isolated from local pedestrian focal points, or, when hierarchy is retrofitted to traditional towns, where a bus station is sited on a distributor road away from the central, pedestrian-intensive streets, since public transport is equated with (high) vehicular function, not pedestrian function. Dividing pedestrians and public transport in this way is a recipe for car orientation (Figure 7.16). And this is the structure built into conventional hierarchies since *Traffic in Towns*.[8]

Overall, car orientation can be seen as a combination of compositional, configurational and constitutional factors. This is seen in the promotion of spread-out, coarse-grained, impermeable layouts that are 'encouraged' by tributary or tree-like structures with poor connectivity, that are in turn 'encouraged' by dendritic constitution. Together, the conventional approaches to configuration and constitution combine to make a 'structure of car orientation' (Figure 7.17).

7.16 • The constitutional structure of car orientation. Public transport confined to arterial routes cannot easily penetrate down into pedestrian territory (A–Z). If pedestrian networks are discontinuous this makes it difficult to get directly from X to Z via Y, but necessitates going via A. The journey X–A–Z is hardly convenient or even feasible for the pedestrian or public transport – or even the two combined.

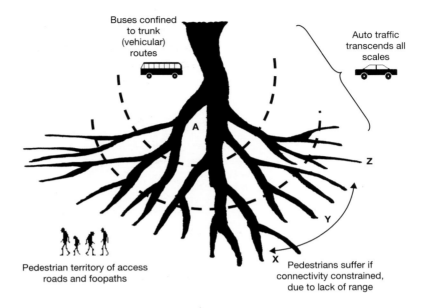

Buses confined to trunk (vehicular) routes

Auto traffic transcends all scales

Pedestrian territory of access roads and foopaths

Pedestrians suffer if connectivity constrained, due to lack of range

THE STRUCTURE OF DISURBAN CREATION

> **The source is at the heart of the built-up area; tiny streams, the narrow local roads, link up to the tributaries, the main road system in the built-up areas. These in turn link up to the main river, the roads running between the built-up areas. As water gathers in volume and the river becomes wider and bolder in scale, so does the traffic increase in volume, the roads becoming wider and broader in scale, and their intersections fewer and fewer.**
>
> Frederick Gibberd[9]

> **Walker and his team set out to create islands of urbanity within the amorphous sea of the grid roads.**
>
> Tim Mars[10]

New towns such as Gibberd's Harlow and Walker's Milton Keynes, alluded to in the above quotations, exhibit or even epitomise the road hierarchy-driven urban structure of much modern development. As well as appearing to be car oriented, conventional road hierarchy has also applied the dendritic constitution in such a way that leads to the disurban layouts bemoaned by many urban designers and planners – and bemoaned, presumably, by

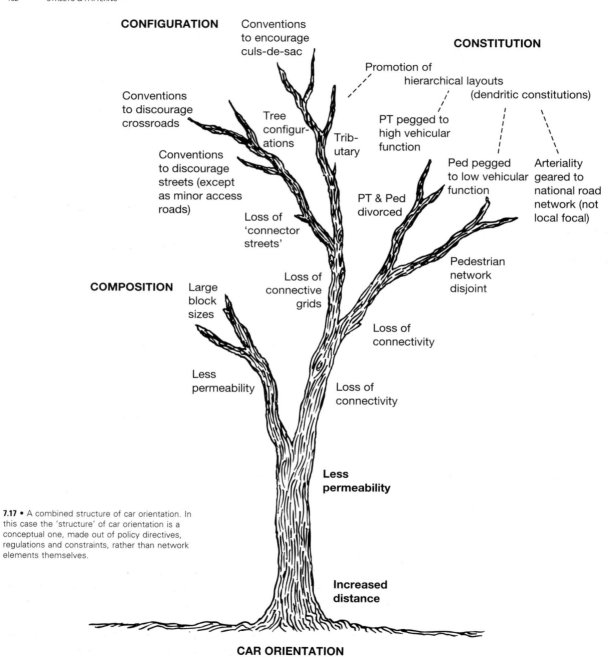

CONFIGURATION

Conventions to encourage culs-de-sac

CONSTITUTION

Conventions to discourage crossroads

Promotion of hierarchical layouts (dendritic constitutions)

Tree configur- ations

Trib- utary

PT pegged to high vehicular function

Conventions to discourage streets (except as minor access roads)

Ped pegged to low vehicular function

Arteriality geared to national road network (not local focal)

Loss of 'connector streets'

PT & Ped divorced

Pedestrian network disjoint

COMPOSITION

Large block sizes

Loss of connective grids

Less permeability

Loss of connectivity

Less permeability

Loss of connectivity

Less permeability

7.17 • A combined structure of car orientation. In this case the 'structure' of car orientation is a conceptual one, made out of policy directives, regulations and constraints, rather than network elements themselves.

Increased distance

CAR ORIENTATION

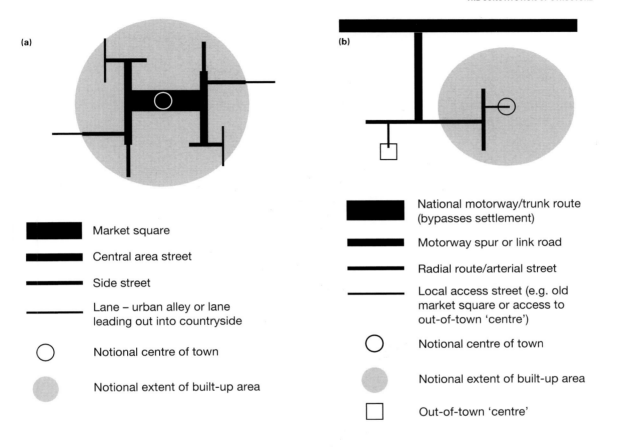

(a)

▬▬▬ Market square

▬▬ Central area street

━━ Side street

──── Lane – urban alley or lane leading out into countryside

◯ Notional centre of town

⬤ Notional extent of built-up area

(b)

▬▬▬ National motorway/trunk route (bypasses settlement)

▬▬ Motorway spur or link road

━━ Radial route/arterial street

──── Local access street (e.g. old market square or access to out-of-town 'centre')

◯ Notional centre of town

⬤ Notional extent of built-up area

☐ Out-of-town 'centre'

7.18 • Inversion of status of historic and modern routes. The relationship between notional centre and main routes is reversed. Arteriality now relates to national road traffic network, not the local centre. (a) Historic structure. (b) Modern structure.

the users of the bleak, dysfunctional landscapes that result. This section explores how the dendritic constitution equates with the 'structure of disurban creation'.

Disurban creation and the dendritic constitution

At the outset of this book, road hierarchy was implicated in the cataclysm of Modernism. The way that conventional road hierarchy treated roads and streets in relation to each other and to urban structure was associated with turning the urban fabric inside out, from the scale of settlements to the scale of street blocks.

Conventional road hierarchy – the kind of 'bad' hierarchy that has been criticised by urban designers and planners – equates with the dendritic

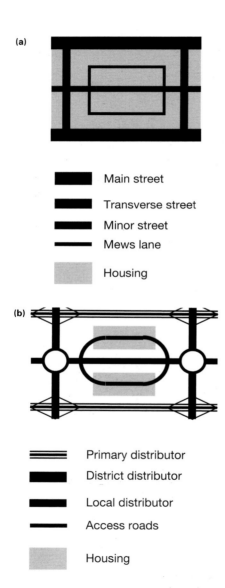

(a)

■ Main street

■ Transverse street

■ Minor street

— Mews lane

Housing

(b)

═══ Primary distributor

■ District distributor

■ Local distributor

— Access roads

Housing

7.19 • Dendritic new towns. (a) Urbanistic grid of a historic 'new town'. (b) Supergrid of a modernist new town.

constitution. Having said that, the dendritic constitution itself is simply an abstract set of relationships between types. What becomes significant is what those types represent.

For example, the urban structures originally shown in Figure 1.3 – reproduced as Figure 7.18 – could both represent dendritic structures. The distinction between the historic structure (Figure 7.18(a)) and the modern one (Figure 7.18(b)) is that in the first case, it is the urban streets that are pegged to 'Tier I', the prime position of arteriality, and inter-urban roads are the lowest rung; whereas in the second case the reverse applies. In the historic structure (a), arteriality is geared to the local high street – a 'people place' – whereas in the modern structure (b), arteriality is geared to the national road traffic network.

The key issue is what it is that is being ranked by arteriality. In the traditional case, it is urban streets: all the main streets connect up, focusing on the central square. In the modern case, arteriality ranks traffic routes; it is the national traffic network that links up contiguously.

The effect of this system is most strongly observed in new development and new towns built according to modernist principles. Here, the dendritic constitution is built in from the start. This means that streets only feature where they are allowed to fit into the hierarchy – which is at the subordinate level of the access road.

So, while Edinburgh's Craig Plan employed a dendritic constitution, all the component types were *streets* of one sort or another (squares, lanes, mews). As the tributaries gather together, they lead towards the most important streets, which form the 'heart' of the system (Figure 7.19(a)). But in a modern new town, the street appears – if at all – only as an access road, at the lowest hierarchical level (Figure 7.19(b)). There is no coherent focus for these streets. As the tributaries gather together, they lead only to the non-place disurban realm of the distributor road. In terms of Gibberd's quotation at the start of this section, the 'heart' of the urban area, such as it is, is not directly connected to the main arteries (Figure 7.20).

The position of streets in the overall scheme of things is, of course, something that is controlled by hierarchy, through the 'inverse relationship' between mobility and access.

Traffic in Towns' *tree-like hierarchy*

In the light of the analysis of this chapter, we can interpret *Traffic in Towns'* reference to the 'trunk, limbs, branches and twigs (corresponding to the access roads) of a tree' as referring to:

(a)

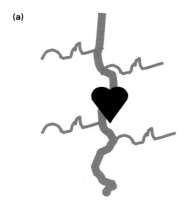

(b)

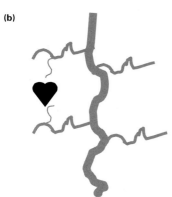

7.20 • The heart and the arteries. (a) Traditional: 'heart' directly connected to main arteries. (b) Modern: 'heart' and main arteries remote from each other.

- the progression from a small number of high ranking roads to a multitude of low ranking roads;
- the progression from strategically connecting roads to local roads;
- the progression from vehicular 'roads' to all-purpose 'streets'.

The key point here is the association of the last two factors, in particular:

- since streets can only be access roads, they must be hierarchically subordinate; and
- since ranking is determined by arteriality, hierarchically subordinate means spatially disjointed.

We can see the spatially disjointed nature from the diagrams in *Traffic in Towns* (Figure 7.21). The lack of connectivity of the minor route network is quite deliberate: Buchanan emphasised that movements between the environmental 'cells' and the interlacing network of distributor roads would be 'canalised *without choice*'.[11]

Buchanan remarks that it is 'interesting that it was basically a Venetian arrangement which emerged in our comprehensive redevelopment study of the Tottenham Court Road area'.[12] Apart from the obvious differences of form and context (and, not least, the use of roads rather than canals), there is indeed a structural similarity between the networks of Venice and

7.21 • *Traffic in Towns'* treatment of road hierarchy. Streets occupy a hierarchically subordinate rank (a), that equates with a spatially disjointed position (b).

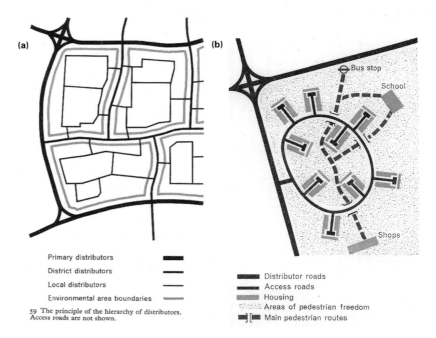

(a)

Primary distributors ▬▬▬
District distributors ▬▬
Local distributors ▬▬
Environmental area boundaries ▬▬▬

59 The principle of the hierarchy of distributors. Access roads are not shown.

(b)

Bus stop
School
Shops

▬▬ Distributor roads
▬▬ Access roads
▬▬ Housing
░░ Areas of pedestrian freedom
▬▌▐▬ Main pedestrian routes

7.22 • The structure of disurban creation. Streets are isolated by a disurban territory of distributor roads.

Buchanan's Fitzrovia. However, what counts most here is not the abstract structure, but what the component elements represent.

Effectively, Venice works where Modernist layouts have failed because in Venice the urban public places are contiguous, while the components forming the 'islands' – or the 'urban rooms' – are private buildings; whereas in Modernist layouts is it the public places constituted by streets that tend to be isolated and separated by a sterile territory of distributor roads.

Within an urbanistic grid like Edinburgh's New Town, it does not matter so much if mews lanes form a disjointed scatter, because they all connect immediately upwards to more urban streets. But it does matter if *all urban streets* form the lowest rung, leading to a scatter of urban oases separated from each other by a desert of distributors. *This* is the structure of disurban creation (Figure 7.22).

The result of this is that the only place for the 'street' in the hierarchy promoted in *Traffic in Towns* is that of a 'twig'. This does not necessarily mean that the street is configurationally a cul-de-sac – although in modern layouts this has often been the case. Rather, it is in a *constitutional* sense that a street is a twig: meaning, the street occupies a hierarchically subordinate and spatially disjointed position in the road network. But, to echo Christopher Alexander, one can suggest that *a street is not a twig* – or at least should not be, if it is to fulfil its urban role.

CONCLUSIONS

This chapter has suggested that, just as a network is a 'structure of routes', a hierarchy is a 'structure of types', and that the system of types and their relationships can be recognised more generally as a system of constitution.

Route types such as arterials and trunks roads may be regarded as constitutional types, and we can distinguish different kinds of constitutional structure, based on a combination of arteriality and access constraint. For example, the conventional 'tree-like' hierarchy has been equated with the dendritic constitution. However, other constitutions, such as the conjoint and the mosaic, may also be identified: these appear to equate more with the kinds of 'good hierarchy' that urban designers and planners tend to favour.

The dendritic constitution may be equated with 'bad hierarchy' to some extent. However, the dendritic constitution is not of itself the problem – since dendritic constitutions can be applied in a variety of ways, including the creation of more traditional, pedestrian-friendly grids. What matters is how and where streets – and routes for different modes – fit into the resulting structure.

The 'structure of car orientation' is revealed as the dendritic structure where pedestrian routes are pegged to the lowest rung in the vehicular hierarchy, while public transport uses the higher tier roads. A stratified hierarchy is fine for cars, which can negotiate up and down the hierarchy with ease, but disbeneficial to the public transport and pedestrian system.

A constitutionally defined 'structure of disurban creation' may also be identified. With conventional road hierarchy, which applies an inverse relationship between 'mobility function' and 'access function', streets are pegged to the lowest rungs in a hierarchy. Since this hierarchy is ordered by arteriality, then 'hierarchically subordinate' equates with 'spatially disjointed'. This spatially disjointed scatter of 'urban public places' constituted by streets is the essence of disurban creation.

Overall, this chapter has revealed the structural conditions underlying some of the problems of urban layout. This has helped to diagnose and pinpoint some of the issues thrown up at the outset of the book. This chapter has also clarified the differences between constitution and configuration, and the relationships between the definition of street type and position in the hierarchy (Chapter 2).

The principal analytic investigation into the nature of structure is now more or less complete. The remainder of the book now turns attention to the design debate, to apply what has been learned about concepts of structure in the preceding chapters to create a new system for the design and layout of streets and patterns.

NOTES

1 MoT (1963: 44).

2 Alexander (1966a).

3 There are also at least two further connotations to do with structural connection, not detailed here: (1) *transition-termination conditions*: a trunk has transition into limbs and branches, whereas (only) twigs terminate; (2) the *trunk-twig gradient*: the condition by which each branch has a definite 'trunk' (or 'ground') end greater than or equal to its own rank, while any other connection must be to an element less than or equal to its own rank.

4 This has been described in terms of peeling off layers of width to reduce a section of street to a skeletal element of nominal width (Asami *et al.*, 2001).

5 *Traffic in Towns* (MoT, 1963: 43).

6 The word 'stratification' comes from the same Latin root as street and structure, relating to construction (Rykwert, 1978: 14). 'Strategic' comes from Greek, relating to military planning.

7   It may be that, in the analytic process, street patterns (or sub-networks) with distinct character – reflecting intrinsic coherence – are those most likely to be defined for analysis in the first place.

8   That is to say that, in *Traffic in Towns*, public transport routes are not necessarily contiguous, since they are not specified in the hierarchy. Routes specified for pedestrian use (i.e. access roads) form the lowest rung in the hierarchy, implying a discontiguous scatter of routes. This, in itself, is not necessarily a problem; it depends what those pedestrian routes connect 'upwards' to.

9   Gibberd (1967: 36).

10 Mars (1992).

11 MoT (1963: 42).

12 MoT (1963: 180).

8 MODES, STREETS AND PLACES

> [T]he subtopian sprawl of edge-of-town housing estates, with sound but dull
> two-storey semis or terraces stretched out along roads wide enough for two
> dustcarts to pass at 50 mph, boarded by pavements wide enough for two
> prams to pass at 20 mph . . . and the lifeline to town an expensive, infrequent,
> inconvenient bus.
>
> *Urban Villages*[1]

Movement ushers in the fourth dimension of urban design, as objects in
motion create linear paths in space through time. These tracks of movement trace out the basic organisational structure of urban topology.
Whatever else streets are used for – as public places or social spaces – it
is movement that demands the continuous thread that links one section of
street to the next, stitching each part into a single whole.

Just as patterns and structures are shaped by their constituent roads
and streets, the design of roads and streets is strongly influenced by the
modes of movement that use them. The quotation above sums up some
of the symptoms of disurban creation, related to the 'overdesign' of roads,
where the concern for the hypothetical possibility of particular types of
vehicle passing each other at unlikely speeds becomes a controlling influence on the layout of development. Those who lay the blame for disurban
creation at the door of highway engineering are criticising a form of design
that appears to serve the needs of vehicles uncritically – the villains variously being cars, 'phantom dustcarts' and even the heavy debris-shifting
vehicles required to clear up neighbourhoods after a nuclear strike.[2]

The conventional Modernist solutions were well intentioned towards
the aims of road safety, but always seemed – implicitly or explicitly – to be
based on the assumption of expediting vehicular traffic flow.

Although the core principles in *Traffic in Towns* could be applied to a
variety of transport contexts, the report did not seem particularly interested
in what we would call sustainable modes: public transport was barely paid
lip service, and bicycles almost written off. In the futuristic manner of its

day, *Traffic in Towns* devoted as many column inches to personal jet propulsion and air cushion craft as it did to the prospects for better use of bikes and buses.[3]

While cities and towns have gained from the legacy of Tripp and Buchanan as far as vehicular flow and road safety are concerned, today's urban agenda demands more from its streets, as urban places as well as routes, serving more 'sustainable' modes of movement and a more holistic kind of functional urbanism. Those who today wish for more traditional streets rather than bleak distributors do not want unsafe roads, but would like a better balance between the needs of those who would like to travel on urban roads safely in fast, noxious vehicles, and the needs of those who wish to safely and healthily occupy those same roads as part of their local street environment.

For a more balanced solution to movement in towns and cities, we need to take account of not just a few extreme design scenarios (phantom vehicles) but a whole spectrum of modes of movement, focusing on the needs of people, whether inside vehicles or not.

Earlier chapters have analysed the nature of structure and hierarchy in connection with streets and patterns. We now look at approaches towards the onward design of streets, addressing the role of streets first as conduits of movement and then as urban places. This requires looking initially at the different kinds of modes which may be considered favourable or worthy of promoting, and then at how a new kind of hierarchy can fit those modes with the other roles of streets.

THE MODAL KALEIDOSCOPE

All around the world, we can find a rich diversity of modes of movement – especially in cities and towns that are not too strictly regulated in terms of street type or vehicle type. Cars, vans, taxis, jitneys, jeepneys, coaches, buses and minibuses are joined by trams, trolleybuses and heavy goods vehicles, not to mention motorised bicycles, mopeds, motor scooters and motorcycles, not forgetting motorised three-wheelers such as *becaks* and autorickshaws. To these we can add 'non-motorised modes' such as bicycles, tricycles and trishaws, rickshaws, wheelchairs, prams and pushchairs, trolleys, handcarts and wheelbarrows, and not to forget rollerblades, roller-skates, skateboards and scooters. And to these human-powered modes we can add transport using horses, oxen, donkeys, llamas, sled-dogs, camels and elephants.[4]

Design to provide for different modes starts with a recognition of the existence of those modes. Today there is much talk about green modes and sustainable mobility, and equity and accessibility for all ages and social groups. If we are serious about 'sustainable transport', we should take care to consider how any or all of the above modes of movement might contribute to sustainability and equity objectives, and not start from an assumption that the central part of every street has precedence given to motor vehicles with four or more wheels, and that everything else that does not walk on two feet must be ignored or banned.

To help to understand and cater for a diverse 'modal kaleidoscope' suggests the need for recognition and classification of different modes. Just as street types have 'multiple personalities' – an overlapping set of simultaneously present attributes – so too do modes. Each mode of movement could be classified by form (e.g. size or weight), by use (e.g. speed or occupancy) or by designation (legal status). To these we can also add means of propulsion, guidance, passenger- or freight-carrying function and public or private transport operation. But how might we arrange these modes in a useful sort of classification?

Transport hierarchies are contrived for a purpose, and that is to manage relationships between modes. A modal hierarchy should be able to help to identify which modes might be compatible for coexisting on the same road or street type, and which 'favoured' modes might be worthy of promotion through street type and network structure. To address the issue of favourability, we first turn to a most influential consideration of contemporary policy, that of sustainability.

Sustainability

While the car may often be cast as the arch-villain in the sustainability equation, there is nothing intrinsically virtuous about buses and trains. Transport enthusiasts steaming around in their own private vehicles are still burning fossil fuels, whether these run on railway tracks or rubber tyres. Even electric trains have an energy bill, which may exceed that of the diesel bus. But, if the swish trains manage to prise more people away from their cars, the overall energy benefit may swing in their favour.

Similarly, cycling may use less energy than walking, but production of the bicycle itself consumes energy – and bikes have their own little oil fix from time to time. The cycle versus walk verdict also depends on whether one counts the environmental cost of the land required to grow the extra cereal the cyclist consumes in order to power the bike.[5] However, this begs the question of whether one should also count the diet and appetite of the person who drives to the gym – or the drive-in – and just eats more anyway.

In other words, recognising environmentally 'sustainable' outcomes is not at all straightforward. And if we expand sustainability to include social and economic as well as environmental concerns, then we head into even more debatable territory. We start to question who is sustaining what for whom – not only what kind of environment, but what kind of society, and what kind of economy. Once social and economic considerations are factored in, sustainability could mean almost anything, from conservatively 'sustaining' traditional societies at their present subsistence level to liberally 'sustaining' growth in GDP through a combination of technological progress and carefully selected exploitation of natural resources. And when the hypothetical needs of future generations are thrown in, we are in danger of losing the plot entirely, as we could end up questioning absolutely everything from the purpose of procreation to post-human evolution and the heat death of the universe.

This book does not presume to give a definitive account of sustainability, but simply attempts to provide a basis for understanding the case for favouring 'greener' modes of transport, while also being aware of the social equity and efficiency benefits of having an integrated range of different modes available to suit different needs. This is done in the first instance by considering the environmental impact of movement at street level.

Motion in the urban room

Imagine an urban square as a habitat, or local 'environment' created to satisfy human needs. It could be a tranquil formal setting, like London's Fitzroy Square, framed by fine buildings, with people strolling by or sitting beneath the shady trees. Or it could be a hectic bustling space in a rapidly developing country, where people are walking, talking, bustling, trading, cooking, eating, sleeping. All urban life is here: a whole mixture of 'land uses' contained in a single 'urban room'.

Now, imagine the presence of a vehicle in the square. At rest, the vehicle represents a certain amount of displacement: it uses up land and causes a visual obstruction. If the vehicle is a bicycle, it takes up hardly any space, and you can see right through it; but a car takes up about the size of a market stall, perhaps, or a fountain. If the vehicle is a lorry or a bus, the displacement is still more substantial.

Now, imagine this vehicle is a motor vehicle, and starts up its engine. This causes noise, some vibration, and if it is a conventional petrol or diesel vehicle, it will emit poisonous gases and particles. The vehicle – with its engine running – is now a nuisance and a health hazard.

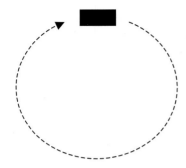

8.1 • Circling the Square. A vehicle causes a variety of environmental impacts in a locality. The degree of displacement, disturbance and danger is essentially related to the type of vehicle and its motion. The impacts arise whether the vehicle is part of a 'flow' or not, or whether the vehicle is performing any social or economic function.

Table 8.1 **Environmental impacts relating to vehicle and spacetime factors**

Environmental disbenefit	Vehicle and spacetime factors
Landtake	Area (m^2) and velocity (ms^{-1})
Visual obstruction	Profile or overall size (m^2 or m^3)
Noise	Engine type
Poisonous gases and particulates	Engine type
Vibration	Engine type; mass (kg) and velocity (ms^{-1})
Path obstruction (severance)	Vehicle length divided by velocity = time (s)
Risk of injury and death	Mass (kg) and velocity (ms^{-1}); momentum ($kgms^{-1}$)

Finally, imagine that the vehicle starts to move, and begins circling round the square, burning up energy at a certain rate (Figure 8.1). The motion of the vehicle means that it claims extra space in front of it, which cannot be used for other purposes.[6] The motion also blocks the paths of other users of the square, imposing delay on others: the longer and slower the vehicle, the greater the delay. And finally, the faster and heavier the vehicle – the greater its momentum – the greater the accident impact, if it were to collide with a person or anything else.

Every kind of vehicle – whether car, bus or bicycle – can be seen as a displacement of other urban activities; and any moving vehicle is a potential danger to life and limb. The degree of displacement, disturbance and danger will depend on the kind of vehicle: larger, faster and motorised vehicles are typically the worst offenders (Table 8.1, Figure 8.2).

Some scientific-looking items are used in Table 8.1 (velocity: ms^{-1}) in order to 'dehumanise' the vehicle: to emphasise that to the person in the street, a moving vehicle is just a nasty package of physics and chemistry: a potentially dangerous projectile, as well as a potentially noxious chunk of hot metal.

Of course, if we are *in* the vehicle, that vehicle can be a marvellously useful contrivance, and a comfortable, person-friendly environment in its own right. Without vehicles, towns and cities as we know them could not function.

No one is seriously suggesting bringing back the law that required every motor vehicle to travel at walking pace behind a man with a red flag.[7] For a start, that is sexist. Second, the labour cost might make road travel uneconomic. Finally, the concern that a flag-bearing employee might sue for health damages might make the whole venture prohibitive. The point is that being on a street shared with vehicles can be a risky and unpleasant experience, to a degree that we would not necessarily tolerate in other walks of life.

Mixed blessing

The presence of a vehicle in a particular locale is almost entirely negative. The basic value of vehicles is not the metallic capsules themselves, but the people and goods within them. Whether it is the social or economic function of people going about their business – or the 'surveillance' value of having traffic and pedestrians visible to each other – it is the people inside that count. More or less all the benefits of vehicle flow are effectively embodied in the flow of people and goods; or rather, the ability of those people and goods to access their required destinations. More or less all the

(a)

(b)

8.2 • Displacement and danger. (a) A bus can carry more people using less space and energy. But might a big fast bus pose more of an accident risk than a rank of slow moving cars? (b) Non-motorised modes pose less of a health risk than motorised modes. A handful of bikes can fit the space of one car. But does a pack of bicycles present more of an accident risk than a single car? It will depend on circumstances – not least, speed.

disbenefits of vehicle flow relate to the *presence* and *motion* of vehicles in a locale, whether or not these constitute a 'flow' or not.

The reason we tend to think of vehicular flow as important is because expediting traffic flow has traditionally been equated with the very objective of traffic engineering. Flow is equated with economic vitality, the lifeblood of a city. But the benefit of traffic flow is not in the hardware. A vehicle is just a vessel. Empty, it is just an obstacle (Figure 8.3).[8]

It is the people getting to places that supplies the positive part of the equation. But those people, when travelling in vehicles, will simply appear in a particular locale as a passing chunk of hot metal: merely a disbenefit to others. This is why traffic is, of course, a 'mixed blessing'. Vehicle flow is a 'beneficial evil' that comes in a single package of people flow plus vehicle motion; but the benefit is in the people, and the evil, such as it is, in the motion of the vehicle. The more people carried, using fewer vehicles (especially, with fewer vehicles of the more hazardous types), the greater the benefit. This formulation may appear stark, even simplistic. But it is no more simplistic than either considering vehicle flow as intrinsically 'beneficial' (the lifeblood of cities) or intrinsically 'evil' (disturbing and dangerous).

The above arguments have drawn attention to certain properties of modes of movement with respect to the urban environment, which are not necessarily directly aligned with concepts of vehicle type or vehicle flow.

8.3 • Patterns of vehicular use. The benefit is in the abstract nature of people reaching destinations, rather than the physical presence of vehicles. But it is easier to count cars than trace people.

This is not to say that vehicle type is not important – it is clearly important for some purposes, such as vehicle licensing or driver qualifications; and vehicle flow is important for some things, such as junction layout or signal timing. However, these are not necessarily the best places to start when considering the design of streets or the layout of towns and cities.

Instead, it might be as well to focus on accessibility (people getting to places), and the impacts of vehicle motion. Rather than being anti-car, as such, we can consider the modes of vehicle use on their individual merits. Expressing modes as permutations of other things (speed, weight, people-carrying capacity) can help to remove the baggage of private versus public operation, and get away from the fetishisation of particular vehicle types. Instead, we can concentrate on the factors that affect which modes go together in which types of street, and, ultimately, how these types of street fit together in different patterns.

Modal favourability

Table 8.2 shows some possible 'modal hierarchies'. In each case, example modal categories are chosen to illustrate points on a spectrum of favourability.

Table 8.2 **Possible hierarchies of mode**

Physics	Chemistry	Economy	Energy (per head)	Geography (range)
1. Fast-heavy	1. Motor vehicle with direct noxious emissions	1. Taxi	1. Motorised solo occupancy	1. Motorised modes with unlimited range at urban scale
2. Slow-heavy or fast-light	2. Motor vehicle powered by source with noxious implications	2. Motor vehicle	2. Motorised HOV (high occupancy vehicle)	2. Bicycle (medium range)
3. Slow-light	3. Other vehicle (manufacture and disposal)	3. Human-powered vehicle	3. Bicycle	3. Walk (short range)
	4. Pedestrian	4. Walk	4. Walk	

The categories in Table 8.2 relate to what makes modes more favourable from the perspective of society and sustainability. That is, from the point of view of accident risk, health, affordability (equity) and ecology, each spectrum reads downwards from 'worst' to 'best'. However, seen from the individual user's perspective, the favourability tends to be the other way around. In other words, very generally speaking, the most convenient modes are the least 'sustainable': hence the challenge for policy-makers.

The modegram

In fact, it is possible to draw different kinds of spectrum together, and express the 'modal kaleidoscope' as a single triangular construct with walking at one vertex, public transport at another, and the car (or individual motorised transport) at the third. The resulting 'modegram' can be used to map out any mode relative to any other (Figure 8.4).[9]

Although triangular, there are effectively two independent axes implied. The first, along the right-hand bound, is the spectrum from the pedestrian to the car. This is a spectrum of mechanisation, from unassisted human locomotion to full motorisation (Figure 8.5). The second, along the left-hand bound, could be vehicle occupancy, from the solo car (or motorcycle, etc.) to the high occupancy train (Figure 8.6). In this sense, the axes of the modegram relate roughly to equating favoured modes with those which carry more people in fewer 'offensive' vehicles.

Operational complementarity

The issue of 'greenness' versus 'convenience' is not just a matter of which individual modes are considered favourable, but how modes link to each

8.4 • The modegram. Each mode is plotted according to a spectrum of locomotion (power/speed/range) and a spectrum of vehicle occupancy (individual to collective transport). Modes on the right-hand bound have door-to-door access; those on the left-hand bound have range and speed. Position A has both: it is the apex of automobility.

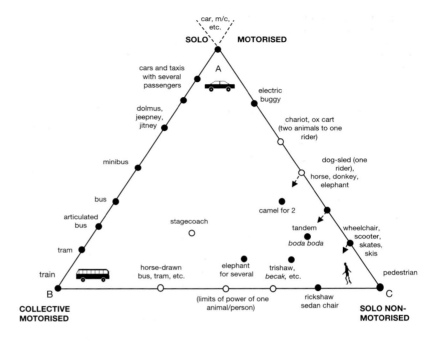

other. Basically, cars are convenient because they are generally able to provide both the benefits of motorisation – high speed and range – with the benefits of individual transport – direct routeing and door-to-door access. The combination of effortless range and door-to-door access means that this mode of movement traverses all scales.

Public transport is effectively set at the macro scale, in the sense of having unlimited range (at the urban scale) while confined to coarse networks of fixed routes which do not penetrate the micro scale (lack of door-to-door access). In contrast, walking is constrained by slow speed, effort and limited range, and is effectively confined to the micro scale; but within the limits of that micro scale, the pedestrian has the greatest accessibility (not only door-to-door, but right inside buildings).

This demonstrates two points. First, public transport and 'non-motorised modes' (such as walking and cycling), although often considered together as 'green' modes, are in fact at the opposite ends of a modal spectrum based on 'scale'. Second, and consequently, from an operational point of view, they need to complement each other to be competitive with the car. This means that to promote these 'favoured' modes, any hierarchy

(a)

(b)

(c)

(d)

must take into account how they must connect up with each other – either by direct connection, or via intermediate modes such as the car.

A NEW FORMULATION FOR ROUTE HIERARCHY

While most modern development planning uses the road network as the key structural element, a sustainable design takes the circulation of people on foot and bike, and the effectiveness of public transport as starting points.
Sustainable Settlements [10]

So far we have acquired some gauge of modal favourablility, and explored possibilities for recognising hierarchies of modes. The question now becomes: how might a *route* hierarchy be employed to promote those favoured modes? In other words, whatever other policy levers might be used to influence the attractiveness of different modes (e.g. regulation, pricing, etc.), the focus in this book is on what kinds of 'route types' and 'network structure levers' may be used to promote the more favoured modes or modal combinations.

The first concern here is to sort out what modes may coexist along a particular route, before determining how these might connect up structurally, according to the principles of arteriality and access constraint.

The speed differential

One of the most basic forms of street management is the fundamental distinction between carriageway and footway. This can be seen not simply as a matter of separating vehicles from pedestrians, but also as a distinction of speed, where the kerb line separates the faster moving traffic in the central portion of the street from the slower movement on the margins. Similarly, the fundamental device of ordering opposing traffic flows into separate streams can be seen not simply as a separation by direction, but as a division between movements of high *speed differential*. And the highest speed differentials on urban streets are usually firmly separated or segregated, by means of a central reservation (dual carriageway) or separate tracks (tramway). The discouragement or banning of vehicle types on certain parts of roadway is often based on speed: whether it is to prevent slow, animal-hauled vehicles or trishaws from impeding cars and lorries, or to prevent fast-moving rollerbladers or skateboarders from

8.5 • The spectrum of power. Equates with energy, speed and range. (a) Human power. (b) Pedal power. (c) Animal power. (d) Motor power.

(a)

(b)

(c)

(d)

(a)

(b)

8.7 • Shared surfaces in low-speed environments, Japan. (a) Bicycles share public plaza area. (b) All modes share the same surface.

terrorising pedestrians. Although these last examples are effectively discriminating against some of the more energy-efficient modes, this is not so much an unfortunate consequence of speed discrimination, as a *failure* to discriminate according to speed, by simply banning vehicle types.

It is only in determinedly low-speed environments that mixed-mode shared surface roads have become more commonplace, where speed *differentials* are kept to a minimum (Figure 8.7).

Taken together, we can see that speed is a key determinant of which modes may coexist along a street. Speed is important because it relates to safety and efficiency of movement, whether relating to public or private vehicles. It is either unsafe or inefficient (or both) to have mixed speeds on the same road or street, without some degree of separation or segregation. In general, it makes sense to bundle together flows of similar speed bands along a particular road type, and to separate those where there is any substantial differential. The general principle of minimising conflicts of speed is an important and positive aspect of having a hierarchy, and should be retained.[11]

Table 8.3 shows a possible hierarchy based on eight speed bands. Such a hierarchy could be divided as finely as desired, to fit local context, as far as is meaningful and manageable.

8.6 • The car–train spectrum. Equates with private to public, vehicle occupancy, network coarseness or 'nesting'. (a) Private car. (b) Taxi. (c) Bus. (d) Tram or train.

Table 8.3 **Stratification by speed**

Speed		Examples of modes of movement
S5.	Very high speed	Train, fast motor movement on motorway, busway, etc.
S4.	High speed	Speeds attained on partially segregated rights of way, and on free flowing suburban main roads; the highest speed for a carriageway associated with a footway or urban street
S3.5	Medium-high speed	Medium-high speed motor transport movement
S3.	Medium speed	Medium speed motor transport movement
S2.5	Medium-slow	Running; cycling; medium-slow motor movement
S2.	Slow	Jogging; slow cycling or very slow motor movement
S1.5	Very slow	Walking pace; cycling or parking at walking pace
S1.	Walking speed	Slow walking pace

The stratification by speed will apply to separation of speeds along a given street, or across a street in cross-section (Figure 8.8; Figure 8.9). Suggested compatibility of speed bands is shown in Table 8.4.

The stratification implies that a particular lane or carriageway can only accommodate a maximum of (in this case) three speed bands (or a difference of one integer value between coded types). The coding by speed rather than mode means that the cyclist of the cycle lane (d, e) may well be going as fast as a tram in a transit mall (f). This system could accommodate types such as Crawford's 'Bicycle Boulevard'.[12]

Stratification by speed

The principle of stratification by speed can be applied not only to different modes along a street, but also to the allowable connections between streets of different speed bands. In other words, there is a clear logic in preventing minor roads with slow moving traffic directly joining major roads with fast moving traffic. This arrangement can cut down the speed differential between interfacing road types, and it also goes hand in hand with minimising the number junctions on the major road (where there are more minor roads than intermediate roads).

Therefore, speed can be retained as a basis for differentiating route type, such that access constraint is applied between route types that are not adjacent in speed band. This will particularly apply to the vehicular part of the spectrum; at the lower end of the spectrum, it will normally be acceptable for a pedestrian path to connect to a medium speed road where this

(a)

(b)

(c)

8.8 • Stratification by speed, by segregation, kerb separation, markings, buffer zone. (a) Servicing manoeuvre speed/walk and cycle speed/parking manoeuvre speed/drive speed/tram speed.
(b) Slow motor speed/walk speed/cycle speed/ fast motor speed. (c) Motor speed/cycle speed/parking manoeuvre speed/walk speed.

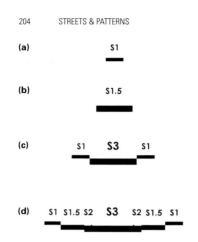

8.9 • Street cross-section, with stratification by speed. (a) Footpath. (b) Woonerf. (c) Standard street. (d) Street with parking and cycle lane. (e) Street with central tramway.

has a footway provided. Example types, employing the speed bands in Table 8.3, are illustrated in Figure 8.10.

Transit-oriented hierarchy

Having obtained a rationale for application of access constraint, we now turn to application of arteriality. Here, instead of relating arteriality to general traffic considerations, or traffic capacity, or trip length, or being pegged to the hierarchy of speed, arteriality can be applied as a new independent dimension, related to public transport orientation. This is because it is public transport that is most in need of strategic contiguity, and for all access modes to systematically connect 'upwards' to it – including cars (park and ride) as well as cycles and pedestrians.

However, we have still to classify public transport modes in a way suitable for a hierarchy. A problem with using vehicle occupancy as a criterion of a modal hierarchy is that it is hard to pin down – a vehicle may vary in occupancy over the course of a single journey. This echoes the difficulty of classifying routes by use (e.g. traffic flow) encountered in Chapter 3.

In effect, what separates the convenience of private transport from the convenience of public transport is not so much vehicle occupancy, but flexibility of routeing. For example, a private touring coach can carry as many people as a scheduled bus, but it goes from point to point by the most direct available route. In contrast, the smallest scheduled bus plies a fixed route with fixed access points (Figure 8.11).

Not only does this fixed-route nature of public transport separate it from 'free range' modes such as cars, lorries and bicycles, but the relative strategic 'scale' of their networks can be used to distinguish *between* public transport modes – for example, between trunk and feeder services. The Japanese *Shinkansen* – known popularly as the 'bullet train' – is a fast, long distance, high capacity (and premium fare) train. However, *shinkansen* means literally 'new trunk line': the trains are defined by the network function of the lines they run on (Figure 8.12).

In fact, this kind of network function can be used to rank *all* modes. Generally speaking, the mode with the finest geographical scale is the pedestrian, followed by the wheelchair, bicycle, motorcycle, then the motor car, then (if certain routes or areas are off-limits) the tour coach or goods vehicle, then a variety of public transport modes.[13] This means that the car–train spectrum of Figure 8.6 can be reinterpreted as one of network coarseness – part of a single pedestrian–train spectrum in geographical terms (i.e. Figure 8.5 plus 8.6). The railways provide the trunk routes or main arteries, and the pedestrian paths are the 'twigs' or finest 'capillaries'.

Table 8.4 Suggested examples of stratification by speed along a street

Example type	S1 Walking speed	S1.5 Dead slow	S2 Slow speed	S2.5 Medium-slow	S3 Medium speed	S3.5 Medium-fast	S4 High speed
(a) footpath for walking and wheelchair access only	■						
(b) woonerf for dead slow movement, as in a parking yard where children may play	■	■					
(c) standard street which might include a tramway moving in the S3 speed band	■		■	■	■		
(d) parked cars help provide speed buffer between footway and main carriageway/tramway in central reservation	■	■	■	■	■	■	
(e) partially segregated median strip which could be for fast motor traffic or reserved for public transport use	■	■	■	■	■		
(f) divided walkway/cycle way, where the 'cycle way' also allows for running and rollerblading	■		■				
(g) transit mall, shared between street-running bus or tram and pedestrians	■	■	■				
(h) footway separated by a verge from a parallel distributor road	■				■		
(i) segregated motorway, busway, tramway or railway						■	■

(a)

(b)

(c)

(d)

BOX 8. TRANSIT-ORIENTED ARTERIALITY

Modes can be arranged in a spectrum according to the strategic contiguity of their networks. This can be termed 'transit-oriented' arteriality. The term 'transit' may be used to move away from the 'public' connotation; here 'transit' can be taken to include the whole intermodal 'food chain'; it is 'oriented' because it is not just a hierarchy of public transport modes, but concerns relationships between all modes.

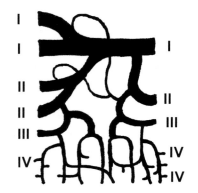

The trunk represents strategic public transport (which could be anything from a bullet train to a bus)

The limbs represent routes used by more local public transport

The branches represent routes used by modes on point-to-point journeys (e.g. car, lorry, coach)

The twigs represent progressively finer scale networks for motorcycles, bicycles, wheelchair-accessible routes and finally pedestrian-only routes

---

Strictly speaking, this ranking is not based on the actual physical coarseness of a network (e.g. linear route length per area) but is based purely on relation, by what may be termed *transit-oriented arteriality* (Box 8).

As with conventional road hierarchy, this public transport hierarchy tends to relate to geographical scale of coverage. In Chapter 3 we saw how a network – or a leaf pattern – divides an area into progressively smaller areas. This relates directly to public transport service penetration. The trunk routes imply the fewest routes with the coarsest networks and most widely spaced access points. At the other end of the spectrum, we have the finest scale networks.

In effect, this hierarchy can be regarded as a system of 'distributor roads' and 'access roads', where the distributors are ranked by spatial scale (Chapter 3). The difference here is that the distributors relate to public

8.10 • Route types stratified by speed. (a) Fast motor speed (S5). (b) Urban traffic speed (S3). (c) Cycle or jog speed (S2). (d) Window-shopping speed (S1).

(a)

(b)

(c)

(d)

Table 8.5 **Transit-oriented hierarchy**

Ref.	Types	Typical examples of modes of movement					
		Foot	Bike, etc.	Car, etc.	Mini-bus	Bus	Tram/rail
A	Arterial/trunk route	●	●	●	●	●	●
B	Sub-arterial route	●	●	●	●	●	
C	Local distributor	●	●	●	●		
D	Access road	●	●	●			
E	Narrow lanes	●	●				
F	Footpaths	●					

Notes

Car, etc. = private motor including car, taxi, goods vehicle, coach.

Bike, etc. = bicycle and other human-powered vehicles.

In some countries, motorcycles and mopeds may use routes for two-wheelers in general; in others they are confined to networks used by private motor traffic in general.

transport serving different spatial scales (from national to local distribution), and the 'access roads' refer to 'access modes' – all modes that may potentially be used to access public transport. Those access modes may themselves be further subdivided by the spatial contiguity of their networks.

The result is that the most strategic public transport routes (arterials or trunk routes) all connect up contiguously, and the set of all routes from the top down to any given level forms a complete contiguous network.[14]

As well as being a useful systematic way of constructing a single ranked hierarchy, out of all possible ways of classifying modes, this form of hierarchy is expressly intended to promote public transport, in such a way that the coarse nature and fixed routes of the public transport services are compensated for by ensuring that they are all contiguously connected up. This should also tend to assist the promotion of the higher capacity modes (although not systematically so).[15]

A possible transit-oriented hierarchy of routes based on six levels, from arterial (A) to footpath (F), is shown in Table 8.5. Selected examples are illustrated in Figure 8.13.

Arteriality is implied in the vertical direction: that is, all A routes should connect up, as should the set of (A + B), and so on. The lowest rungs imply

8.11 • Odd one out. In network structural terms, the scheduled bus is the odd one out because it follows a fixed route. This is independent of vehicle shape or occupancy. (a) Private vehicle. (b) Heavy goods vehicle. (c) Touring coach. (d) Scheduled bus (postbus).

8.12 • *Shinkansen*. The trains are named after the network function of the routes they run on: the 'new trunk line'.

a scattering of access modes to public transport: walking, cycling and driving (park and ride access).

Each route's rank is defined by its 'highest ranking' mode; it does not mean that all the 'lower' modes in public transport terms are necessarily present – including private modes such as cars. Private motor vehicles such as cars may use any level down to the local road level (D); this level is the finest scale network accessible to motor vehicles.

Overall, although termed a 'transit-oriented' hierarchy for convenience, this is not a separate specialised classification just for public modes, divorced from the concerns of 'private' travel and traffic engineering, but includes all modes that play a role in the public transport 'food chain' – that is to say, *all modes.*

The combined 'articulated' route hierarchy

We have arrived at an articulated hierarchy, so-called because each route is considered *separately* in terms of the speed and transit-oriented arteriality. Each route is then connected to other routes according to access constraint (according to speed) and arteriality (according to transit-orientation). Examples of street types interpreted in terms of this hierarchy are given in Figure 8.14.

The articulated route hierarchy decouples the conventional assumption (implicit or explicit) that high speed, high flow, long distance travel and arteriality go together. Arteriality is instead prioritised overall for strategic public transport routes – and, further down the scale, ensures contiguity of routes cumulatively for all motor vehicles, all vehicles and all modes. There is room in the hierarchy to accommodate a variety of modes implicitly, without necessarily formally writing their specification into the system. *Allowable* connections are simply assessed in terms of compatible speeds; *necessary* connections are assessed in terms of transit-oriented arteriality.

This system echoes the logic of 'favourability' of the modegram (Figure 8.4). However, rather than promoting low power vehicles as such – which can be achieved through other policy levers – the hierarchy promotes low *speeds*, through provision of slow-speed streets. These would naturally favour walkers and cyclists, while encouraging those with cars to use them in a people-sensitive and environmentally-sensitive manner. Similarly, rather than promoting high occupancy vehicles as such, the hierarchy promotes those modes most disadvantaged by inflexibility of their access and routeing.

So, our two 'network structure policy levers' are to make sure that those modes that are able to and allowed to access the finest scale have

8.18 • Streetspace classification applied to selected London streets. Arteriality tends to be continuous along a street, but urban place value tends to vary along it. Here, one can recognise the 'vertical' spectrum of arterial significance from Marylebone Road to the most local streets; or the 'horizontal' spectrum of urban place significance varying along Marylebone Road from the almost 'non-place' of Marylebone Road at Edgware Road to the district centre of Marylebone Road at Baker Street.

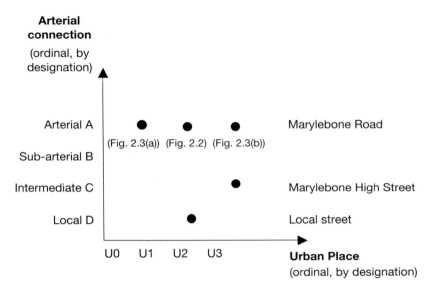

The trade-off

The consideration of the relative importance of arterial connection and the sense of urban place of a specific street area can assist in determining the extent to which it should be occupied by vehicles (moving or otherwise), or used by people for other urban activities. The trade-off is not one of 'traffic versus people', or 'safety versus vitality'; but the relative significance of route and place in terms of geographical scale.

This 'hierarchy' of geographical scale does not mean that the national interest will always override the local interest. It will depend on which has the best claim to use a specific area of streetspace. For example, the larger the strategic scale of a route (e.g. national), the more flexible it should be in terms of which particular links it uses; whereas a local route might be the most constrained to claim use of that particular link.

If the arterial and urban place roles are incompatible, then this suggests reducing arterial status (e.g. rerouting the strategic artery), or reducing urban place status (e.g. shifting the high status urban activity off the line of the route). Once the roles of arterial connection and urban place have been set, then the design of streetspace – for appropriate vehicular motion – can be implemented.[22]

Since public transport vehicles carry more people in fewer vehicles, there is less conflict between vehicles and use of the street by people for other urban activities. A tram or a few buses are more compatible with high

8.19 • High arterial connection and urban place significance. Tram street, Strasbourg.

intensity use of space than a stream of cars carrying an equivalent number of people. This means that it is more feasible to have a street that *combines* both a strategic public transport role and a significant urban place role. Hence, the conjunction of high status arterial connection and high urban place status does not necessarily represent a problem area, but could represent a *solution* area (Figure 8.19).

A particular street will tend to have a constant arterial status, while having a varied urban place value along its length. The resulting pattern of streets as *routes* (in terms of arterial connection) will be the familiar topology of arteriality. The distribution of urban place will be more a 'mosaic' of different qualities.

However, we can set a minimum standard of contiguity applying to all areas possessing 'positive urban place' – almost any public streets and spaces – such that none is isolated by swathes of 'non-place' (e.g. bleak distributor territory). Hence, the system of all streets becomes contiguous. This 'minimum standard' echoes Buchanan's desire for minimum environmental standard, but does so by employing a definite topological property (the same property that is conventionally assumed for roads). This can therefore help to overcome the structure of disurban creation.

URBAN STREET TYPOLOGY

Finally, we round off the discussion of street type by considering the fully three-dimensional character of a street. The last sections suggested classifying routes or streets independently in terms of speed, transit-oriented arteriality and urban place status. This means that any number of street types could be generated, by overlaying other factors such as road width, building type, frontage function, and so on. In fact, there is a great flexibility in types of street allowable, since their crucial design parameters are either already accounted for (e.g. design for speed) or are intrinsic to any designation subsequently overlain (e.g. width of street).

Unlike conventional typologies based on a single criterion (or set of bundled criteria), there is *no need* to keep the number of types down on the basis of providing a manageable set of allowable and necessary connections, since the allowable and necessary connections are already accounted for. Therefore, architects, urban designers, planners and engineers can all devise different kinds of street type according to taste (Figure 8.20). Looking back, this could accommodate both the engineering-oriented road types of Table 3.1 and the 'urbanistic' street types of Table 3.2. As long as these street types are coded in terms of speed and transit-oriented arteriality, they will automatically fit the classification relating street type to spatial structure.

The significance of the typology in Figure 8.20 is two-fold. First, and most obviously, it expresses an architectonic appreciation of form and space: it is not simply the raw skeletal constitution of conventional hierarchy which sees all 'streets' fated to be lumped together in the unloved access road category. Second, although it may look like any other collection of urbanistic types, it also builds in the network-structural parameters of stratification and strategic contiguity. The types here are not just expressions of wishful thinking, floating adrift of road hierarchy, but have a clear rationale for connection to network structure.

The result is that terms like 'mews', 'square' and 'boulevard' can feature explicitly and unashamedly in authoritative classifications as serious options for creative urban structuring, rather than the current situation with two sets of guidance: one set of urban design guidelines (featuring streets) and another set of road layout ones (featuring an unappetising choice of distributor or access roads).

CONCLUSIONS

This chapter has considered a variety of modes of movement, and how these might be compatible with each other, bundled together along different kinds of routes; how these routes might connect with each other (arteriality and access constraint); and how these may be reconciled with the role of the street as an urban place.

In doing so, the chapter has suggested retaining some conventions, altering others, and letting others fall by the wayside. It has been suggested

(a)

(b)

(c)

(d)

(e)

(f)

(g)

(h)

(i)

(j)

(k)

(l)

that neither 'traffic flow' nor 'vehicle type' need be used directly in mode or street classification, but we can focus instead on certain key 'active ingredients' such as speed and transit orientation, that most directly relate to design problems of street type and urban structure. Focusing on modes as 'modes of movement' – rather than vehicle type *per se* – not only enables design for compatibility of a diversity of existing modes, but also allows the possibility of creating favourable niches for novel emerging modes without having to expressly rule them in (or inadvertently rule them out).

On this basis, it has been possible to generate an 'articulated' route hierarchy based on two independent dimensions: first, a stratification by speed band, and second, a 'transit-oriented hierarchy' organised according to strategic contiguity. The resulting hierarchy promotes an integrated public transport–pedestrian system. This route hierarchy is offered as an alternative to the 'structure of car orientation'.

This chapter has also suggested an 'urban streetspace classification' which allows a rationale for the reconciliation between the role of a street as an arterial connection and its role as an urban place. As anticipated in Chapter 3, arteriality is not necessarily incompatible with urban place. Both may be considered on comparable terms – based on geographical scale of significance. Real streets treated in this system may still throw up conflicts, but these can be handled in a transparent way. The proposed system can ensure contiguity of the street system (positive urban place) and therefore provide an alternative to the 'structure of disurban creation'.

Finally, a variety of street types incorporating spatial or built form properties is possible. As long as the coding for speed and transit-oriented arteriality are part of the designation, any proposed street type can be fitted structurally within the hierarchy. This addresses the challenge of Chapter 2, and could be considered beneficial in combining the need for an ordered, structured classification that addresses concerns for traffic compatibility and safety, with the desire for a flexible, diverse, street-oriented classification.

The diversity of street types is possible because the hierarchy is 'articulated' – the underlying dimensions of classification are independently

8.20 • A diverse street typology. Any number of street types may be classified according any kind of form, use, relation or designation. As long as each street type is integrally coded for speed and arteriality, it will automatically fit the 'articulated' route hierarchy. There are two rules: (1) Each route type must connect to another route of the same or higher transit orientation; (2) Routes are stratified by speed: there is no direct connection between S4 to S2 except via S3. For all streets (roads with a non-zero value of urban place) urban contiguity can also be assured. (a) Tram Mall, Amsterdam (A2). (b) Tram boulevard, Tashkent (A3). (c) Tram artery, Hong Kong (A3.5). (d) Classical square, Edinburgh (D3). (e) Central traffic street, Richmond (B3). (f) Suburban through road, Richmond (C4). (g) Gravel promenade, Richmond-upon-Thames (E1.5). (h) Mews, London (D2). (i) Residential street, Poundbury (D2). (j) Alley, Jaffa (F1). (k) Arcade, Leeds (F1). (l) Walkways, Leeds (F1).

specified, rather than being forced into fitting predetermined combinations of movement and place function. This avoids foreclosing the possibility of potentially viable but unanticipated types.

Indeed, the 'tyranny of hierarchy' can be reinterpreted as a tyranny of rigid typology, rather than one of rigid hierarchical structure. In this perspective, conventional road hierarchy is uncomfortably rigid not because it has a constraining order *per se*, but because it constrains things it does not need to constrain, in the specification of road type. It demands combinations such as frontage-free-distributor-bus-route or short-local-all-purpose-frontage-access-road. The possibilities of a tram-served-arterial-connector-boulevard or the slow-speed-shared-surface-woonerf are foreclosed. The solution, it is suggested, is to deal with individual characteristics – such as arterial connection, speed or urban place – in an articulated hierarchy, and let the resulting streets 'work themselves out'.

The system of classification suggested in this chapter is certainly not the only way of classifying streets, but it does provides a systematic means of classifying streets in a way that usefully relates to urban structure and patterns. That is, the network-structural role is effectively 'coded' into the definition of each street type. The nature of the resulting structures and patterns is the subject of the next chapter.

NOTES

1   Aldous (1992: 23).

2   ITE (1999); Easterling (1999: 76); 'nuclear strike', ITE (1999: 4).

3   MoT (1963). Dedicated paragraphs on personal jet propulsion, p. 24; air cushion vehicles, p. 25; the future of cycling, p. 64, the future for buses, p. 195. See also commentary in Marshall (2003b).

4   Rare attempts to harness zebras for transport are noted by Diamond (1998: 171).

5   Wackernagel and Rees (1996).

6   Roberts (1990).

7   Locomotive Act (MoT, 1963: 9).

8   Similarly, transport infrastructure in itself is not beneficial; it is only the use by vehicles – and in turn people – that makes for a net benefit. A road that simply tore through the countryside, but on which no traffic materialised, would rightly be considered a waste and a gross disbenefit. In this respect, an empty or almost empty vehicle is wasteful, just like an empty or almost empty road.

9   See Marshall (2004) for further exploration of the modegram. Data informing the modegram and Table 8.2 on space occupation, speed, energy, vehicle occupancy, stop spacing and range of different modes, including non-motorised modes and modes in developing countries from Ritter (1964), Hathway (1985),

Harwood (1992), Dimitriou (1995), Marshall (2001), Richards (2001), Njenga and Davis (2003), Potter (2003).

10   Barton *et al.* (1995: 105). A related point is made by Battle and McCarthy (1994): 'The key to a sustainable transportation system is the implementation of a transport hierarchy which gives priority to the pedestrian and public systems above the car.'

11   Stratification by speed is considered by Bartlett (2003a, 2003b); Smith and Freer (1999); and speed used to rank some existing statutory classifications, e.g. Danish (Appendix 3).

12   Crawford (2000: 176).

13   A route usable by a wheelchair could be physically used by a bicycle, but not necessarily legally so. Similarly, for a cycle route being used by motorcycles.

14   The 'strategic' designation is relative to context, and is independent of vehicle type. In one city there might be a 'clear hierarchy' from rail to tram to bus, but in another there might be a distinct hierarchy of trunk and feeder services all operated by buses.

15   For example, a private touring coach would be lower in the hierarchy than a postbus. However, although a coach might use less energy per head than a postbus or half-empty service bus, the coach is well adapted to the kind of road system geared to private motor traffic in general, and already benefits from conventional hierarchy and all its trappings.

16   The Copenhagen/Denmark classification system has two dimensions: speed and traffic-oriented arteriality; the Portland classification system has two dimensions: traffic role and public transport role (Appendix 3). In retrospect, the articulated route hierarchy proposed in this chapter could be seen as combining the advantages of both systems (speed, arteriality and public transport orientation).

17   As called for by the ICE (2002).

18   Hall (forthcoming).

19   Smailes (1944); Smith (1968); Hall, Marshall and Lowe (2001).

20   Marshall (2002b); Marshall, ed. (2003).

21   This term 'arterial connection' avoids the 'motion' connotation of movement (which, of itself, has no intrinsic value), but instead connotes network function. The word 'access' is avoided since this suggests a street's value is in being a 'trip end', rather than a place in its own right. The term 'environmental area' is also avoided, since it seems to imply an all-embracing zone like a district or quarter, and not some specific square-metres'-worth of streetspace. In contrast, the term urban place could apply to a city, building or a specific area of contested tarmac.

22   In particular, the design for speed can be adjusted so that speed is compatible with the kind of urban place. There may well be effectively an 'inverse relationship' between speed and urban place, although this is not advanced here as a fixed principle to be followed. Local circumstances will dictate: as is done in any case, for the accommodation of safe design for vehicle motion in a particular locality. Like urban place, speed will vary from section to section of a route, whereas arteriality tends to be continuous along a route.

9 FROM STREETS TO PATTERNS

Neo-traditional urbanism has provided one of the main stimuli for this book: the challenge of how to base urban design on a framework of streets, rather than the Modernist framework of point blocks or 'development pods' appended off a skeletal network of distributor roads.

As discussed in Chapter 2 (and also demonstrated in Chapter 6) neo-traditional street patterns are not necessarily structurally faithful to actual traditional patterns. Moreover, they are not necessarily created in a 'traditional' manner – in other words, how those original patterns grew up themselves. Indeed, neo-traditional solutions may be imposed in a rigid manner of formal drawing-board design, in a process not unlike the kind of top-down, imposed solutions that were criticised as Modernist dysfunctionalism by the likes of Jane Jacobs and Christopher Alexander. Therefore, while much of today's urban design and planning draw inspiration from Jacobs and Alexander in principle, many of today's neo-traditional design solutions seems to go against the spirit of their arguments in practice.

The term 'neo-traditionalism' implies a curious juxtaposition: something at the same time old and yet new. While there is a clear logic to creating anew old-fashioned 'new towns' such as Edinburgh's Craig Plan, there is less obvious rationale to creating anew old *unplanned* towns.[1] While re-creating traditional planned layouts is a relatively straightforward matter of taking the relevant plan and applying it to a new site, the same cannot be said for the attempt to recreate the more 'organic' patterns of traditional urbanism.

That is, there is a challenge to consciously recreate patterns that were never consciously created in the first place; how to provide design guidance for forms that had no formal design in the first place. The last chapter addressed the issue of street type. This chapter now considers how streets might form patterns, within which the central challenge is effectively to find a way of creating a diversity of patterns through a system of generic design guidance.

DESIGN APPROACHES – GENERATIVE PROCESSES

First, we need to consider how, in principle, patterns may be generated. For the purposes of addressing neo-traditional design, a particular angle to consider is how traditional patterns were generated.

The *New Theory of Urban Design* of Christopher of Alexander and associates suggests an approach to design where specification is in the form of a program or process rather than prescription of pattern *per se*. Indeed, the *New Theory*'s self-proclaimed most controversial feature is 'to generate urban structure without a plan' such that '*in some fashion*, the large-scale order will emerge, organically, from the co-operation of the individual acts of construction'.[2]

This has a resonance with bottom-up approaches to creation of form. With this kind of approach, there may be an underlying program, but no final pattern is preconceived. Indeed, in the design exercise illustrating the *New Theory*, the street pattern unfolds in an incremental way, giving rise to a textbook example of characteristic structure.

A comparable approach may be found in Michael Sorkin's *Local Code*, in which local rules may be used incrementally to build a city:

> The code recognises that a vision already concretised pre-empts the greater possibilities of an incitement to open many interpretations . . . it seeks a city designed not simply through the deductions of a dominating generality but also via induction from numberless individual points of departure.[3]

Local Code is written like an abstract manifesto – there is deliberately no illustration suggesting any design outcome. Rather, it comprises a systematic set of rules covering a vast range of city-building concerns; patterns of routes are built up using explicitly defined branching algorithms. This is a very pure case of a constitutional approach.

Sorkin describes his code as a 'kind of utopia'. However, such a code need not be some remote or fanciful ideal. A constitutional approach is right here with us. It is, after all, the approach of the highway engineer.

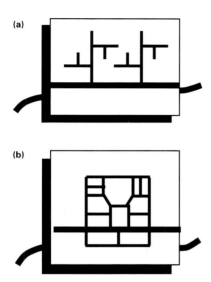

9.1 • 'Bad' and 'good' pattern replication. Layout design considered as if whole pattern template 'copied and pasted' on to site. (a) Stereotype of 'standardised tree-like' pattern. (b) Neo-traditional grid.

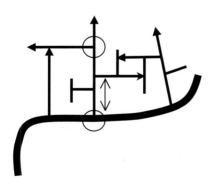

9.2 • A constitutional approach only specifies elements and connections, not final patterns. A dendritic constitution need not result in a tree-like configuration.

Design debate revisited

At the outset of the book, the design debate was considered in terms of the contrasting approaches of conventional highway engineering and neo-traditional urbanism. Figure 9.1 shows how these approaches may often appear to manifest themselves in resultant patterns.

Case (a) represents the 'problem': this is the kind of layout for which engineers are blamed, and which neo-traditional urbanists would like to replace. Their solution is often something like case (b), in which conventional road hierarchy is rejected, to be replaced by a 'best practice pattern' based approach, with grid-like configurational or compositional exemplars (for example, Poundbury, or 'preferred' and 'discouraged' exemplars: Figures 2.7 and 2.8).

However, when looking more closely at the generation of urban structure, things are not what they might appear at first sight. The highway engineers' actual rules relate only to local connections, and therefore allow a local, incremental approach where no single configurational outcome is prescribed (Figure 9.2).

This approach also allows flexibility of application by individual designers and allows emergent forms. In principle, the rules of hierarchy can be used to synthesise structure without specifying any overall pattern. This is a constitutional, rather than a configurational approach. Seen this way, the apparent lack of design guidance for overall pattern, encountered in Chapter 2, is perhaps better interpreted simply as an *absence*.

The case shown in Figure 9.1(a) is more of an impression of the *perception* of replicating 'standardised' loop-and-cul-de-sac layouts, in which hierarchy (dendritic constitution) is perceived to be inevitably entwined with tree-like configurations. While these may often have been associated in practice, it is not an inevitable outcome in principle.

As seen in Chapter 7, Colin Buchanan explicitly rejected the notion of road types such as 'ring roads' which presupposed the final layout of a road with respect to overall network structure. Instead, he opted for route types defined only by their immediate rules of relation. In this sense, Buchanan's system was a flexible mode of pattern generation. It is tempting to suggest that this is part of the reason why Buchanan's 'code' has been so resilient, and its descendants live on today, albeit in an adapted form, almost four decades later (while *Traffic in Towns'* physical planning and urban design solutions have fallen out of favour).

In other words, it is not the constitutional (hierarchy-driven) approach of highway engineering that is at fault, but the rigid application of the hierarchical structures conventionally employed. In principle, a constitutional

185 m   150 m

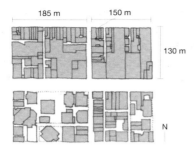

130 m

N

Adelaide, Australia

100 m

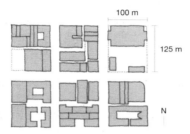

125 m

N

Chicago, USA

180 m   180 m

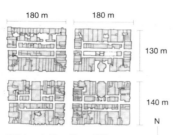

130 m

140 m

N

Edinburgh, New Town, UK

65 m

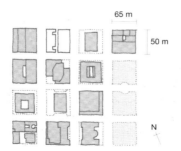

50 m

N

Portland, USA

approach should be capable of being more flexible, with the ability to generate a broader and deeper 'solution space' of possible patterns, than is currently apparent from existing design guidance (whether based on hierarchy or desired pattern templates).

Design by composition, configuration and constitution

The different approaches to design may be associated with different ways of presenting design guidance.

Composition

A compositional exemplar would be one using an existing site plan to inform onward design of a new site more or less directly (Figure 9.3). An example of this is the process of 'tissue analysis' where existing scale plans are used to inspire and evaluate possibilities for application to a new site.[4]

   While tissue analysis can remind us of what works – by directly replicating both the structure and scale of existing town plans – it may be hard to generalise as a generic rule system. However, a hint of flexibility is seen in Figure 9.3, taken from the *Urban Design Compendium*, which depicts a selection of grids to choose from. This appears to suggest the general term 'grid', without implying mechanistic replication of any particular composition. In effect, the designer is being invited to abstract the concept of 'grid' intuitively – this being, in effect, a kind of configurational 'lowest common denominator' – from these four diagrams.

Configuration

A configuration-led approach would more directly and explicitly abstract the target kind of configuration (e.g. grid) and present that as the object of design guidance (Figure 9.4).

   A configurational template should in principle be a more flexible approach than a compositional template, since there is some flexibility in applying a given configuration to a particular site: its shape and orientation can bend to the contours of the ground and respond to enhance or avoid conflicting with existing site features. In contrast, the direct transplanting of a particular composition, with all its lengths, areas and angles intact would imply a more rigid application, which would be likely to overwrite any existing site features. Having said that, the composition might more faithfully reproduce the functional urbanistic qualities of the exemplar site, which a configuration could lose, if stretched out of all proportion.

9.3 • Compositional exemplars. Each plan could be interpreted as a 'template' used to inform the design of a new site.

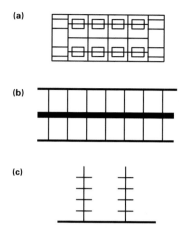

9.4 • Configurational exemplars. These have no metric dimensions, only topological properties and relationships. (a) Craig Plan. (b) *Ciudad Lineal.* (c) Hilberseimer's *New City.*

Design by replicating a given configuration or composition could be described as being 'broad but shallow'. This is in the sense that a relatively broad range of patterns may be allowable (e.g. grids as well as loops and culs-de-sac), but the superficial level at which the patterns are reproduced in principle limits the potential solution space (Figures 9.5 and 9.6). Overall, there is a danger here of using templates to churn out typecast patterns that are insensitive to individual sites.

Constitution

Using a constitutional approach can theoretically deepen the solution space further, broadening it in the process, since a given constitution can generate a multitude of configurations, each of which may in turn generate a further multitude of compositions. Figure 9.7 represents a possible theoretical diverse generation from a constitutional approach.

However, in practice, in the *de facto* case of conventional road hierarchy, this range of theoretical possibilities is pruned. This is due to explicit constraints: both configurational (such as the rejection of crossroads) and compositional (such as the adoption of the sweeping geometry of motorised movement). It is also due to a lack of creativity, where a dendritic constitution is unimaginatively applied as a tree-like configuration. The *de facto* conventional case is therefore limited to a 'deep but narrow' slice of the solution space (Figure 9.8). It therefore *appears* to be more standardised than the neo-traditional menu.

A more permissive rule system – that is, a constitution whose particular rules are more permissive than conventional road hierarchy – could allow the generation of more diverse, connective layouts. This could realise the full potential gain in depth and breadth of a constitutional approach, whose solution space could potentially include both the favoured neo-traditional layouts and conventional layouts, as well as other, unknown forms. In such a way, the present narrow scope of road-based hierarchy can be unfolded – indeed evolved – into a broader, street-based constitution.

Constitution for network generation

A constitution-led approach is one based on the specifications of elemental types (links, routes or junctions) and their relationships, without specifying any particular overall configurational (or compositional) outcome. A constitutional code for street design would specify constitutionally designed road or street types, their necessary and allowable connections (i.e. arteriality and access constraint), as well as specification for allowable junction type (e.g. use of T-junctions, X-junctions, etc.). Through the specification of different

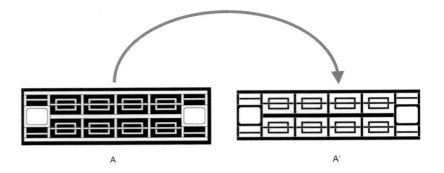

9.5 • Application of composition. A 'preferred' exemplar (A) is simply applied to a new site. Here we imagine Edinburgh's admired Craig Plan being 'copied and pasted' to a new location – the whole layout with all dimensions intact (A').

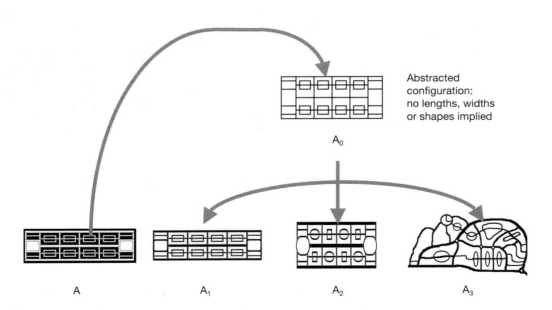

Abstracted configuration: no lengths, widths or shapes implied

9.6 • Application of configuration. An abstract configuration (A_0) is extracted from the exemplar (A). This configuration is used to generate a set of compositional alternatives (A_1, A_2 and A_3), each of which differs in shape and size but has the same topology. The solution space is, in a sense, broader and deeper than in Figure 9.5.

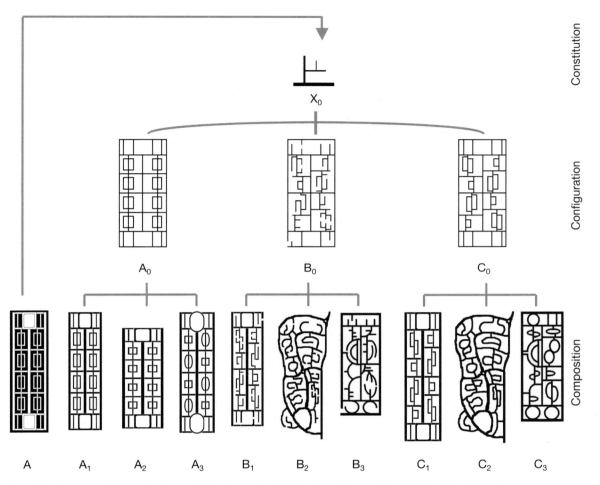

9.7 • The full breadth and depth of a permissive constitutional approach. An abstract constitution is abstracted (X_0), and may be used to generate a large number of configurational alternatives (A_0, B_0, C_0, . . .). This can create a large solution space of possible compositions, within which the solution spaces of the previous Figures (9.5, 9.6) may be nested.

kinds of local relationships and connections between elements, network connectivity can be influenced, without prescribing the connectivity at the network level.

An advantage of a constitution-led approach is that it builds into it the desired relationships of structure between local and strategic routes and route types, without presupposing any particular final form. This makes it particularly suitable for use in design guidance, since a single 'code' or

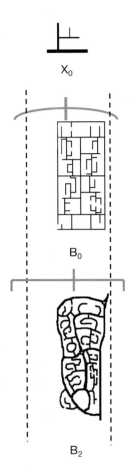

X_0

B_0

B_2

9.8 • Deep but narrow. In practice, conventional hierarchy limits the potential diversity of layouts by: (1) ban on crossroads; (2) standardised application of modern curvilinear composition.

'program' can generate a diversity of layout patterns which can themselves be adapted to local circumstances. And, although the final pattern is not prescribed, when a pattern does emerge, it should be coherent, legible and functional, because the parts that are put together embody the relationship with the whole.

Towards a street-based constitution

A constitutional approach to urban layout can use the *street* as the fundamental building block of urban structuring. The core element of the street type is the route type, to which building frontages or other land uses may be appended. Effectively, the buildings and frontage uses are the 'flesh on the skeleton'; it is the skeleton of the route network that forms the principal organising structure, that relates each part to the whole.

The route type is, in turn, based on the different modes of movement; and those modes are based on attributes such as speed and 'transit-oriented arteriality' (Box 8) (i.e. trunk mode, feeder mode, access mode).

The issues of mode type, route type and street type have all already been addressed in Chapter 8. (In fact, Chapter 8 contains all the necessary ingredients to go out and create street patterns and urban structures.) The remainder of this chapter is simply concerned with helping to demonstrate how these could be realised in terms of design guidance and pattern outcomes.

A STREET-BASED CONSTITUTION

As suggested in Chapter 7, hierarchy is more than just a 'ranked list' or a 'table of road types', but is a kind of structure. Where the component types in a hierarchy are ranked according to their structural connection, a hierarchy can also be used as a means of structuring, and the basis for a constitutional approach to design. In other words, in any organisational context, if a Type A is defined as 'a Type that must at least connect to another Type A, and may also connect with a Type B', then the definition of the type builds something of the structure of the whole into the individual element. This is the key to a constitutional approach.

Constitutional code[5]

A constitutional code for road network structure will include a series of route types based on factors such as speed and transit orientation (Chapter 8). A constitutional code for the structure of *street* pattern will also include factors to do with the physical nature and character and use of the street, addressing non-transport issues.

The components of a constitutional code will reflect the first four structural conditions of the tree analogy (Figure 7.3), to which we can add in connection type (junction type).

1.   Different types – e.g. street, square, transit mall.
2.   Ranked order – e.g. 20 km/h, 30 km/h, 40 km/h.
3.   Arteriality – based on transit-oriented arteriality.
4.   Access constraint – based on speed differential.
5.   Allowable junction type for given connecting road types.

Since the combined specification of arteriality and access constraint generates a ranked order of different types, this actually boils down to a minimum of just three considerations (3, 4 and 5) for a transport route constitution, although, for a street-based constitution, it is likely that some variations in type or ordering that go beyond network connection factors would also be helpful.

First, we will look at individual street types expressed in constitutional terms, and then look at example constitutional structures demonstrated using a graphical device that will be referred to as a constitutional archetype.

Street type

Figure 9.9 depicts a graphical code specifying necessary and allowable connections for two street types (I and IV) in a conjoint constitution. For each street type (expressed at the left-hand side) one can read along which other types *may* be connected to, and which type *must* be connected to.

Figure 9.10 gives another example, this time of a dendritic constitution. Here, access constraint applies as well as arteriality, and so there will be a reduced number of allowable connections.

Any street type can be graphically depicted in this way. As well as individual streets being coded in this way, we can also depict a whole street typology (constitution) in a single diagram, which will be referred to as a constitutional archetype.

Constitutional archetype

An archetype is a general model that embodies the features of all individual cases. In biology, the concept of an archetype was used to try to explain the diversity and similarity between different species and body plans. Philip Steadman has applied the concept of the archetype to buildings, where any building can be expressed as a combination of variations from a basic 'archetypal building'.[6]

9.9 • Examples of street code depicting constitutional logic for a conjoint constitution for two types of street (a) Type I; (b) Type IV.

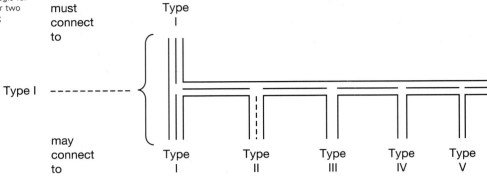

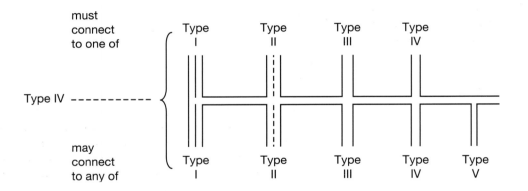

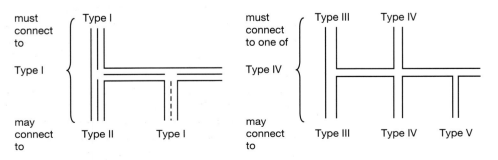

9.10 • Street code for two types of street in a dendritic constitution (arteriality and access constraint).

BOX 9. CONSTITUTIONAL ARCHETYPE

This is a graphic device that expresses the prescribed connections between different route types, in terms of arteriality and access constraint.

The graphic says:

- Type A must (and may) connect with another type A; it may (also) connect with a Type B or C.
- Type B must (and may) connect with either a Type A or B; it may (also) connect with a Type C.
- Type C must (and may) connect with either a Type A, B or C.

Note: logically, if a type *must* connect with another, it simultaneously *may* connect with it, i.e. a necessary connection implies an allowable connection.

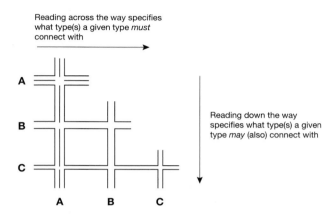

Reading across the way specifies what type(s) a given type *must* connect with

Reading down the way specifies what type(s) a given type *may* (also) connect with

Here, a 'constitutional archetype' for road network structure is demonstrated. This expresses a basic theoretical structure which may be transformed into any number of individual site designs by expressing (selecting) or suppressing different components in different proportions and sequences. A basic form of suggested constitutional archetype is shown in Box 9. This expresses allowable and necessary connections of all street types (in a given code), in a single diagram.

Any kind of constitution can be graphically expressed in this way (Figure 9.11). The constitutional archetype can even build in compositional guidance, on absolute geometric standards, such as typical width or road standard, or minimum junction spacing between types. This information could be expressed individually for each route type, as well as in a full archetype (Figure 9.12).

Figure 9.13 demonstrates one interpretation of the 'articulated' route hierarchy of Chapter 8 as a pair of constitutional archetypes: first, based on transit-oriented arteriality, and, second, based on stratification by speed. The hierarchy is effectively a superposition of a conjoint constitution for the public transport-plus-access system (Figure 9.13(a)), and a serial constitution for modes of movement based on speed (Figure 9.13(b)). Figure 9.14

(a)

Boulevard

Street

Lane

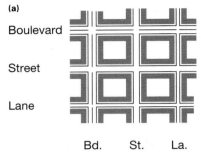

Bd.   St.   La.

(b)

Boule-
vard

Street

Lane

Bd.   St.   La.

(c)

Boule-
vard

Street

Lane

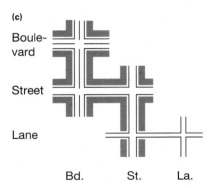

Bd.   St.   La.

9.11 • Examples of archetypes for different kinds of constitution. (a) Mosaic. (b) Conjoint. (c) Dendritic.

shows an interpretation of the urban streetspace constitution of Chapter 8, in which contiguity of the combined urban street–urban place system is guaranteed.

Intersection type

In addition to expressing necessary and allowable connections between types of route, a constitutional code can also express the *type* of connection or intersection. This could be a purely engineering consideration of allowable intersections between different route types. Figure 9.15, for example, demonstrates allowable junction types, among other things suggesting that crossroads are only permitted either for very slow speed streets, or must be signalised. Intersection type can also be expressed in terms of land use (e.g. high-intensity development at a public transport node) or urban design treatment (e.g. use of squares or 'rond-points' at major intersections) (Figure 9.16).

Overall, the constitutional archetype therefore represents a concise graphical depiction of a possible basis for design guidance, essentially combining allowable street type, allowable connections and allowable type of junction; with the possibility of also expressing dimensions, frontage uses and building forms.

Application to design guidance

The constitutional archetype can be used as a basis for design guidance. Indeed, the diagrams in the *Essex Design Guide* shown in Figures 2.11 and 2.12 may be interpreted as *de facto* constitutional archetypes, albeit without explicit articulation of arteriality. The archetypes presented in this chapter therefore can be seen to build on an existing tradition, but introducing new elements to systematically generate alternatives. They therefore combine a degree of novelty with a degree of continuity.

In other words, the kinds of constitutional archetype expressed here can be seen to be evolvable from existing conventional road hierarchy. The graphic form and logic of the archetype are simply an expressive tool that could represent any kind of constitutional structure, from a conventional road hierarchy like that in *Traffic in Towns* to some onward evolution from it (Figure 9.17).

Since the 'constitutional' or 'archetypal' approach can accommodate and contain the conventional approaches within it, it could even be adopted in principle prior to making any changes to the individual design rules or recommendations. In other words, a 'constitutional code' with 'archetypal' graphic format could be introduced to design guidance first – prior to

(a)

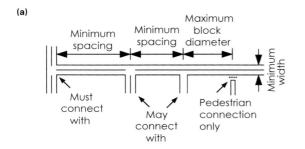

(b)

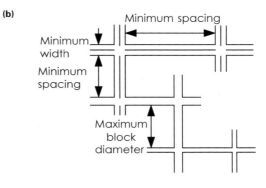

9.12 • Dimensioned archetypes. (a) Single street type. (b) Structure of streets.

(a)

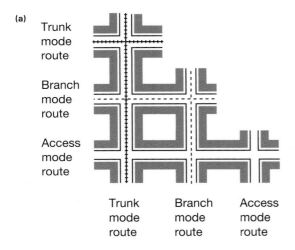

(b)

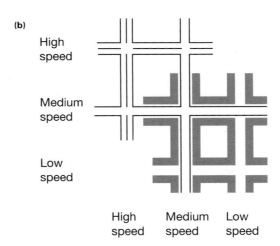

9.13 • Archetype for the articulated route hierarchy of Chapter 8. (a) Transit-oriented hierarchy. (b) Speed hierarchy.

changing any actual rules of necessary or allowable connection – followed by progressive changes in content. Revised rules for street type, necessary and allowable connections, and intersection type might be generated independently of one another and added incrementally to the archetype.

Although the form of these archetypes may appear sparse or 'mechanistic' – like building up a structure similar to an engineering structure, with different kinds of members, connections, nuts and bolts – this does not mean that the form of generation is rigid or need create 'utilitarian' patterns (except in the positive sense of functional structures). The more abstract the diagram, the more flexible, allowing a diversity of outcomes and styles. If the style looks unadorned here, it is not because the product should be

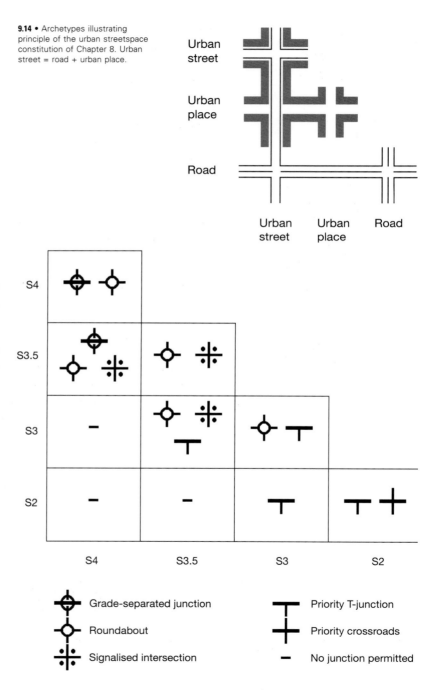

9.14 • Archetypes illustrating principle of the urban streetspace constitution of Chapter 8. Urban street = road + urban place.

Urban street

Urban place

Road

Urban street   Urban place   Road

S4

S3.5

S3

S2

S4   S3.5   S3   S2

9.15 • Allowable junction types. This demonstrates a possible example of specification of allowable junction type for junctions between different tiers of route, graded by vehicle speed. Note that the blank cells – indicating no junction type – are a consequence of access constraint.

Grade-separated junction

Roundabout

Signalised intersection

Priority T-junction

Priority crossroads

—   No junction permitted

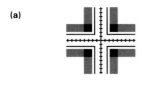

(a)

■ High intensity development

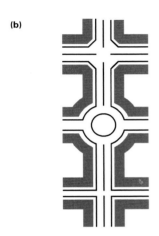

(b)

9.16 • Urban expressions of intersection type. (a) Land use. (b) Urban design.

bare and unadorned, but because the adornment is added at the site design stage, by the individual designer. The bare elements may be 'fleshed out' with architectonic form. In other words, good architecture is desired, but this is not (yet) part of the specification for the street layout.

EXAMPLE PATTERNS

So far this chapter has illuminated what this constitutional approach means in the sense of street type being the basis of constitutional design guidance. While this is sufficient in principle, drawing towards the close of a book on 'Streets and Patterns' seems to demand something that goes beyond the catalogue of street types presented at the end of Chapter 8 – or the 'constitutional archetype' presented so far, in this chapter. It seems to demand the demonstration of possible or desirable patterns, to demonstrate more effectively how the abstract constitution can indeed create actual street patterns.

Therefore, a few illustrations of actual patterns are now suggested. This exercise requires care, since, having opened up a range of diversity and variety for different kinds of street type and pattern, we do not wish to throw that all away by narrowing down to a few particular patterns. There is the danger that expressing any actual configurations or compositions here is open to misinterpretation – for example, by only showing grid-like layouts.[7] Having said that, it now seems appropriate here to suggest how a few potentially desirable patterns could be generated by the constitutional approach described in this chapter.[8]

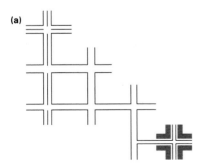

(a)

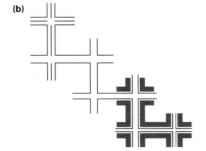

(b)

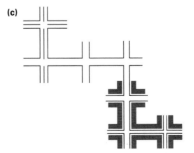

(c)

9.17 • Expression of a conventional constitution, and possible onward evolution. (a) An interpretation of the hierarchy of *Traffic in Towns*. (b) An evolution of the original, that allows the 'local distributor' to become a frontage street. (c) Further evolution that allows for arterial streets (i.e. frontage streets forming network with arteriality).

(a)

(b)

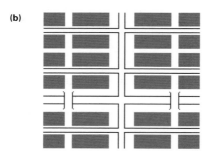

(c)

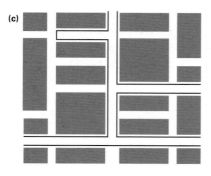

9.18 • A 'tartan constitution' (a) could generate either a tartan grid (b) or a 'tartan tree' (c).

Relationship to desired properties and patterns

We saw earlier some of the desired properties of patterns, including permeability, connectivity, legibility, coherence, clear typology and 'good' hierarchy. Desired patterns could be expected to feature a variety of block shapes and sizes, curvilinear alignments, and so on; and should cater for different modes, including fast and slow movement of private and public transport.

A suitable form of pattern that easily demonstrates these features is some kind of grid, but not a uniform grid; rather, one with a differentiation of street types based on different modes and speeds. These, together, point to a kind of form recognisable as a sort of 'tartan grid'.

Tartan grid

The tartan grid combines a variety of features of pattern from Chapter 4. It is 'hierarchical' by having different types of route; this may be equated with 'directional' or 'differential' grid types. It may also be differentiated in terms of block type (even if all streets are more or less the same) – as in the case of the gridiron or oblong grid. The tartan grid can be seen to embody elements of linear systems – single, double or triple strands – as well as those of grid systems. The tartan grid can be curvilinear, rather than a pure rectilinear form. It also need not be a pure grid in a configurational sense, but may have tree-like components – for example, a cul-de-sac and bollards to separate a minor street from a main boulevard (while allowing pedestrian connection to remain). Or incompatible connections may be dealt with by grade separation.

In fact, the flexibility of the tartan grid points us to the realisation that the term 'tartan' is effectively a mark of a constitution – independent of configuration or composition. If a grid can be regarded as a particular combination of composition (rectilinear orthogonal) and configuration (cell), then a 'tartan' grid is a grid with a certain kind of tartan as a constitution (or, a given 'tartan' constitution in the form of a grid). A given 'tartan' constitution could similarly generate tree-like patterns, or 'characteristic' patterns (Figure 9.18).

Therefore, the following examples are set up to demonstrate how each tartan grid is the result of a given kind of constitution (or a particular kind of 'tartan'), which could apply either to a grid form or to some other form.

Figure 9.19 shows three possible kinds of pattern expressed as tartan grids. Figure 9.19(a) shows a most basic case, the 'uniform' tartan. Although this has a regular street type throughout, it is a 'tartan' pattern in the sense that it is made up of two distinct components: route and block, where the route is a three-strand assembly of footway, carriageway and footway.

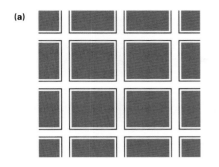

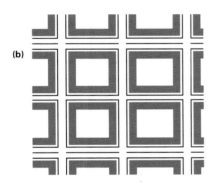

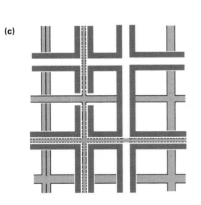

9.19 • Kinds of tartan grid of different degrees of complexity. (a) Uniform tartan. (b) Craig tartan. (c) Buchanan tartan.

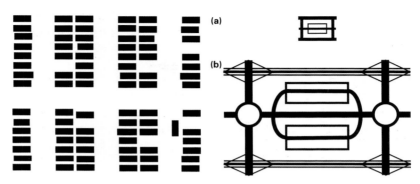

9.20 • Car park as interlocking intermodal tartan grid.

9.21 • Two 'New Town' solutions for different modes. Both have similar structures – but at different scales. (a) 'New town' for human and horse power. (b) 'New town' for motor traffic.

These are merely indicative illustrations of the possible diversity of patterns obtained by just a few street types. The 'Buchanan tartan' here is intended to be as far removed as possible from the tree-like pattern of conventional hierarchy which often followed.

The tartan grid as transport 'modulor'

Le Corbusier's modulor used the dimensions and reach of the human body as the basic units of space for the design of buildings. Transport extends the human reach to the scale of cities, creating patterns from different modes of movement. Streets and patterns are based on the dimensions and attributes of the modes of movement that use them, from the human-scale pedestrian to fast motor traffic.[9]

A tartan grid may be compatible with providing different connectivities for different modes of movement, providing different scales of articulation for different modes (Figures 9.20 and 9.21).

In a 'transport modulor', fast-moving modes will tend to have a more coarsely spaced network – as with urban motorways and railways – while slow-moving modes will benefit from a finer scale network – such as routes serving pedestrians, which will include not only pedestrian-only alleys, but all normal pedestrian-accessible streets. Figure 9.22 suggests some examples of possible 'tartans' based on differentiation of mode.

A tartan grid allows good accessibility to blocks by different modes. A rectangular grid supports a block being served by up to four different kinds of route. This means, for example, that pedestrians do not need to

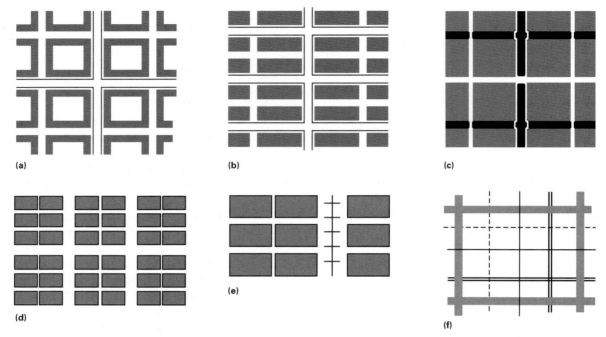

(a)

(b)

(c)

(d)

(e)

(f)

9.22 • Kinds of tartan grid differentiating mode. (a) Alexander tartan – motor traffic/pedestrian. (b) Radburn tartan. (c) Venetian tartan – canal traffic/pedestrian. (d) Car park tartan. (e) *Ciudad Lineal* tartan. (f) Japanese tartan.

be confined to isolated precincts, nor buildings left marooned away from vehicular access.

Pedestrian routes can be continuous. This does not just mean new-town style walkways, but old-fashioned alleys. Instead of mews just being back courts, these could be continuous, woven through the urban fabric. A 'mile-long mews' could be a distinctive street type that takes its place within the urban pattern – a pedestrian-friendly artery that weaves its way through the urban fabric with long-distance continuity.

In the case of the 'Japanese tartan', the interior of the block can be served by different kinds of traffic-calmed street.[10] In some cases these streets may be roofed over to create pedestrian arcades. These arcades can continue, block after block, providing a pleasant continuous environment for strolling and shopping, that can form an extensive network (for example, reaching out across a central area), rather than having a solid block of vehicle-inaccessible territory. This retention of a degree of penetration by motor vehicles may fall short of the aspirations of those advocating car-free cities, but it allows a gradual selective introduction, rather than insisting that a solid chunk of a district become suddenly bereft of private motorised mobility.

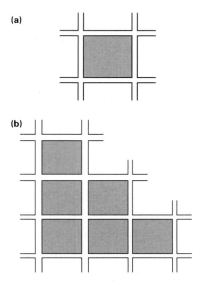

9.23 • Different block types generated by different route types. (a) A single street type generates one intersection type and one block type. (b) Two street types generate three types of intersection and six types of block.

The tartan grid as a generator of diversity

A street-based code that builds frontage function into street type thereby ties land use pattern into the transport pattern. A tartan grid can generate a diversity of mixed-use land use blocks. The number of block types generated will depend on the number of street types present, the kinds of allowable connection, and how distinct block types are recognised in relation to these street types and connections (Figure 9.23).

A system of three street types – boulevard, street and minor lane, say – generates a maximum of six types of intersection and 21 types of block (Figure 9.24).

If access constraint is applied to disallow connection between the boulevard and the minor lane, then the number of block types reduces to twelve (and the number of intersection types reduces to five). If we were to introduce a condition that ruled out boulevards being on consecutive parallel alignments (i.e. ruling out blocks with boulevards on opposing sides); and a similar condition that ruled out minor lanes on consecutive parallel alignments (i.e. ruling out blocks with minor lanes on opposing sides), then the number of block types reduces to just six (Figure 9.25).

This rationalisation exercise is done for the purposes of illustration, to demonstrate a manageable-looking number of block types (i.e. six instead of 21). There is, however, no practical need to reduce the number of allowable permutations (the number of allowable block types) for the purposes of having a manageable typology for design guidance, because the design

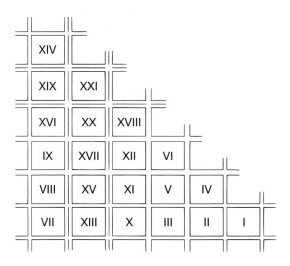

9.24 • Twenty-one block types generated by three street types.

guidance need not be specified at the level of the block. In other words, one does not start with the idea of 21 block types, and start fitting these together in different patterns. Here, block type is an emergent feature of different street types in combination. It is street type that is the basis for specification.

The implication is that a constitutional street code can generate a mixed use land use pattern, without specifying (or 'zoning for') mixed use zones. The mix of uses arises as a result of the interplay between street types (Figure 9.26).

The conventional planning practice of zoning was, of course, devised to separate incompatible land uses. This positive aspect of town planning need not be lost. All that is required is that block types as they emerge are checked for internal compatibility of land use. This will be a purely relational rule of adjacency, i.e. which land use may or may not adjoin which other land use. How this differs from conventional town planning is that it does not pre-suppose a final distribution of land uses at the macro scale. It does not specify that residential or industrial areas should be kept as separate zones, simply that certain land uses might not share a particular block.

The resulting kind of mixed use pattern is the sort of pattern that may arise naturally, as demonstrated by Richard MacCormac's domino theory, based on observation in inner London, in which compatibility of different land uses is resolved within blocks. Other cases, where a tartan pattern of routes is associated with a mixed pattern of land uses, are seen in the examples of London's Bloomsbury with its streets and mews, in Kevin Lynch's alternating net and the concept of the 'transit corridor district'.

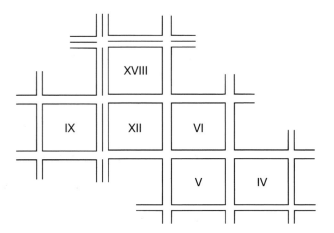

9.25 • Selection of six block types generated by three street types.

9.26 • Mixed land use pattern generated by interplay of different street types.

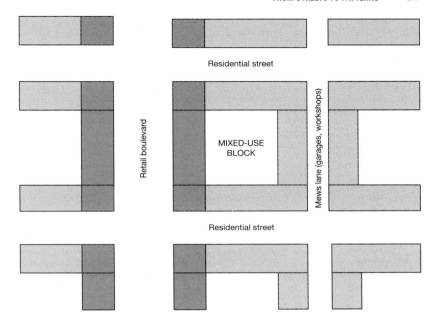

These cases indicate that the idea of the 'tartan constitution' – although perhaps given a distinct new emphasis here – actually ties back into a variety of existing and proposed urban forms.[11]

The tartan pattern, to sum up, combines linear continuity of route types with diversity of land uses or block types. The route types can also be made as diverse as desired, to accommodate 'sustainable' transport modes, so that the resulting urban pattern has both modal choice and mixed land uses. The tartan grid is not the only way of achieving this. But it presents a clear and simple schema for at least including these desired features. It is up to designers in individual circumstances, and real sites, to make use of the full complexity and creativity that a constitutional approach affords.

CONCLUSIONS

This chapter has laid out the basis for a constitutional approach to the design of urban structure and layout, using the street as the fundamental building block. While it is not a completely detailed system of design guidance, as such – that would need to tie into a specific context of application – the chapter has demonstrated the basic principles, some tools for expressing alternative constitutions and suggestions for resultant patterns. The specified elements of the resulting constitutional code are shown in Table 9.1.

Table 9.1 **Elements of an integrated street-based constitutional code**

Sphere	Code rule	Explanation
Transport/route network	1. Modes	Allowable modes coexisting along a street
	2. Arteriality	Necessary connections between route types
	3. Access constraint	Allowable connections between route types
	4. Connection type	Allowable junction types between route types
Land use	5. Frontage use	Allowable compatible uses to adjoin each route type, to create street type
	6. Block composition	Allowable compatible uses to adjoin each other, to create block type
Urban design	7. Building and spatial relations	Overall arrangement and assembly of buildings, form and massing within blocks, across blocks and shaping of street space

The first four create a system for transport network management – which could apply to any urban or inter-urban network. The fifth ties in frontage use to create street type, so that the first five together create a system for generating street pattern. This relates back to Chapter 1, and the 'lost art' of street grid design. The sixth creates a system of land use planning. The seventh and final completes an urban design code: this then relates to the fully three-dimensional aspect of the street (Chapter 1).

These seven rules seem to represent a minimum of design/planning conditions to generate urban layout. Different aspects could be used independently, or in a single system. The latter possibilities do not need to be pursued for the road layout part to work, as a simple updated system of 'hierarchy'. This system could be used, at least, as a basis for road layout guidance; at most, the system envisaged – with rules suitably fleshing out the skeleton – could even be sufficient to form a 'code' for urban design or even 'town planning'.

As it turns out, then, we have seen how desired urban layouts might be achieved not only by the prescription of particular compositions or configurations, but might be generated by the means of constitutional rule systems. In doing so, we have seen how road hierarchy may be reformulated as a kind of urban street constitution. Rather than rigidly prescribing preferred configurations or compositions, it is possible to synthesise street pattern using a series of constitutional rules. In this way, the incremental application of rules of constitutional connection (arteriality and access constraint) can lead to emergent forms. By a few modifications to existing rules of street type and connection, it is possible to open up a greater diversity of possible patterns.

Such a kind of 'constitutional' system of structural generation – already used by the highway engineering tradition – may therefore turn out to be capable of, if not preferable for, generating the elusive emergent properties of coherence and organised complexity, found in traditional settlements, which are desired or appreciated by 'urbanists' of whatever profession. Perhaps surprisingly, then, the engineer may already have the rational foundations for generating urban structure, from which a variety of urban design creations may arise. The constitutional approach can unite both the 'road hierarchy' of the engineer and the 'local urban code' of the urban designer. So, the point 'where urbanism meets hierarchy' (opening Chapter 2) need not be a disurban rupture, but can be a seamless urban creation.

NOTES

1   Arguably, any town or city contains a mixture of planned and unplanned features. Here, 'unplanned' means 'not wholly planned' rather than 'wholly not planned'.
2   Alexander *et al.* (1987: 37).
3   Sorkin (1993: 127).
4   Tissue analysis is described by Hayward (1993) and Cowan (2002: 36).
5   This term coincidentally is the name of a classic work by Jeremy Bentham (1830).
6   Steadman (1998).
7   Just as Buchanan's principles of hierarchy did not require megastructural architecture nor cul-de-sac layouts, the principles of a constitutional approach to urban structure do not require the use of the grid, or neo-traditional street types – or even the street. The approach here could be applied to create a Buchanan-style quartet of primary distributor, district distributor, local distributor and access road if desired.
8   Rather than creating too many new patterns, we choose to tie back where possible into existing types or proposals, to demonstrate the diversity achievable by the basic constitutional form, that does more than promote one single type of preferred pattern peculiar to this book.
9   Le Corbusier (1951); a similar idea of articulating speed and scale has been suggested by Smithson and Smithson (1968).
10   Odani and Yamanaka (1997).
11   MacCormac (1996); Deckker (1998) and Hillier (1996) on mix of uses according to different streets; Lynch (1981); Beimborn and Rabinowitz (1991) on transit corridor districts.

10 CONCLUSIONS

This book opened with a bit of futurism from the 1960s. It was noted that under today's inherited conventions for urban layout, we could not easily recreate an urban quarter like London's Bloomsbury or an urban street such as Tottenham Court Road. Yet the analysis of this book suggests that it should be possible. How?

Looking back, we can see that, potentially, the difference that the findings of this book can make (or, the reason the book can uncover possible answers) is by a combination of going back to first principles, and unpicking entrenched conventions – the 'unchallenged truths' of conventional theory. Looking back, we can see instances where relationships that were previously assumed to be fixed are seen not necessarily to be so.

We have seen that there is not just one kind of street – that is, a street is not just an 'access road'. Nor is there just one kind of 'main road' or 'strategic road' – but many ways of recognising what should be top of the hierarchy. There is not just one kind of hierarchy – and not even just one kind that employs the conventional 'dendritic' hierarchical structure. There is not just one way of dividing up transport modes by vehicle type. There is not just one way of conceptualising transport networks, as links and nodes. There is not just one kind of grid layout – nor even just one kind of 'tartan grid'. There is not just one way of achieving desired patterns through certain processes of generation or particular kinds of design guidance.

When we unlock the fixed assumptions within each of these topics individually, we also unlock the potential for unleashing new permutations across the board, and the possibilities of new relationships between people, activities, streets, patterns and settlements.

10.0 • Tottenham Court Road.

The book's analysis has, on the one hand, clarified distinctions between compositional, configurational and constitutional properties, where these were previously tangled up; and on the other hand has shown that the issue of structure ties street type and pattern type rather closely together. On the one hand, we can see that it is quite possible to have an 'arterial connector boulevard' street type – where arterial, connector and boulevard are not mutually exclusive; or, for that matter, a 'dendritic tartan gridiron' type of pattern. On the other hand, we have seen how closely connector streets are bound up with connector networks; and arterial streets bound up with arterial networks.

By scrutinising all of these, it has been possible to analyse which conventional relationships are valuable and should be kept, and which are not necessarily so, where there could be room for reform, on which to base future revisions to design practice.

TOTTENHAM COURT ROAD REVISITED

The realisation that today's Tottenham Court Road prevails as a reasonably successful, functional street – despite not fitting with the Modernist vision of *Traffic in Towns* or the engineering conventions that grew out of it – says two things. First, it demonstrates the justification for revisiting and reviewing existing theory and conventions – this was a stimulus to the book in the first place. Second, it demonstrates that if we can supply a new framework that can accommodate within it the existing reasonably good practice, then this demonstrates that the new framework is not some outlandish or abstract innovation, but is grounded in a viable context. Therefore, the workability of the book's suggestions is demonstrated not least by checking how the streetgrids of contemporary Bloomsbury or Fitzrovia could now be accommodated.

For a start, by abandoning the presumed 'inverse relationship' between mobility and access, it is not necessary to insist that Tottenham Court Road must either be a primary distributor or an access road. Tottenham Court Road can be recognised as being both a strategic arterial – with a significant public transport role – and an important frontage street. This combination can allowably be embodied in a single street type on the assumption that the traffic is kept to tolerably low 'urban' speeds, as indeed it should do on any urban street.

It is only fair that the 'urban place' role of Tottenham Court Road is recognised, since its role as a bustling commercial street is clear to anyone on the ground, whereas 'strategic' designation, as we have seen, is based on somewhat abstract and subjective considerations of network topology.

Therefore, although the research for this book has involved detailed and, at times, abstruse structural and conceptual investigations, the findings can be used to expose and support the right for the immediate, tangible use of streets for people, against the supposedly unassailable 'traffic engineering' rules for strategic roads, which turn out not to be based on traffic, but more to do with the way lines connect up on the map. This allows the bus stop to be located on the same street (and at the same level) as the grocery store (Chapter 10 opening image).

Having revisited Tottenham Court Road, we can now revisit Bloomsbury and Fitzrovia. Here, the crossroads intersections that are a feature of this part of inner London are permissible where there is appropriate junction treatment – such as a combination of low speed and/or signalisation. The combination of frontage streets and crossroads intersections allows the traditional form of the streetgrid to be positively designed, rather than being, at most, tolerated. The permeability of traditional street grids that allow ease of walking can be maintained. And the pub on the corner can be spared the bulldozer.

As high speed and traffic flow are decoupled from the arterial role, it is also possible for side streets to connect up directly with the main street, Tottenham Court Road. Put simply, 'main street' is, in effect, redefined as something like 'continuous street with side road off it', rather than 'big road' or 'busy road' or 'high-speed road'. It then becomes acceptable for minor side streets to have direct access to the main street, again with appropriate junction treatment. This allows the most direct access possible between the bus stop on the main street and its catchment area in the adjoining urban quarters.

Effectively, this means designing the urban structure with the traditional urban archetype of the 'main street with side roads off it' in mind, and then devising traffic engineering solutions that work, to fit around it. This puts the 'town' ahead of the 'traffic'. It puts traffic engineering in a valued supporting role – as is usually the case, in existing urban areas; rather than in a leading formative role, out of its depth as far as urban formation is concerned – as sometimes occurred, in cases where it was allowed to be a primary influence on the form of new developments or whole new settlements.

The supporting role of traffic engineering was always one envisaged by Colin Buchanan in *Traffic in Towns*. He always intended that standards for environmental quality should be unassailable, and fixed first, before fitting around this provision for accessibility. This intention was stated in conscious contradistinction to previous approaches that had appeared to put traffic first.[1] However, in practice, the kind of environmental quality supported by *Traffic in Towns* was effectively the kind of quality retained in the set piece of Fitzroy Square (Figure 8.16), that works as an architectural composition, but is divorced from the surrounding context – the rest of Fitzrovia that would go under the bulldozer.

If urban design has taught us anything over the past 40 years, it is the importance of how things connect up across boundaries. Urban design is not just 'architecture writ large' – but necessarily deals with *relationships* between professions and their products and processes, and *relationships* between buildings, spaces and land uses, that cross site boundaries, cross public and private spaces, and even stake a claim to some of the surface of the Earth normally reserved for highway purposes.

If, despite best intentions, the legacy of *Traffic in Towns* has appeared to put traffic considerations ahead of urban design considerations, it is perhaps because there was always a clear prerogative for ensuring the connectedness of arterial roads, whereas there was no particular priority, far less guarantee, that urban places should all connect up in any particular way. In other words, the 'structure of disurban creation' was always a likely – if not inevitable – outcome of the logic that ensured that strategic traffic routes were the 'trunk' and the streets became isolated as 'twigs'. This book has now suggested a possible way of redressing the balance, by recognising the significance of arteriality, and by using this to ensure that the contiguity of 'urban place' is prioritised at least as much as any priority afforded to the contiguity of traffic routes.

CODING FOR STREETS AND PATTERNS

This book suggests that it should be possible to reformulate design for streets and urban layout, using the street as the basic building-block of urban structure. The proposed approach combines two fundamental things: first, the use of the street (as opposed to the road or traffic conduit) as the primary element; and second, the system of generating structure by the constitutional connection of skeletal elements (streets or routes). In other words, this effectively uses engineering means – albeit a broader, more flexible constitutional form than road hierarchy *per se* – to address urbanist ends.

Expressed in this manner, it can be seen that the two components – streets and constitution – were never mutually exclusive. The adoption of a constitutional approach to layout (specifying types of route and connection) never required this to be fixed rigidly to a system that prioritised vehicular considerations (speed, flow) with strategic routes; conversely, adopting a traditional-streets-oriented urban design agenda never meant the need to abandon a rational, generic system of design guidance.

The envisaged system, in its fullest extent, is based on the following premises:

- rather than design guidance being based on a limited typology of desired patterns, patterns can be generated by a 'program' or 'code' of types and relationships;
- for urban application, the street can be the fundamental building block of urban structure; so, patterns are created from combinations of street type;
- street types, of whatever form, are in turn based on route type, and 'coded' for their constitutional relationships, in terms of allowable and necessary structural connections between route types;
- those constitutional route types are based on mode of movement, where mode of movement refers to speed and 'transit orientation', not vehicle type *per se*.

The resulting system of regulation has been set out earlier, in Table 9.1. In essence, the system comprises a 'transport code' (route type; necessary connections; allowable connections; connection type), a 'land use' component (street type incorporating frontage use; block land use mix) and an 'urban design' component (three-dimensional relationships) that, together, comprise a full 'urban design code'.

While the foregoing is a possible system of general design principles and approaches, there has been no scope in this book to prescribe solutions to particular design situations, nor to recommend specific revisions to particular design codes. For onward application, the system would need to be fully fleshed out with detailed rules set, tailored to individual contexts of geography or professional specialism. This implies, ultimately, a plurality and divergence of possible approaches – just as the most basic principles such as hierarchy have been applied (similarly yet differently) in a variety of contexts over the past decades.

Having said that, it is hoped that sufficient detail has been provided to demonstrate the applicability of the principles. Where possible, links can be seen to existing cases, whether in terms of existing conventions, applications or speculations. For example, principles such as arteriality or stratification by speed are already practised, albeit not necessarily in these terms. And as new possible permutations open up new areas of solution space, these may be found already to be inhabited by existing speculative ideas for new forms of street (e.g. Alexander's Green Street, or Crawford's Bicycle Boulevard) which effectively exist in isolated pockets, waiting to be engaged or activated by mainstream practice.

What the system proposed in this book does is effectively to tie the traditional street into a conceptual framework, where before the street has seemed to 'float free' of official practice. As noted in Chapter 2, the street seems to float free typologically in the sense that it habitually crops up in urban design advocacy and guidance, yet without being tied back to a specific role in road-based engineering guidance. Additionally, the street also *topologically* 'floats free' in the sense that under the conventional principles, the only role for the street is as an access road, habitually in a disjointed position in the urban layout: isolated within development pods (or environmental *areas*). This book allows the street to reclaim its rightful place centre stage; it shows how the contiguity of urban streetspace can be guaranteed, by insisting on arteriality (strategic contiguity) for urban streets.

The significance of this is that where currently we see a raft of urban design guides and street design guides, these still do not wholly tie up with the core engineering guidance, to which, sooner or later, they must connect. This book shows a way of uniting the different traditions of urban design and engineering in a single framework, so that we do not necessarily have to have two separate sets of documents. It means that we do not need to suspend our belief in the existence of streets whenever we delve into engineering guidance that admits of only 'distributor roads' and 'access roads'; nor need we suspend belief in the existence of those official road layout conventions when dreaming up urban designs that propose grids of 'boulevards', 'mews' and 'streets' with not a standard highway type in sight.

Although the investigation has been 'radical' in the sense of going back to first principles and digging around the foundations of conventional practice, the application of the resulting principles does not rely on some leap of faith, some unproven technological fix, nor require any radical change in human nature. For example, when choosing which modes of movement to use, there is no need to assume that some new benign mode will be invented, nor that the public will choose to put the good of the planet ahead of their own personal convenience. What is proposed is that viable alternatives are not ruled out at the outset, simply because they are never offered as choices in the first place.

IMPLICATIONS FOR PRACTICE

Overall, this book has proposed a combination of analytic and generative processes. These can perhaps help to satisfy Hillier's criteria (quoted at the end of Chapter 2) of precise diagnosis and permissive creation.

The general principles of the book's proposed street-based constitution have been given above. Some specific changes to existing practices are now suggested.

Urban analysis

The book has proposed a number of concepts and devices for identifying, analysing and expressing different kinds of street type, pattern, hierarchy, and so on. These include route structure analysis, and the graphical devices of the netgram, modegram, constitutional archetype, and so on. All of these could be further refined and developed. Their basic application is to help specify structure more effectively: where better specification of different kinds of urban spatial phenomena can allow testing for desired performance and hence prescription.

Urban design

The findings of this book can inform future urban design guidance, by plugging directly into those parts of urban design guidance addressing street type and layout structure (street pattern). Street pattern is just one area of urban design concern, but sets the spatial framework for other aspects of urban design. In particular, the affinity between street type and pattern or topology has been demonstrated. A number of specific interpretations of desired properties for street layout have been suggested, including interpretations of 'connective networks', 'clear hierarchy' as well as other properties such as 'legibility' and 'coherence' (Chapter 7).

As well as addressing urban patterns, this book also suggests design processes, in the form of the constitutional approach. This suggests the possibility of generic coding for structure, as an alternative to 'desired pattern' templates. It suggests the possibility of an approach that is both 'rational' and 'organic'.

The next steps would be to work towards combining different types of street with different kinds of spatial composition and built form: a more detailed typology of squares, terraces, etc.; design codes for building types, and planning codes for frontage use, in a single system of design guidance. This could be developed for different cities and countries.

Highway engineering and road layout

The approach of this book builds on the principle of hierarchy, but adapts and 'evolves' it to suit contemporary needs. Conventional road hierarchy always made sense for general traffic, and the approach of this book allows the logic and rationale of hierarchy (e.g. arteriality and access constraint) to be adapted to better suit public transport and pedestrians as well as private motor traffic.

Basically, the system proposed decouples the issue of arteriality from factors such as vehicle flow, trip length and speed. This does not alter the prerogative for the safe design of road links or junctions. Specifications for the detailed design of links and junctions for different speeds and flows would still prevail as a parallel but separate exercise, just as current design standards for the construction of roads (subgrade, surfacing materials, and so on) are determined by local (per link) factors such as flows and axle weight. What the reformulated hierarchy does is to prioritise the strategic contiguity of the public transport–pedestrian system ahead of the strategic contiguity of high-speed, high-volume vehicular routes, as the primary formative basis of structuring urban areas.

Rather than abandoning hierarchy, a reformulated 'hierarchy' based on the street is placed at the core of an integrated system of urban design. This reflects the topological centrality – or skeletal role – of transport relative to other land uses. In any case, the application of hierarchy has traditionally been associated with development control, as much as with traffic flow. The result would be revisions to national and municipal guidance on road and street types. These could be crystallised into a single 'manual for streets' covering all engineering and infrastructure aspects of street design.

Transport planning and policy

The proposed system consciously uses urban structure to serve a diversity of transport modes. The result can boost alternatives to car use, but is not anti-car as such. What the system prohibits is those people travelling in fast, noxious vehicles from mixing with other people going about their urban business on foot. This does *not* mean we permit only roads that cater for only one or the other; that would represent one of the kinds of simplistic jumping-to-conclusions sometimes found in Modernist theory that one would hope to avoid repeating this time around.[2]

And, just because we need van-shaped vehicles to move household appliances from warehouse to home, or estate-car-sized vehicles to take a climbing party to the foot of a mountain at dawn, or secure metal-and-glass-encased vehicles to transport lone individuals home safely at night does not give the right for any person to use any car-like vehicle anywhere at any time. Nor is this a justifiable basis for an 'idealised' transport system.

Rather, the proposed system promotes maximum accessibility for slow modes (or modes at slow speed) and strategic contiguity for coarse-network modes (such as public transport). By focusing on key 'active ingredients' such as speed and network coarseness, rather than on individual vehicle type, this is intended to accommodate and even promote (rather than exclude or discourage) participation of unconventional and novel modes. This should increase choice, and potentially boost efficiency and attractiveness of more 'sustainable' modes.

The resulting system effectively integrates walking (and other access modes) with the public transport system, as a priority, rather than simply being the lowest rung in the vehicular hierarchy. To operationalise the 'transit-oriented hierarchy' implies optimising public transport patterns with respect to the urban street network (and the inter-urban network beyond). This book has suggested a possible starting point in principle, with suggestions for levels in such a hierarchy. To realise this will mean taking the theoretical concept of arteriality and interpreting and expressing this in practical terms for the purposes of planning the public transport service network. This will mean ensuring that strategic routes and services connect up; this is not only a matter of road layout, of course, but implies coordination across modes, infrastructure providers and operators.

Town planning

The general topic of town planning has been somewhat peripheral to this book, since the main focus has been on certain topics relating to transport and urban design (and, even then, substantial areas of transport and urban design have not been addressed at all). In one sense, therefore, town planning is perhaps a discipline barely touched by the concerns of this book. However, in another sense this book could present a challenge to town planning orthodoxy, perhaps precisely because the investigation has suggested the possibility of generating urban structure without reference to the overall urban outcome – in other words, creating towns *without* plans.

What is at stake is the basic organising unit of spatial structure. The street-based approach suggested in this book effectively puts the topology of the line of movement ahead of the topology of the area – such as the land use parcel, zone or neighbourhood – which has been the conventional spatial basis for town planning. In effect, it would be possible to have a system of spatial organisation based wholly on the structural organisation of routes, where route types had land uses built into them – rather than the other way around. In this sense, the primary determinant of land use would be the street type, not the land use zone.

Moreover, the street-based generation of urban structure is a constitutional approach, in which only local elements and relationships are specified. This is a bottom-up approach, that starts with streets and builds up urban structure, rather than a top-down approach which presupposes the idea of a whole town as the unit of design. This has resonance with existing approaches of Christopher Alexander and others, in their *New Theory of Urban Design*, and with critics of planning orthodoxy from Jane Jacobs onwards. The challenge to town planning therefore lies in the level at which design intervention takes place: and whether there is a need for 'town' planning at all. That investigation would effectively take us beyond the scope of 'streets and patterns', and is the subject of another work.[3]

THE FUTURE

Planning, and to an extent any form of design, are in a sense an exercise in futurism. A potential problem with futuristic visions comes if too narrow a frame of reference is envisaged. We are tempted to extrapolate a single variable, such as traffic growth or city size, without considering the circumstances in which overall scenarios would develop or evolve. This can limit the ability to visualise solutions. For example, it is difficult to imagine the car-free city of tomorrow, if we simply try to imagine the city of today without the cars. So, while it is easy to imagine cities of tomorrow, it is not so easy to imagine viable ones – or the path to get from here to there.

This book has demonstrated novel or uncustomary permutations of existing things – existing modes, street types, hierarchical structures. These may now be used to anticipate possible developments for the city of the future, at least in terms of streets and patterns, transport and urban design. The city of the future envisaged here is not so much a projection of trends into the future, but just a glimpse of different permutations of existing forms.

Future modes

Transport modes can be seen to be part of a succession of types going back through history: today's articulated lorry can be seen as an 'evolutionary descendant' of the ox-cart. Sometimes, modes will diverge, as the horse and carriage branched out on the one hand to become the horse-drawn omnibus, and on the other, to become the 'horseless carriage' or motor car. These modes are to some extent 'co-evolutionary' with the urban environment. This means there is a two-way dynamic relationship between transport and urban form, and a combination of continuity and change over time.[4]

If current legislation makes it difficult for new modes to evolve, then we will be stuck with the city of today. The role of policy need not be to fix urban geometry and form to existing modes, but could be to provide spaces and channels to protect and encourage more favourable modes of movement. This could include encouraging the 'speciation' of new modes, that is, the evolutionary divergence from existing lineages.

For example, instead of having the car as a single monolithic mode, that means so many things to so many people – some would say *too* many things to *too* many people – there could be a technical and legislative division of different facets of the car into different roles. This would let people make their own trade-offs – the conventional family saloon for long motorway journeys, a compact 'clean technology' car for nipping through the inner city.

This idea is not new – Lewis Mumford argued for a similar approach, back in 1961. It seems that four decades later, what with the advances in vehicle technology and the progressive environmental prerogative for 'greener' transport, the time might be ripe for looking into the idea again.[5]

This division between city car and inter-urban car would not require a zonal ban – sealing off inner cities from modes that access the outside world – but could be effected by a conversion of selected streets over time, gradually coarsening the network of routes used by inter-urban vehicles, and gradually accustoming people to the idea that they have alternatives to their conventional mode of choice, that are both green and convenient.

For example, a coarser network of routes for 'highway cars' would provide access to parking garages – so that these would have an accessibility profile more akin to the bus network and bus stops (or coach parking) than for conventional cars. This would be complemented by a finer scale network of access and parking for small clean two-seaters – 'compact cars for compact cities'. This in turn allows the development of further compact centres, with narrow streets and scaled-down, end-on parking spaces.

In effect, it is possible to imagine a hierarchy of private modes based on their permitted network penetration – large fast 'A-road cars' for inter-urban travel, that would penetrate the strategic (A-road) network of urban areas, and park in designated parking garages; smaller 'B-road cars' that would penetrate the more local (B-road) network, with parking on-street in conventional parking spaces; and finally 'C cars' – the clean, calm compact 'city cars' that would access all areas currently accessible to motor vehicles in today's cities, travelling at slow speeds on a fine network of traffic-calmed streets, and parking end-on as close to their destination as possible. By providing a more finely graded spectrum of modes from 'compact car' to conventional car to public transport, a better 'modal fit' between vehicles and urban places could be effected.

Future streets

Whatever future vehicles will be like, they are likely to be human-shaped on the inside. Similarly, the city of tomorrow is likely to be in some way street-shaped on the inside – whether enclosed cities on the Earth's surface, underground or in space.

Streets shared by trams and pedestrians could be covered over to provide a system of arterial arcades, like elongated shopping malls or 'crystal palaces' that could form the backbone of one possible kind of future city.[6]

The streets of tomorrow would do well at least to accommodate the modes of today, never mind the modes of tomorrow. The so-called all-purpose street of today hardly caters for the full range of human-powered vehicles that might be more popular if they had a legitimate running space set aside for them. At present, modes such as rollerblades, skateboards and scooters are systematically ignored or discriminated against. Yet a system that encouraged citizens to burn up their own energy could beat today's combination of obesity, walking-pace congestion and toxic emissions. If we can have bicycle boulevards – or fan-assisted cycle tunnels[7] – then why not rollerblade arcades?

Perhaps there never was and never will be a viable evolutionary path to reach the city of human-powered locomotion.[8] But, if we are serious about a 'green' transport future, can we really afford to write off human-powered modes as fanciful? What other innovative modes could be encouraged, if there were an infrastructural niche for them to occupy?

Future patterns

The different types of streets plied by different modes of movement should be able to permeate the whole urban area, rather than being confined to isolated pockets. The tartan grid, already demonstrated in Chapter 9, is a suitable medium for this purpose. In a rectangular grid, each block can be served by up to four street types, each with a different modal combination. A block could be attached to an arterial arcade on one side, a canal to another, a conventional all-purpose street on another, and a human-powered street on another.

Such a system could be introduced gradually, with selective conversion of streets: perhaps every fourth street in each direction converted for use by clean or slow modes. This can gradually build up networks of 'green' streets as linear 'habitats' favourable for 'green modes'. It can also lead to the gradual closing off and covering over of streets and squares to form sequences of arcades and atria, gradually extending a continuously connected temperate environment for human passage.

Phasing in the future

Traffic in Towns may have been revolutionary; but the revolution was not generally realised by the immediate sacking of inner cities, by the construction of urban motorways and megastructures. The urban revolution happened mostly gradually, incrementally and progressively over years, applied by footsoldiers in traffic and planning departments up and down the land, as each development decision reinforced the status of certain roads as distributors, and each road's status confirmed the allowable development patterns, to create the urban structure we see today.

The approach of this book also suggests a kind of gradualism, a kind of onward evolution, albeit with a slightly different underlying code. But this change builds on measures that have been part of a change in direction already well underway: all the counter-measures that have sprung up in the most recent decades – the traffic calming, the bus lanes, the bus priority signals, the cycle lanes, the shared surfaces and *woonerven*. These are all now quite firmly installed in practice, although they not do necessarily fit with the purest forms of theory based on free-flowing vehicular roads separate from buildings, that still prevail in principle. In a sense, what is needed is for theory to catch up with practice. This book has provided some ways of addressing this so that the conceptual basis better fits the reality. (Here, 'reality' either means expressly stated policies and practices which do not fit conventional theory, such as policies for 'streets', although streets may not be recognised officially; or, it means intuitive practices that get by without reference to conventional theory, such as common-sense designing for streets, in the absence of official guidance for 'streets' as such; or intuitively designing according to arteriality, without explicitly saying so, etc.)

Phase 1 would be to adopt the general conceptual framework, within which existing progressive practice may be located. This phase does not necessarily mean changing any actual content of practice, but it will 'legitimise' a lot of existing good practice.

- Express existing modes of movement that are
  - (a) promoted;
  - (b) provided for;
  - (c) expressly permitted;
  - (d) neither expressly permitted nor expressly prohibited;
  - (e) expressly prohibited.
- Express existing street types in terms of the above modes of movement, and assumptions about speed, and transit orientation, and allowable frontage access.
- Express existing road hierarchy explicitly in terms of arteriality and access constraint in terms of 'constitutional archetypes' (for individual route types and

the whole hierarchy). This exercise can promote thought on what types are actually being used, how and why.
- Express existing land use compatibility and urban design relationships.

This can assist thinking about which street and block types, patterns and combinations are available, which are actually not prohibited, and which new creative combinations are possible – all within the existing rules.

Phase 2 would then be to phase in new good practice: to start selectively changing rules and relationships to move in desired directions. This could include the following, for example:

- Switch priority of arteriality to public transport.
- Enforce speeds to meet requirements of street and junction type.
- Legislate for 'speciation' of vehicle category, to split the car into two or more classes.
- Provide streets and lanes for diversity of modes (human-powered streets, streets for clean/compact vehicles, slow streets, etc.).
- Apply network coarsening for fossil-fuelled modes.
- Apply land use regulation (or liberalisation) with respect to street types.

Phase 3 would then be 'letting go' – phasing out unnecessary and redundant uses:

- Ban unclean vehicles from urban areas altogether. There will have been sufficient time for people to get used to choosing appropriate alternatives.
- Weed out unnecessary regulations of zoning, planning, etc.

This system will not solve all problems, but it points a way forward for tackling several issues, not least problems created by existing practices and conventions of typology, hierarchy and planning. Unlike urban problems such as congestion, pollution, poverty, disease or danger, the raft of engineering and planning regulations and zoning practices, typologies and hierarchies are all rational human constructs, put there expressly to serve human purposes. We should tailor them so that they are not part of the problem, but part of the solution.

NOTES

1   MoT (1963: 52).
2   This has been characterised as the 'fallacy of singularity' of conventional Modernism (Robbins, 2000).
3   Marshall (forthcoming – *Cities Design and Evolution*).
4   Marshall (2004).
5   Mumford (1961; 1964). For discussion of current prospects for battery electric vehicles, hybrid electric vehicles and fuel cell electric vehicles, see, for example,

Kemp and Simon (2001), Banister (2002), Hoogma *et al.* (2002), Khare and Sharma (2003), Johansson (2003), Sperling (2003).

6   For example, a version of Joseph Paxton's proposed 'Great Victorian Way' (see, for example, Evans *et al.*, 1986) for the twenty-first century – a grand arcade with trams running along it. See Richards (2001) for further ideas for future transport in cities, including covered-over streets.

7   Turner (1996).

8   This is for a similar reason that there maybe never was and never will be an evolutionary opportunity for six-legged horses. On the difference between logical possibility, biological possibility and evolutionary history, see Daniel Dennett's *Darwin's Dangerous Idea* (1996).

APPENDICES

APPENDIX 1 SOURCES OF CRITICISM (FIGURE 1.10)

Almost all the blame for the amount of disappointing bland housing estates can be laid at the door of highway engineers
>   Thorne (LTT, 1998)

Destructive orthodoxies
>   Cowan (1997: 8)

Excessive road standards promoted by Le Corbusian architects and traffic engineers
>   Schurch (1999: 5)

Fanatical highway promoters
>   Mumford (1964: 180)

Imposition of rigid traffic engineering standards
>   Gosling and Maitland (1984: 13)

Over-regulation
>   Baxter (1998)

Rigidity and standardisation
>   DTLR and CABE (2001: 24)

Hosts of supposed experts, many of whom, like sinister Departments of Transportation everywhere, have played major roles in tearing the environment to bits and encouraging its most cancerous aberrations
>   Scully (1994: 225)

Slavish adoption of mechanistic standards
>   Jenkins (1975: 17)

Standardised, often uniform, solutions to layout
    Carmona (1998: 180)

Tree-structured road hierarchies, . . . a freak of central government imposition
    Simmonds (1993: 101)

Tyranny of highway standards
    Punter and Carmona (1997: 23)

Unimaginative, standardised road layouts
    CPRE (Carmona, 1997: 18)

Unsympathetically imposed road hierarchies and standards
    Davies (1997: 27)

APPENDIX 2 DESIRED PATTERNS AND PROPERTIES (FIGURE 2.6)

Clear articulation of public space	Urban Task Force (1999: 54)
Clear (hierarchy of) connections	DTLR and CABE (2001: 25)
Clear hierarchy (of transport modes)	Urban Task Force (1999: 88)
Clear hierarchy of spaces	DETR (1998a: 31, 34)
Clear movement hierarchy	Urban Task Force (1999: 53)
Clear network	DETR (1998a: 26)
Clear network of streets . . . squares	SUNI (1997: 2)
Clear network/hierarchy of streets	ICE (2002: 27)
Clear pattern (of roads)	Smithson and Smithson (1967: 63)
Clear public transport structure	Averley (1998)
Clear sense of direction	Evans (1996: 2)
Clear street pattern	Unwin (Hall, 1992)
Clear structure and identity	Southworth and Ben-Joseph (1997: 121)
Clear structure of accessible routes	Urban Task Force (1999: 90)
Clear and coherent system of sequences	Lynch (1990: 93)
Clear and coherent routes (for cycling)	Thorne (LTT, 1998: 9)
Clear and legible structure	Keeble (Taylor, 1998: 31)
Clear, legible and articulating structure	Essex Planning Officers' Association (1997: 10)
Clear destination of pedestrian routes	Chatwin (1997: 15)
Clear, simple and legible street pattern	Ross (1997: 23)
Clearer and more explicit spatial structure	Butina Watson (1993: 71)
Clearly defined public spaces	Cowan (1997: 25)

Clearly defined hierarchy of routes	Essex County Council (1973: 13)
Clearly defined hierarchy of routes	Essex County Council (1980: 10)
Clearly defined hierarchy of roads and public transport routes	IDC (1971: 82)
Very clearly defined urban structure	DTLR and CABE (2001: 40)
Clearly distinguishe[d] street network	Western Australia (1997: 20)
Clearly recognisable hierarchy of streets	Ross (1997: 23)
Coherent network of streets	Beauvais (1996: 78)
Coherent structure	Davies (1997: 29)
Coherent urban form	Carmona (1998: 180)
Coherent urban structure	DTLR and CABE (2001: 40, 41)
Coherent and easy to remember pattern	Lynch (1990: 215)
Coherent, logical and efficient street system	Southworth and Ben-Joseph (1997: 142)
Coherent, meaningful system of spaces	Stones (1997: 31)
Differentiated but well patterned flow system	Lynch (1990: 61)
'Hierarchical' layout	Lerner-Lam *et al.* (1992: 21)
Highly memorable structures	Evans (1996: 2)
Interconnected networks of streets	Morris and Kaufman (1998: 219)
Interconnected pedestrian network	Southworth and Ben-Joseph (1997: 126)
Interconnected network of streets	Lerner-Lam *et al.* (1992: 19)
Inter-connected (framework of) routes	DTLR and CABE (2001: 40)
Inter-connected local street system	Calthorpe (1993: 64)
Inter-connected movement routes	DTLR and CABE (2001: 41)
Interconnected streets	ITE (1999: 6)
Interconnected streets	Lerner-Lam *et al.* (1992: 19)
Legible network of public spaces	TRL (1997: 18)
Legible pattern of pedestrian routes	Chatwin (1997: 15)
Memorable network [of streets]	Krieger and Lennertz (1991: 22)
Open-ended layouts	DTLR and CABE (2001: 25)
Permeable grid	Urban Task Force (1999: 90)
Recognisable, formalised local street system	Calthorpe (1993: 64)

Regular, geometric pattern (of streets)	Lerner-Lam *et al.* (1992: 19)
Robust street pattern	Ross (1997: 23)
Straightforward street pattern	Ross (1997: 23)
Well connected patterns	Lerner-Lam *et al.* (1992: 17)
Well connected layouts	DTLR and CABE (2001: 25)

APPENDIX 3 CATALOGUE OF STREET CLASSIFICATION SYSTEMS

A3.1 *Catalogue of street typologies/road hierarchies*

Roman planning
(Dickinson, 1961)
Cardo
Decumanus
(Hill, 1996)
Colonnade street

Act for the Rebuilding of the City of London (1667)
1. High and principal streets (40 ft wide)
2. Streets and lanes of note (35 ft wide)
3. By-lanes (14 ft wide)
4. Narrower alleys (9 ft wide)

Edinbugh New Town
('Craig Plan')
1. Squares
2. Major streets
3. Transverse streets
4. Minor streets
5. Mews

Ebenezer Howard (1904)
Boulevards
Avenues
Streets

Le Corbusier's 7V
(Spreiregen, 1965: 171)
V1 – Cross country
V2 – Branch to city
V3 – Sector dividers
V4 – Sector connectors
V5 – Local spines
V6 – To buildings
V7 – Pedestrians

Tripp's Classifications
(1950), (1942: 41)
General
Arterial roads
Sub-arterial roads
Local or minor roads
Subdivision of local roads
Town:
    Shopping
    Business industrial
    Amusement
    Residential
Country:
    Village streets
    Country lanes
Other or special types
1. Major shopping or business streets
2. By-pass roads
3. Ring roads
4. Parkways
5. Road tunnels
6. Roads above railways

Suggested nomenclature
(Min. of War Transport, 1946)
1. Arterial roads
2. Through roads
3. Local through roads
4. Local roads
5. Development roads

Other types:
By-pass roads
Radial roads
Ring roads
Shopping streets and arcades
Local roads
Boulevards and parkways
Sub-surface and elevated
The single-purpose road

A hierarchy of street types
(Tunnard and Pushkarev, 1963)
1. Local
2. Collector
3. Arterial

Four levels of facility of the circulation network:
Freeway
Arterial street
Collector street
Land service street

Traffic in Towns, **UK**
(MoT, 1963: 44)
1. Primary distributor
2. District distributor
3. Local distributor
4. Access road

Traffic in Towns, Glossary
(MoT, 1963)
Access road

By-pass
Corridor street
Distributor road
Freeway
Motorway
Motor road
Precinct
Relief road
Ring road
Street
Tangential road

Four-Criteria Classification Formed by Complete Subdivision of All Classes
(Morrison, 1966)
Trunk roads v. Other roads
Straight v. Winding
Very wide v. Wide
Fairly wide v. Narrow
Hilly v. Flat

Five-Criteria Classification Formed by Sub-Division of Successive Remainders
(Morrison, 1966)
1 Motorways
2 Others:
2.1 Dual carriageways
2.2 Others:
2.2.1 Major traffic routes
2.2.2 Others:
2.2.2.1 Paved
2.2.2.2 Stone-surfaced
2.2.2.3 Cinder track
2.2.2.4 Others:
2.2.2.4.1 Roads not always passable
2.2.2.4.2 Footpath, mule track

Jamieson et al. (1967)
Radial road/route
Ring [road]/route

Essex County Council, 1973
1. Local distributor
2. Major access road
3. Intermediate access road
4a. Minor access road
4b. Minor access road
5. Mews court
6. Private drive

Central area grid roads
MKDC (1974)
City grid roads – 'red' roads
North-south – 'blue' roads
Boulevards – 'green' roads
Small 'yellow' streets
Pedestrian routes

Structural role (configuration)
Potter (1976)
Grid road
Loop road
Radial road/route
Ribbon road

New South Wales, 1980
(Brindle, 1996: 76)
Arterial roads
Sub-arterial roads
Collector roads
Local roads

Channel prototypes
Lynch (1981)
Major:
1. Boulevard
2. Freeway
3. Parkway
4. Pedestrian promenade, street, arcade
Minor:
1. Curving suburban street
2. Cul-de-sac
3. Close
4. Square

Other:
Chaotic commercial strip
Barren arterial
Arid industrial route

Melbourne Hierarchy of Roads, 1981 (Brindle, 1996)
Freeways
Primary arterial roads
Secondary arterial roads
Collector roads
Local access streets

South Australia, 1986
(Brindle, 1996)
Arterial roads
1. Primary arterial roads
2. Secondary arterial roads
Local roads
1. Major collector roads
2. Collect./local crossing roads
3. Local streets

Suggested Categories of Highway (Jones, 1986)
I. Motorway
II. Primary
IIIa. Main distributor
IIIb. Secondary distributor
IVa. Local roads (1)
IVb. Local roads (2)

Roads and Traffic in Urban Areas, UK
(DoT/IHT, 1987)
1. Primary distributor
2. District distributor
3. Local distributor
4. Access road
5. Pedestrian street

Russell (1988)
Traffic roads
Local roads

Shopping streets on major
    urban roads
Major highways through
    villages
Quiet roads

Glossary of urban form terms (Larkham and Jones, 1991)

Alley
Avenue
Back lane/access
Boulevard
Break-through street
Bye-law street
Consequent street
Cul-de-sac
High street
Main street
Major traffic street
Mall
Occupation road
Residential street
Ringstrasse
Ring road
Street

Glossary of street types (AlSayyad, 1991)

Tariq (road)
Maiydan (Public square or open space)
Sikah (Side street)
Darb (Lane)
Zuquq (Lanes and alleys)

Four types of road alignment (McCluskey, 1992)

1. Townscape
2. Flowing
3. Hillroad
4. Countryside

UK residential roads (DoE/DoT, 1992)

1. Major access road
2. Minor access road
3. Shared surface road
4. Shared driveways
5. Driveways

Form of the street (Moughtin, 1992)

Straight or curved
Long or short
Wide or narrow
Enclosed or open
Formal or informal

Avalon Design Code
DPZ architects (Krieger and Lennertz, 1992: 90)

'More urban'	*'More rural'*
Boulevard	Parkway
Boulevard	Highway
Main street	Avenue
Street	Road
Minor street	Minor road
Court	Lane
Alley	Way

Street and circulation system (Calthorpe, 1993)

Arterial streets and
    thoroughfares
Connector streets
Commercial streets
Local streets
Alleys
Pedestrian routes
Bikeways

Public transport related (Wood, 1994)

Bus-only streets
Busways
Public transport malls
Tram street

Urban function (Moughtin *et al.*, 1995)

1. Civic street
2. Commercial street
3. Residential street
4. Multi-function street

Institute of Transport Engineers, USA (Jacobs *et al.*, 1995)

Freeway
Expressway
Major arterial
Collector street
Local street
Cul-de-sac

The AIA Thoroughfare Nomenclature (Culot, 1995)

Highway
Boulevard
Avenue
Drive
Street
Road
Alley
Lane
Passage
Path

ICE proposed tiers (ICE, 1996: 1)

1. International/national
2. Regional
3. Local
4. Access

Constituent parts of the grid, (Brown-May, 1995)

Street
Lane
Right-of-way
Street corner

Carriageway
Footpath

South Africa
(Behrens and Watson, 1996)
Regional distributor
Primary distributor
Multi-functional routes
Activity route/street
Collector route
Service road
Access road
Pedestrian route

Street types
(Greenberg, 1997)
Mews
Minor street
Street
Traditional street/major street
Main street
Grand boulevard

**Classification of arterial
routes and local streets**
(Western Australia, 1997)
Arterial routes
- Primary distributor
- Integrator arterials
- District distributor
  integrator 'A'
- District distributor
  integrator 'B'
Local streets
- Neighbourhood connector
- Access street
- Lane way
- Cul-de-sac

Essex Design Guide
(Essex Planning Officers'
Association, 1997: 56)
Local distributor
Link road
Feeder road

Minor access road
Minor access way (2 types)
Mews (2 types)
Parking square

VicCode, Victoria, (1992)
(Brindle, 1996: 78)
Major arterial
Arterial
Sub-arterial
Trunk collector
Collector street
Access street
Access place
Access lane

**Portland Arterial Street
Classification Policy**
(Dotterer, 1987: 171)
Auto Traffic:
1. Regional trafficway
2. Major traffic street
3. District collector
4. Neighbh'd collector
5. Local service street
Transit:
1. Regional transitway
2. Major transit street
3. Minor transit street
4. Local service transit

Poundbury (DETR, 1998a)
Square
Street
Lane
Courtyard
Mews
Pedestrian street

**Urban Design
Compendium**
(Llewelyn-Davies, 2000: 75)
Mews
Residential street
High street

Square
Boulevard

Urban function Machón
et al. (in Marshall, 2002a)
1. Residential street
2. Industrial street
3. Commercial or office
   street
4. Other predominant use

UK national guidelines
(IHT, 1997)
1. Primary distributors
2. District distributors
3. Local distributors
4. Access roads
5. Pedestrian street
6. Pedestrian route
7. Cycle route

*Bristol City Council
(2000)*
1. National primary
   routes
2. City primary routes
   (i) Links to national
   primary routes
   (ii) Principal public
   transport corridors.
3. Local distributor roads
4. Roads within
   'environmental cells'
5. 'Transport greenways'

Lillebye (2001)
Main street
Residential street
Industrial street
Park street
Stair street
Through street
Boundary street
Sequence street
Fond street

Biddulph (2001: 51)

A. Mews
B. Circus
C. Crescent
D. Close
E. Square
F. Arcadia
G. Street

Erickson (2001: 24, 26)

Armature
Vista street

Urban role of arterials
(Marshall, 2002a)

1. Spine
2. Separator
3. Seam

Belgium
Functional classification
(Marshall, 2002a)

1. Motorway
2. Metropolitan road
3. Trunk road
4. Inter-District road
5. Through street
6. Local street

Belgium
Administrative
classification
(Marshall, 2002a)

1. Regional network roads
   (Brussels Capital Region)
2. Local network roads
   (Communes)

Germany
EAHV and RAS-N
(Selected from wider series)
(Marshall, 2002a)
B III+IV Non-frontage
arterial streets

C III Arterial streets
C IV Main collector streets
D IV Collector streets
D V access street
E V access street
E VI access way

Denmark
Road Directorate – Road
Standard Committee (1991,
2000) (Marshall, 2002a)
Traffic roads

1. TR-High speed
2. TR-Medium speed
3. TR-Low speed

Local roads

4. LR-Medium speed
5. LR-Low speed
6. LR-Very low speed

Copenhagen
Municipality Plan (master
plan) for The City of
Copenhagen 2001
(Marshall, 2002a)

1. Motorway
2. Regional roads
3. Primary roads
4. Distributor streets
5. Local streets

Greece: Ministry of
Environment and Public
Works (Marshall, 2002a)

1. Freeway
2. Arterial street
3. Collector street
4. Local street

Hungary
Road Planning Technical
Guidance, public roads in
built-up areas
(Marshall, 2002a)

1. Motorway

2. Semi-motorway
3. I. class main road
4. II. class main road
5. Collector road
6. Service road
7. Bicycle road
8. Footpath

Portugal
(Marshall, 2002a)

1. Collector roads
2. Main distributor road
3. Local distributor road
4. Access roads
5. Pedestrian streets

Spain
(Marshall, 2002a)

1. Motorways
2. Arterial street
3. Distributor
4. Local street

Sweden/ Malmö
(incorporating
national and local roads)
(Marshall, 2002a)

1. Throughfare/radial road.
2. Main street (arterial street)
3. Collector street
4. Local street
5. 'Woonerf'
6. Pedestrian street

Mayor for London/Transport
for London
(Marshall, 2002a)

1. National roads (M/ways)
2. Transport for London Road
   Network (TLRN)
3. Borough roads

London Borough of Camden
(Marshall, 2002a)

1. Strategic roads
2. London distributor road

3. Borough distributors
4. Access roads

India (Bartlett, 2003a)
National highways (NH)
State highways (SH)
District roads (DR)
Major district roads (MDR)
Other district roads (ODR)
Village roads (VR)

Nepal (Bartlett, 2003a)
National highways (NH)
Feeder roads (NR)
District roads (DR)
Urban roads (UR)
Village roads (VR)

Lebanon (Bartlett, 2003a)
International roads
Primary roads

Secondary roads
Local roads

Italy (Bartlett, 2003b)
Motorways
Principal inter-urban roads
Secondary inter-urban
    roads
Urban roads (connectors)
District urban roads
Local roads

**Road classification related
to design speed** (Bartlett,
2003b)
0   Footway
10   Pedestrianised street
20   Residential street
30   Traffic-calmed street
40   Local street
50   Local road

60   Urban/highway
70   Urban traffic-way
80   Urban expressway
90   Trunk road
100 Expressway
110 Freeway
120 Motorway
130 Fast motorway
140 National motorway
150 Autobahn

A3.2 Classification themes (from Marshall, 2002a)

1)   Systematically applied classification themes
Themes used to categorise the whole spectrum of route types in a given country's or city's typological set.
1. Traffic speed
2. Trip length
3. Destination status
4. Strategic role
5. Circulation v. access
6. Administration

2)   Partially developed classification themes
Themes used to categorise individual route types in various typologies
7. Network role
8. Access control
9. Traffic volume
10. Transport mode
11. Other urban users

12. Environment
13. Built frontage
14. Road width

3) Diverse themes
Other actual or potential themes (outside official typologies)
15. Street name
16. Street in cross-section
17. Frontage form
18. Planting
19. Street character
20. Urban character
21. Spatial shape or character
22. Visual axis
23. Civic role
24. Space syntax and 'spatial integration'
25. Urban morphology (formation)
26. Structural role
27. Corridor role
28. District role
29. Land use or frontage function
30. Commercial role
31. 'Towncentredness'
32. Intensity of use
33. Urban uses and users
34. Living space
35. Neighbourliness
36. Pedestrian use of streets
37. 'Diverse' vehicular classification
38. Public transport
39. Sustainability

A3.3 Summary of route types suggested in this book

Configurational	Constitutional	Transit-oriented hierarchy	Stratification by speed
Spine	Arterial or trunk	A. Arterial	S4. High speed
Stem	Sub-arterial	B. Sub-arterial	S3.5. Medium-high
Corridor	Local	C. District	S3. Medium speed
Cantilever		D. Local	S2.5. Medium-low
Collector		E. Bicycle access	S2. Low speed
Connector		F. Foot access	S1.5. Very low speed
Cross-connector			S1. Dead slow

APPENDIX 4 CATALOGUE OF PATTERNS

A4.1 Catalogue of pattern typologies

Sitte ([1889] 1945)
1. Rectangular system
2. Radial system
3. Triangular system
4. 'Bastard offspring'

Unwin (1920)
Irregular (various, not based on
    street pattern)
Regular
    1. Rectilinear
    2. Circular
    3. Diagonal
    4. Radiating lines

Abercrombie (1933)
1. Gridiron
2. Hexagonal
3. Radial
4. Spider's web

Tripp (1950: 328)
Rectangular
Gridiron with superimposed
    diagonals
Radial
Concentric

Topographical-informal
Irregular-medieval
Radials blended with
    gridiron
Combined rectangular and
    irregular

Dickinson (1961)
1. Irregular
2. Radial-concentric
3. Rectangular or grid

Mumford (1961)
1. Street village (=)
2. Cross-roads village (+)
3. Commons village (#)
4. Round village (O)

Lynch (1962: 34)
1. Grid
2. Radial (inc. branching)
3. Linear

Jamieson *et al*. (1967)
1. Cartwheel
2. Linear
3. Ring and radial

4. Single strand
5. Double strand, etc.

Farbey and Murchland
(1967)
1. Radial and circumferential
    system
2. Grid system
3. Hyperbolic grid system

Morlok (1967: 65)
1. Spinal or tree
2. Grid network
3. Delta network

**Colin Buchanan and
Partners** (1968)
1. Centripetal
2. Linear
3. Grid

Moholy-Nagy (1968)
1. Geomorphic
2. Concentric
3. Orthogonal-connective
4. Orthogonal-modular
    clustered

Clifford Culpin and Partners
(1969)
1. Centralised
2. Linked radial
3. Radial
4. Web
5. Figure of eight
6. Radial-linear
7. Centripetal net
8. Centripetal grid
9. Ringed spine
10. Spine
11. Triangular net
12. Hexagonal net
13. Regular grid
14. Directional grid
15. Nucleated corridor
16. Dispersed
17. Honeycomb
18. Uniform grid
19. Canalised grid
20. Linear grid
21. Linear

Abrams (1971)
City linear
Gridiron plan
Linear system
Radial street pattern

March and Steadman
(1971)
Radio-axial city
Cellular city

Echenique *et al.* (1972)
1. Axial grid
2. Loose grid
3. Radial cross-shaped
4. Semi-radial

Stone (in Potter, 1977)
1. Linear
2. Rectangular
3. Star (inc. X and Y shapes)

Lynch (1981)
1. Axial network
2. Capillary
3. Kidney
4. Radio-concentric
5. Rectangular grid

Lynch (1981)
1. Star (radial)
2. Satellite cities
3. Linear city
4. Rectangular grid city
5. Other grid (parallel,
   triangular, hexagonal)
6. Baroque axial network
7. The lacework
8. The 'inward' city (e.g.
   medieval Islamic)
9. The nested city
10. Current imaginings
    (megaform, bubble,
    floating, underground,
    undersea, outer space)

Pressman (1985)
1. Dispersed sheet
   (orthogonal gridiron)
2. Spider web (radio-
   concentric) or (ring radial)
3. Star (finger)
4. Satellite (cluster)
5. Linear
6. Ring
7. Galaxy
8. Polycentred net

O'Flaherty (1986)
1. Gridiron
2. Linear
3. Radial

Rickaby (1987)
0. Existing configuration
1. Concentrated-nucleated
2. Concentrated-linear

3. Dispersed-nucleated
   (satellite towns)
4. Dispersed-linear
5. Dispersed-nucleated
   (villages)

DoE/DoT (1992)
Curvilinear (network)
Hierarchical
Rectilinear (grid)

McCluskey (1992)
1. Branching pattern
2. Grid
3. Radial
4. Serial
5. Web pattern

Southworth and Owens
(1993)
1. Fragmented parallels
2. Interrupted parallels
3. Lollipops on a stick
4. Loop and cul-de-sac
5. Loops and lollipops
6. Warped parallels

AIA (Culot, 1995)
1. Curvilinear
2. Diagonal
3. Discontinuous (Radburn)
4. Grid with diagonals
   Organic
6. Orthogonal

Brindle (1996)
1. Grid
2. Tributary

Bell and Iida (1997: 19)
1. Path
2. Tree
3. Cycle
1. Linear
2. Grid

Satoh (1998)
1. Warped grid
2. Radial
3. Horseback
4. Whirlpool
5. Unique structures

Frey (1999)
1. The core city

2. The star city
3. The satellite city
4. The galaxy of settlements
5. The linear city
6. The polycentric net or regional city

Boarnet and Crane
(2001: 86)
1. Grid

2. Cul-de-sac
3. Mixed

DTLR and CABE
(2001: 42)
1. Regular blocks
2. Concentric blocks
3. Irregular blocks

A4.2 Directory of pattern types and sources

Amorphous Keeble (1969)
Asterisk Kostof (1991)
Axial grid Echenique *et al.* (1972)
Axial network Lynch (1981)

Branch-and-twig Stones (1997)
Branching pattern McCluskey (1992)

Capillary Lynch (1981)
Cartwheel Jamieson *et al.* (1967)
Cellular March and Steadman (1971)
Centripetal Colin Buchanan and Partners (1968)
Checkerboard Groth (1981), Larkham and Jones (1991)
Circular Unwin (1920)
Concentric Kostof (1991), DTLR and CABE (2001: 42)
Cul-de-sac network Crane and Crepeau (1998), Boarnet and Crane (2001)
Curvilinear (network) DoE/DoT (1992), AIA (Culot, 1995), Western Australia (1997)
Cycle Bell and Iida (1997: 19)

Deformed grid Hillier (1996), Carmona *et al.* (2002)
Delta network Morlok (1967: 65)
Dendritic ITE (1999: 7)
Diagonal network AIA (Culot, 1995)
Directional grid Colin Buchanan and Partners (1968), MKDC (1974), Houghton-Evans (1975)
Discontinuous network AIA (Culot, 1995)
Dispersed Clifford Culpin and Partners (1969)
Double strand Jamieson *et al.* (1967)

Fragmented parallels: Southworth and Owens (1993)

Grid Lynch (1962: 34), Farbey and Murchland (1967), Morlok (1967: 65),
    Colin Buchanan and Partners (1968), Keeble (1969), Barnett (1982),
    Beimborn and Rabinowitz (1991), Larkham and Jones (1991),
    McCluskey (1992), Jacobs (1993), Brown-May (1995), Bell and Iida
    (1997: 19), Boarnet and Crane (2001)
Grid with diagonals AIA (Culot, 1995)
Gridiron Abercrombie (1933), MoT (1963), Abrams (1971), Scargill (1979),
    Groth (1981), O'Flaherty (1986), Larkham and Jones (1991)

Helix Kostof (1991)
Hexagonal Abercrombie (1933), MoT (1963)
Hierarchical Bentley *et al.* (1986), DoE/DoT (1992)
Hyperbolic grid system Farbey and Murchland (1967)

Interrupted parallels Southworth and Owens (1993)
Irregular Dickinson (1961), DTLR and CABE (2001: 42)

Kidney Lynch (1981)

Lazy grid Lock (1994)
Lazy supergrid Lock (1994)
Linear (linear system) Lynch (1962: 34), Jamieson *et al.* (1967), Colin
    Buchanan and Partners (1968), Tunnard (1970), Abrams (1971),
    Stone (in Potter, 1977), O'Flaherty (1986), White (1995), Bell and Iida
    (1997: 19)
Lollipops on a stick Southworth and Owens (1993)
Loop and cul-de-sac Southworth and Owens (1993)
Loops and lollipops Southworth and Owens (1993), DTLR and CABE
    (2001: 41)
Loopy Crane (1998: 5)
Loose grid Echenique *et al.* (1972)

Modular grid Moholy-Nagy (1968)
Multicentred Banks (1998)

Nebula Kostof (1991)
Net-like Alexander (1966b)

Octopus Keeble (1969)

Organic (organic network) Moudon and Untermann (1987), AIA (Culot, 1995)

Orthogonal (orthogonal grid) Tunnard (1970), Hanson (1989), AIA (Culot, 1995), Hillier (1996)

Ortho-radial grid Hillier (1999)

Path Bell and Iida (1997: 19)

Pseudo-organic Moudon and Untermann (1987)

Quincunx Tunnard (1970)

Radial (pattern, system) Sitte ([1889] 1945), Abercrombie (1933), Abrams (1971), O'Flaherty (1986), Hanson (1989), Kostof (1991), McCluskey (1992), Hillier (1996), Abercrombie (1933)

Radial including branching Lynch (1962: 34)

Radial and circumferential system Farbey and Murchland (1967)

Radial-concentric Dickinson (1961), Kostof (1991)

Radial cross-shaped Echenique *et al.* (1972)

Radial star Kostof (1991)

Radiating lines Unwin (1920)

Radio-axial March and Steadman (1971)

Radioconcentric Lynch (1981), Houghton-Evans (1975)

Rectangular Tripp (1942), Stone (in Potter, 1977)

Rectangular or grid Dickinson (1961)

Rectangular (grid, system) Sitte ([1889] 1945), Tripp (1942), Lynch (1981)

Rectilinear (grid) Unwin (1920), Jakle (1987), DoE/DoT (1992), Handy (1992)

Regular blocks DTLR and CABE (2001: 42)

Ring and radial Jamieson *et al.* (1967), Keeble (1969: 112)

Semi-radial Echenique *et al.* (1972)

Serial McCluskey (1992)

Serpentine Farbey and Murchland (1967)

Single strand Jamieson *et al.* (1967)

Spider's web Abercrombie (1933), Keeble (1969)

Spinal or tree Morlok (1967: 65)

Spindelform Kostof (1991)

Stadtwurst **(sausage city)** Beimborn and Rabinowitz (1991)

Star Stone (in Potter, 1977)

Starfish Keeble (1969)
Sunburst Kostof (1991)

Tangential Ritter (1964)
Tartan grid Azuma (1982), Gosling and Maitland (1984), Mitchell (1990)
Tartan-plaid-like Jacobs (1993)
Topographical-Informal Tripp (1950)
Tree Bell and Iida (1997: 19), Morlok (1967: 65)
Tree-like (network) Ritter (1964)
Triangular system Sitte ([1889] 1945)
Tributary Brindle (1996)
Triple strand Jamieson *et al.* (1967)

Umbrella Keeble (1969)

Warped grid Satoh (1998)
Warped parallels Southworth and Owens (1993)
Web pattern McCluskey (1992)

X shape Stone (in Potter, 1977)
Y shape Stone (in Potter, 1977)

A4.3 Compilation of typologies of pattern and structure suggested in this book

ABCD Typology (Chapter 4)			
A-type	B-type	C-type	D-type

Systematic taxonomy (Chapter 4)			
Linear	Tree	Radial	Cellular

Configurational attributes/ route structure (Chapters 4 to 6)			
T-tree	T-cell	X-tree	X-cell

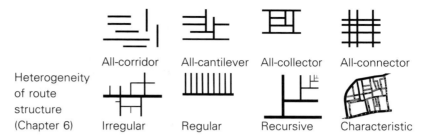

Heterogeneity of route structure (Chapter 6)

| All-corridor | All-cantilever | All-collector | All-connector |
| Irregular | Regular | Recursive | Characteristic |

APPENDIX 5   ROUTE STRUCTURE ANALYSIS

A5.1 Route structure conventions

A *route* comprises a link or a linear aggregation of conjoined links. Linear aggregation means a series of links joined serially, end-on. This outlaws a branching aggregation of links: a **T** shape cannot be a single route. Each route has a definite start and end point (a route forming an **O** shape circuit must have one node at which it starts and ends).

A *joint* is a node with one and only one conjoined route passing through it. (A joint has a minimum of two links and one route.) For example, a joint representing a four-way intersection is deemed to have a single through route, and two side routes.

All joints are formed at *nodes* (usually at junctions), but not all nodes are joints. A junction is usually a joint – an exception would be where routes meet at a node but none is continuous through it.

By the above conventions, the number of routes formed will be directly determined by the number of links and the number of joints present: R = L – J (Box 5). This number of routes holds irrespective of which pattern of aggregation is chosen.

The following notation conventions are applied. Lower case denotes properties of elements (routes, nodes), while upper case denotes properties of whole networks (Appendix 6). Roman symbols denote integer properties that may be read off diagrams, while Greek symbols denote rational numbers obtained by calculation.

A5.2 *Route structure properties*

Route properties		Routegram properties	
l	continuity of a route	λ	relative continuity = c/s
c	connectivity of a route	χ	relative connectivity = l/s
d	depth of a route	δ	relative depth = d/s
s	sum value of a route (= l + c + d)		

Example: Bayswater Road

		Absolute value (Table 5.1)		Relative value (Figure 5.14)
Continuity	l	8	λ	0.50
Connectivity	c	7	χ	0.44
Depth	d	1	δ	0.06
Sum values	s	16		1.00

A5.3 *The Routegram*

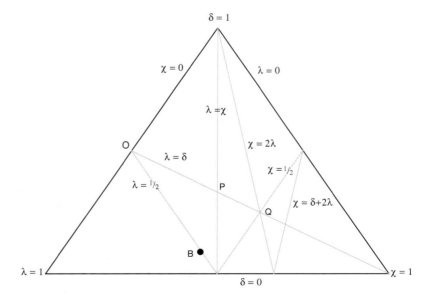

Each plotted point on the routegram represents a single *route*. For each position on the routegram, $\lambda + \chi + \delta = 1$. On the bottom axis, where $\delta = 0$, $\lambda = (1 - \chi)$. Each position on the routegram can be expressed in terms of three parameters (λ, χ, δ) or simply two parameters (χ, δ). The notation (χ, δ) is convenient as it echoes the Cartesian pair of 'along' and 'up' (x, y). Point O $(\frac{1}{4}, \frac{1}{2})$ is the position of a single link route at depth 1 $(l = 1, c = 0, d = 1)$. Point P is $(\frac{1}{3}, \frac{1}{3})$; point Q is $(\frac{1}{2}, \frac{1}{3})$. Bayswater Road lies at position B $(\lambda = 0.5, \chi = 0.44, \delta = 0.06)$ or simply $(\frac{7}{16}, \frac{1}{16})$. This lies on the reference line $\lambda = \frac{1}{2}$. The grid of references lines could be equated with the 'rhumb lines' on a navigational chart (Wilford, 2000) or reseau (reference lines on a star map, etc.) to distinguish these from lines that are routes they represent.

A5.4 Route type

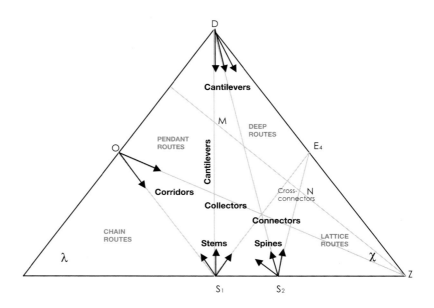

Structural types found commonly as routes in street networks are shown in black lower case. These mostly fall within the bounds of points S_1, M, N, and S_2. The set of stems – routes with all intermediate junctions three-way – radiates from point S_1. The set of spines – routes with all intermediate junctions four-way – radiates from point S_2. Corridors radiate from point O, which is the position of a single one-link datum route. These types are tabulated and explained in Table 5.2.

Types shown in grey upper case represent regions of the routegram containing structural types less commonly found as routes or streets. A chain is a route containing non-junction joints. A pure chain would contain *only* non-junction joints. A pendant route has both ends pendant, i.e. not ending at another route. Here a 'deep route' means routes with high value of depth not commonly found in street networks. 'Lattice routes' have all junctions with more than four arms.

APPENDIX 6 PROPERTIES OF ROUTE STRUCTURES

A6.1 *Street networks used as example cases*

Case name	Location
● Athens Inner	Plaka district, historic core of Athens
○ A-type	'Altstadt' urban core archetype (Figure 4.7A)
● Babylon	Babylon, ancient Mesopotamia (Iraq)
● Bayswater	Inner suburban streetgrid, London W2
● Bloomsbury	Inner urban grid, London WC1
○ B-type	'Bilateral' grid archetype (Figure 4.7B)
○ Chaotic	Implicit negative connotation (Figure 4.2c)
○ Characteristic	Demonstrative layout (Figure 6.8(b))
□ *Ciudad Lineal*	Soria y Mata's vision for linear suburb/city
○ Connector	Based on Calthorpe (1993) (Figure 2.4)
● Copenhagen-Central	City centre grid, Copenhagen
● Copenhagen-Inner	Frederiksberg, inner suburban grid
● Cornhill	Historic core of City of London EC3, 1677 (Hillier, 1996)
● Coventry Tributary	Radburn style, Willenhall Wood, Coventry (Keeble, 1969)
□ Craig Plan	Geometric abstract of Edinburgh New Town (Figure 2.13)
● Crawley Suburban	Wood Green, New Town neighbourhood (Keeble, 1969)
○ C-type	'Conjoint' urban pattern archetype (Figure 4.7C)

○ Discouraged   Neo-traditional anti-exemplar

● Dorchester Central   Central grid, Dorchester (DETR, 1998a)

○ D-type   'Distributory' layout archetype (Figure 4.7D)

● East Finchley   Northern suburb along radial route, London N2

● E.K. Suburban-1   Calderwood, New Town neighbourhood, E.K.

● E.K. Suburban-2   The Murray, New Town neighbourhood, E.K.

● E.K. Tributary   St Leonards, New Town neighbourhood, E.K.

● E.K. Village   Original village of East Kilbride, Scotland, UK

● Elmwood   Inner suburban, Berkeley, CA, USA
(Southworth, 1997)

○ Essex Tributary   Design guidance for road layout (Figure 2.12)

○ Ewing-1   Typological example (Ewing, 1996)

○ Ewing-2   Typological example (Ewing, 1996)

○ Ewing-3   Typological example (Ewing, 1996)

○ Ewing-4   Typological example (Ewing, 1996)

○ Ewing-5   Typological example (Ewing, 1996)

○ Focal Web   Demonstrative layout – traditional
(Figure 5.3(a))

● Glasgow 1790   Historic core of the city, 1790 (Moore, 1996)

● Glasgow-Grid   Blythswood planned grid, city centre

● Glasgow-Southside   Inner city traditional grid, Govanhill

○ Grid   Demonstrative layout (Figure 6.8(c))

● Hamilton   Central grid, Hamilton, Bermuda

● Highworth Village   Village of Highworth, Gloucestershire

□ Hilberseimer   *New City* vision (Hilberseimer, 1944)

● Kentlands   Neo-traditional, peripheral suburban,
Gaithersburg, USA (Southworth, 1997)

● Kirkwall   City of Kirkwall, Orkney, Scotland

○ Laguna West   Neo-traditional peripheral suburban,
Sacramento, USA (Southworth, 1997)

○ Layered Loops   Demonstrative layout – suburban
(Figure 5.3(b))

□ North Bucks New City   'Pod' of residential development, unbuilt new
town (Richards, 1969)

● Poundbury   Neo-traditional suburb, Dorchester, England
(DETR, 1998a)

○ Preferred   Neo-traditional exemplar.

● Reykjavik Tributary-1   Gerdi, periphery of Reykjavik

● Reykjavik Tributary-2   Hamrar and Foldir, periphery of Reykjavik
● Reykjavik-Central   City centre including inner grid, Reykjavik
● Shoreditch   Inner urban grid, 1890, London E2 (Moholy-
                           Nagy, 1986)
● St Andrews-Central   Historic central grid of streets, St Andrews
● St Andrews-   South-west suburbs of St Andrews, Scotland
    Suburban
● Sydney Inner   Surry Hills, inner city grid, south/east of CBD
● Tehran Inner   Inner city, Tehran, Iran
● Thamesmead   Peripheral 'new town' style development,
                           London SE28
● Tokyo Grid   Inner city grid, Iriya area, Tokyo
○ Traditional   Neo-traditional exemplar
○ Tributary   Demonstrative layout (Figure 6.8(a))
● Tunis Medina   Medina – historic city core, Tunis

Note: ● Actual street network □ prototype ○ demonstrative

A6.2 Route structural parameters and equations (for networks)

Basic relationship between routes and links

$$R = L - J \text{ (Box 5)}$$

where R = number of routes in a network; L = number of links in a network; J = number of joints in a network

Permutations of aggregation

Permutational constant for a joint representing a junction with a arms, p_a (i.e. number of permutations of aggregation for a single joint):

$$p_a = \sum_{i=1}^{(a-1)} i \quad \text{for junction with } a \text{ arms, } a > 1$$

Total number of permutations of aggregation for a whole network, P

$$P = \prod_{i=1} p_i{}^{J_i} = p_3{}^{J3} \times p_4{}^{J4} \times p_5{}^{J5} \times \ldots$$

where J_i = number of joints representing junctions with i arms

Network properties

L	number of links in a network; network sum continuity = Σl
C	network sum connectivity = Σc
D	network sum depth = Σd
S	sum value of a network ($= L + C + D$)
R	number of routes
Y	number of types of route
D'	maximum depth value of network

Netgram properties

Λ	relative continuity = L/S
X	relative connectivity = C/S
Δ	relative depth = D/S

$\Lambda + X + \Delta = 1$

Hetgram properties

Ψ	irregularity = Y/R
Φ	regularity = $1 - \Psi$
Θ	recursivity = D'/R
Ω	complexity = (Y − D')/R

$\Phi + \Theta + \Omega = 1$

Properties for Bayswater network

Network properties (Table 5.1)				Netgram values (Figure 6.4)		Hetgram values (Figure 6.12)	
L	73	R	27	Λ	0.28	Φ	0.26
C	112	Y	20	X	0.42	Θ	0.15
D	79	D'	4	Δ	0.30	Ω	0.59
S	264				1.00		1.00

For the Bayswater network (Figure 5.13), there are 41 T-junctions ($J_3 = 41$) and 5 crossroads ($J_4 = 5$). Hence $P = p_3^{J3}$ $p_4^{J4} = (3^{41} \times 6^5) = 283{,}614{,}019{,}828{,}880{,}035{,}069{,}728$.

A6.3 The Netgram

Each plotted point on the netgram represents a whole *network* (route structure). For each position on the netgram, $\Lambda + X + \Delta = 1$. On the bottom axis, where $\Delta = 0$, $\Lambda = (1 − X)$. Each position on the netgram can be expressed in terms of three parameters (Λ, X, Δ) or simply two parameters (X, Δ). The notation (X, Δ) is convenient as it echoes the Cartesian pair of 'along' and 'up' (X, Y). A set of reference lines (shown in grey) may be used to conveniently locate positions on the netgram, using simple relationships between Λ, X and Δ. Point O ($\frac{1}{4}$, $\frac{1}{2}$) is the position of a single link network (L = 1, C = 0, D = 1). Point P is ($\frac{1}{3}$, $\frac{1}{3}$); point Q is ($\frac{1}{2}$, $\frac{1}{3}$). The grid of references lines could be equated with the 'rhumb lines' on a navigational chart (Wilford, 2000) or reseau (reference lines on a star map, etc.).

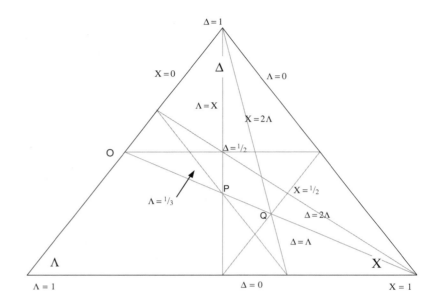

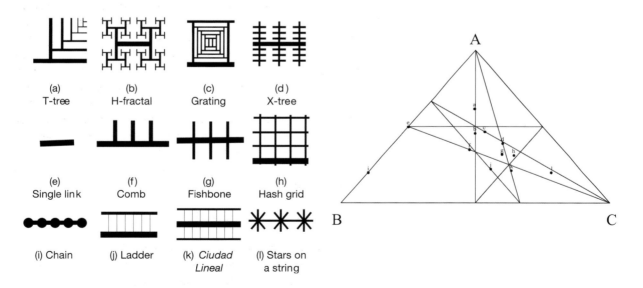

(a) T-tree

(b) H-fractal

(c) Grating

(d) X-tree

(e) Single link

(f) Comb

(g) Fishbone

(h) Hash grid

(i) Chain

(j) Ladder

(k) *Ciudad Lineal*

(l) Stars on a string

A6.4 Exploring 'Netspace'

'Netspace' represents the theoretical 'solution space' of possible network structures. A series of theoretical structures can be used to map out what structures occupy different parts of the netgram. In each case opposite the exact structure shown there is plotted, except for (j) and (k) which are infinitely long versions of the structures illustrated.

Towards the top of the netgram lie deeply recursive (layered or branching) structures such as trees. As more branches or layers are added to structures 'a', 'b', 'c' and 'd', these go off to infinity at point A. The lower left part of the netgram is occupied by long chain structures (such as 'i'); as more links are added, the chain goes off to infinity at point B. The lower right part of the netgram is occupied by structures with high connectivity relative to depth or continuity, such as multi-spoked stars or 'stars on a string' ('l'). A radial pattern with an infinite number of spokes, or an infinitely long chain of 'stars on a string' would be located at point C.

Not all extremely repetitious structures would occur at the vertices of the netgram, since some shape functions, as they tend to infinity, converge on a point in the 'interior'. For example, an infinitely long *Ciudad Lineal* would occupy position 'k' on the netgram. This would effectively correspond to the position of Soria y Mata's suggested *Ciudad Lineal* from Cadiz to St Petersburg, or one from Brussels to Beijing (Soria y Mata, 1892: 22).

This hypothetical *Ciudad Lineal* lies on the same line ($X = 2\Lambda$) as point 'd' representing an X-fractal shape – and Hilberseimer's *New City* (Figure 6.2 (c)). The reason they lie on the same line is that they are both strongly 'spinal', with more or less the same proportion of connectivity to continuity. This line also corresponds to the line on which the 'spine-cantilever' route type occupies on the routegram. Basically, as these structures grow, they are made up of more and more spine-cantilevers (X-fractal) or a longer and longer main spine-corridor (*Ciudad Lineal*).

Structures typically found as street patterns – characteristic structures – occupy the central zone.

APPENDIX 7 CONSTITUTIONAL STRUCTURE

A7.1 Constitutional graph representations of structure

A hierarchy of types may be represented as a *constitutional graph*, where each vertex represents a set of types – as opposed to a configurational graph where a vertex represents an individual route or junction.

Conventional hierarchy
expressed as
constitutional graph

● Primary distributor
● District distributor
● Local distributor
● Access road

- Each vertex represents a street type or set of streets.
- Each line (edge) represents an allowable connection between types.
- The vertical direction represents the necessary connections upwards in the hierarchy: this is vertical order by arteriality.
- A circled vertex represents the 'top tier' type or types. The presence of a circled vertex indicates the presence of arteriality – all streets of the circled type form a single contiguous network.
- Where present, a circled vertex also serves to indicate that the graph is a constitutional graph – as opposed to configurational graph.

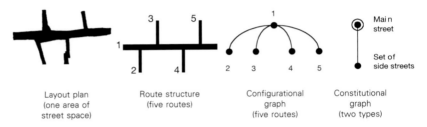

Layout plan
(one area of
street space)

Route structure
(five routes)

Configurational
graph
(five routes)

Constitutional
graph
(two types)

Although the constitutional graph for conventional hierarchy demonstrates a familiar stratification, the levels themselves are associated with arteriality. This is the condition by which all routes down to any level (starting with primary distributors) must form a contiguous system. Here, primary distributors must necessarily form a single network, while pedestrian streets might form a scatter of segments isolated from each other.

Arteriality introduces *asymmetry* into the hierarchy, since it implies different kinds of network connectivity as we move 'up' or 'down' the hierarchy. This intrinsic asymmetry demonstrates why we cannot simply 'invert' the hierarchy – putting pedestrians nominally at the top and cars at the bottom, for example – without implying changes to network structure.

A7.2 Constitutional graphs supporting arguments in text

The significance of the transport land use

Public street system ‑ ‑ ‑ ‑ ‑ ‑ ‑ ‑ 'The Transport Land Use'

Housing   Open Space   Civic   Shops   Industry ‑ ‑ ‑ ‑ ‑. 'Other Land Use'

Road network structure

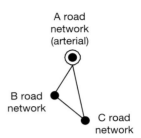

A road network (arterial)

B road network

C road network

Constitutional graphs from Chapter 3

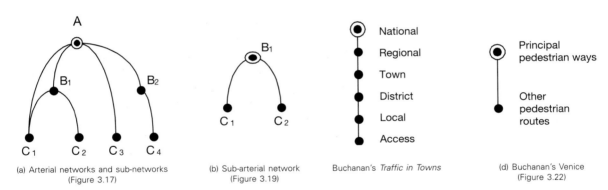

(a) Arterial networks and sub-networks (Figure 3.17)

(b) Sub-arterial network (Figure 3.19)

Buchanan's *Traffic in Towns*

National
Regional
Town
District
Local
Access

Principal pedestrian ways

Other pedestrian routes

(d) Buchanan's Venice (Figure 3.22)

Constitutional graphs for the four basic types of constitutional structure

(a) Mosaic

(b) Conjoint

(c) Dendritic

(d) Serial

Constitutional graphs relating to different modal orientation

Pedestrians pegged to bottom end
of vehicular hierarchy

Public transport separated from
customers (Figure 7.16)

Dysfunctional for public transport
connectivity (Figure 7.14)

Good for public transport (plus walk
access) (Figure 7.15)

Constitutional graphs relating to the structure of disurban creation

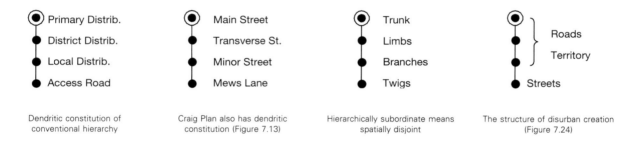

Dendritic constitution of
conventional hierarchy

Craig Plan also has dendritic
constitution (Figure 7.13)

Hierarchically subordinate means
spatially disjoint

The structure of disurban creation
(Figure 7.24)

Constitutional graphs relating to Chapter 8

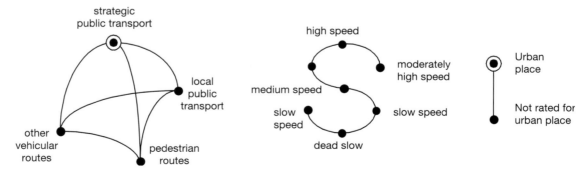

Transit-oriented arteriality

Stratification by speed

Contiguity of urban place

GLOSSARY

Access constraint In a *hierarchical* network, a form of *stratification* by which routes may only connect to other routes of the same or adjacent *tier* (Chapter 7).

Arterial (route) A *constitutionally* defined type of route, forming the uppermost tier in an *arterial network*, such that the set of arterials forms a complete contiguous network (Chapters 3 and 7). An arterial may take different forms (e.g. arterial road, arterial street, etc.).

Arterial network (1) Generally, any network possessing *arteriality*; (2) specifically, the sub-network formed by *arterial routes*, i.e. the uppermost tier.

Arteriality The manifestation of *strategic contiguity* in networks, in which each route must be connected to another route of the same tier or higher tier (Chapters 3 and 7). Arteriality was originally identified by Morrison (1966).

Articulated route hierarchy A proposed *hierarchy* which combines (1) *transit-oriented arteriality* and (2) *stratification* by speed (Chapter 8).

Characteristic pattern (1) Generally, any abstract pattern which appears 'likely' to represent a street pattern; (2) more specifically, a particular kind of irregular structure which is distinctively 'street-pattern-shaped' (Chapter 6).

Composition The geometric formation of a layout, featuring absolute distances, widths, angles of orientation and alignment (Chapter 4). Contrast *configuration*.

Configuration The topological formation of a structure: a road layout considered as an abstract network (Chapter 4). Contrast *composition* and *constitution*.

Conjoint (constitution) A *constitutional structure* possessing *arteriality* but no *access constraint*, typical of traditional street patterns or road networks (Chapter 7).

Connectivity In *route structure analysis*, the connectivity of a route (c) is taken as the number of times routes directly connect to it; the sum of connectivity values over a whole network is denoted by C (Chapters 5 and 6).

Connector A *configurationally* defined route type where all junctions are four-way (Chapter 5).

Constitution An abstract formation of elements (types) and their necessary and allowable connections. Contrast *configuration* (Chapter 7).

Constitutional archetype A graphic expression of the allowable and necessary connections in a *constitutional structure*. It may also express allowable junction types (Chapter 9).

Constitutional graph A kind of graph representation denoting *constitutional structure* (Appendix 7).

Constitutional structure Type of constitution defined by combinations of *access constraint* and *arteriality* (Chapter 7).

Constitutional type Type (of route or structure) defined by constitutional relationships, e.g. *arterial* (route or network) (Chapter 7).

Continuity In *route structure analysis*, the continuity of a route (l) is taken as the number of links constituting the route. The sum of continuity values over a whole network then equals the total number of links (L) (Chapters 5 and 6).

Conventional (road) hierarchy The application of the *inverse relationship* to a *dendritic constitution* in which the highest tiers equate with high 'mobility function'. The classic version of road 'hierarchy' was set out by Buchanan in *Traffic in Towns* (MoT, 1963).

Conventional (transport) network analysis The convention in which links in a transport network are represented directly as the edges in a graph, and nodes are represented directly as vertices. A classic interpretation was set out by Kansky (1963).

Datum (route) In *route structure analysis*, the route or set of routes from which the *depth* of all other routes is measured. By the convention within this book, the datum is a single route, whose depth is taken as 1 (Chapter 5).

Dendritic (constitution) A *constitutional structure* possessing *arteriality* and *access constraint*, typical of modern 'hierarchical' road networks (Chapter 7).

Depth In *route structure analysis*, depth is used as a route-structural property (d) that measures adjacency to a *datum* (route). The sum of depth values over a whole network is denoted by D, and the maximum depth by D' (Chapters 5 and 6).

Hierarchy A kind of *constitution* where there is a clear (especially, asymmetric) ordering of types, as in pyramidal or dendritic structures. The term 'hierarchical' effectively implies the possession of either *arteriality* or *access constraint*.

Inverse relationship The conventionally proposed relationship in which a road's 'mobility function' is inversely related to its 'access function' (Chapter 3).

Joint A node at which two links are conjoined to form a *route* (Chapter 5).

Pattern A recurring structural, spatial or temporal feature; may refer to a composition, configuration or constitution. A pattern may also refer (after Alexander *et al.*, 1977) to an urban set piece, in which case a street type could be regarded as a 'pattern'.

Route A linear element, representing a movement path, comprising one or more *links*. The fundamental element of a *route structure* (Chapter 5).

Route structure The diagrammatic representation of a network as a set of *routes* (Chapter 5). This can be converted to a graph, in which routes correspond to the vertices of the graph, and junctions to the edges of the graph. This forms the basis of *route structure analysis*.

Route structure analysis (RSA) The analysis of the *route structure* of a network, using the *route* as the fundamental element of structure (Chapter 5).

Strategic contiguity The condition by which all strategic elements form (and are defined by forming) a single contiguous structure, and where the set of all elements from the top *down* to any given tier form a single contiguous system. In networks, strategic contiguity is manifested as *arteriality* (Chapter 7).

Stratification The condition by which elements may only connect with other elements of the same or immediately adjacent status. In networks, stratification is manifested as *access constraint* (Chapter 7). Stratification may also apply to a street in cross-section (Chapter 9).

Street (1) Transport – an urban road with built frontages or buildings associated *or* (2) urban design – an urban space or place used for public access and passage.

Structure The arrangement of parts with respect to each other and to the whole. Structure is normally associated with *configuration* or *constitution*.

Structure of car orientation *Dendritic constitution* in which public transport routes are pegged to upper tiers in hierarchy, separated from pedestrian routes pegged to lower tiers (Chapter 7).

Structure of disurban creation *Dendritic constitution* in which *streets* are pegged to lower tiers in the hierarchy, such that they form a fragmented scatter (Chapter 7).

Taxonomy A system of classification in which sets of possible and actual types are organised in a systematic structure of classes and sub-classes (Chapter 4). Compare *typology*.

Tier A set of route types of equal rank or status with respect to *arteriality*. May be designated by ordinals I, II, III, etc. (Chapters 3 and 7).

Transit-oriented arteriality A system of arteriality based on network coarseness, in which the upper tiers are strategic public transport routes; middle tiers are local public transport and lower tiers are routes used by access modes (Chapter 8).

Tree A *configuration* comprising branches but no circuits.

Tributary (1) Generally, a structure in which layers of *depth* are built up by branching and/or loops; (2) specifically, a *route structure* where *relative connectivity* is less than relative depth ($X < \Delta$) (Chapter 6).

Trunk (route) An *arterial* (route), forming part of the top tier in a hierarchy (Chapter 7).

Typology A practically useful sub-set of all possible types (may be regarded as a 'slice' extracted from a fuller *taxonomy*), organised in a pragmatic structure, e.g. a simple listing (Chapter 4).

BIBLIOGRAPHY

AASHTO (1990) *A Policy on Geometric Design of Highways and Streets 1990.* Washington, DC: American Association of State Highway and Transportation Officials.

AASHTO (1995) *A Policy on Geometric Design of Highways and Streets.* Washington, DC: American Association of State Highway and Transport Officials.

AASHTO (2001) *A Policy on Geometric Design of Highways and Streets.* Washington, DC: American Association of State Highway and Transport Officials.

Abbey, L. (1992) *Highways: An Architectural Approach.* New York: Van Nostrand Reinhold.

Abercrombie, P. (1933) *Town and Country Planning.* London: Thornton Butterworth.

Abrams, C. (1971) *The Language of Cities: A Glossary of Terms.* New York: The Viking Press.

Aldous, T. (1992) *Urban Villages.* London: Urban Villages Group.

Alexander, C. (1966a) A city is not a tree, in *Design,* 206, 46–55.

Alexander, C. (1966b) The pattern of streets, in *Journal of American Institute of Planners,* 32(5) 273–78.

Alexander, C., Ishikawa, S., Silverstein, M., Jacobson, M., Fiksdahl-King, I. and Angel, S. (1977) *A Pattern Language: Towns. Buildings. Construction.* New York: Oxford University Press.

Alexander, C., Neis, H., Anninou, A., King, I. (1987) *A New Theory of Urban Design.* Oxford: Oxford University Press.

AlSayyad, N. (1991) *Cities and Caliphs: On the Genesis of Arab Muslim Urbanism.* Westport, Conn.: Greenwood Press.

Anderson, S. (ed.) (1978) *On Streets.* Cambridge, Mass.: MIT Press.

Appleyard, D. (1981) *Livable Streets.* With M. S. Gerson and M. Lintell. Berkeley, CA: University of California Press.

Asami, Y., Kubat, A. S. and Istek, C. (2001) Characterization of the street networks in the traditional Turkish urban form, *Environment and Planning B: Planning and Design,* 28, 777–95.

13.0 • Ludgate Hill, London.

Ashton, W. (1966) *The Theory of Road Traffic Flow*. London: Methuen & Co., New York: John Wiley & Sons.

Averley, J. (1998) From vision to reality: The rebuilding of Manchester city centre in progress. Presentation at the Urban Design Alliance Annual Conference, *Urban Design Makes Better Cities*, London, 15 October 1998.

Azuma, H. (1982) Towards a theory of city form: a study of North Bucks New City and Milton Keynes. Unpublished MPhil thesis, University College London.

Bacon, E. (1975) *The Design of Cities*. London: Thames and Hudson.

Banai, R. (1996) 'Neotraditional' settlements and dimensions of performance, in *Environment and Planning B: Planning and Design*, 23, 177–90.

Banister, D. (2002) *Transport Planning* (2nd edn). London: Spon.

Banks, J. H. (1998) *Introduction to Transportation Engineering*. Boston: W. C. B. McGraw-Hill.

Barnett, J. (1982) *Introduction to Urban Design*. New York and London: Harper and Row.

Bartlett, R. (1995) GIS-CAD and the new urban planning universe. Resource paper for the 1995 ITE International Conference, Fort Lauderdale, Florida.

Bartlett, R. (2003a) Road hierarchy. Highway design notes 1–102. Unpublished working paper (roadnotes@freenet.de).

Bartlett, R. (2003b) Road classification. Highway design notes 1–103. Unpublished working paper (roadnotes@freenet.de).

Barton, H., Davis, G. and Guise, R. (1995) *Sustainable Settlements: A Guide for Planners, Designers and Developers*. Bristol: University of the West of England and The Local Government Management Board.

Battle, G. and McCarthy, C. (1994) Multi-source synthesis: the design of sustainable new towns, in *Architectural Design* profile No. 111, *New Towns*. London: Academy Group.

Batty, M. (1997) Cellular automata and urban form: a primer, in *Journal of the American Planning Association*, 63(2), 266–74.

Batty, M. (1999) A research programme for urban morphology, in *Environment and Planning B: Planning and Design*, 26, 475–76.

Batty, M. and Longley, P. (1994) *Fractal Cities: A Geometry of Form and Function*. London and San Diego: Academic Press.

Baxter, A. (1998) Integrated transport and urban design. Presentation at the Urban Design Alliance Annual Conference, *Urban Design Makes Better Cities*, London, 15 October 1998.

Beauvais, N. (1996) 'Forum' section, in *Places*, 10(3), 78.

Behrens, R. and Watson, V. (1996) *Making Urban Places: Principles and Guidelines for Layout Planning*. Cape Town: University of Cape Town Press.

Beimborn, E. and Rabinowitz, H. (1991) *Guidelines for Transit-Sensitive Suburban Land Use Design*, Washington, DC: US Department of Transportation.

Bell, M. G. B. and Iida, Y. (1997) *Transportation Network Analysis*. Chichester: John Wiley.

Ben-Joseph, E. and Gordon, D. (2000) Hexagonal planning in theory and practice, in *Journal of Urban Design*, 5(3), 237–65.

Bentham, J. (1830) *Constitutional Code; for the Use of All Nations and All governments Professing Liberal Opinions. Volume I.* London: Robert Heward. Edited by Rosen, F. and Burns, J. H. (1983). Oxford: Clarendon Press.

Bentley, I., Alcock, A., Murrain, P., McGlynn, S. and Smith, G. (1985) *Responsive Environments*. Oxford: Architectural Press.

Berge, C. (1958) *The Theory of Graphs and its Applications*. London: Methuen.

Biddulph, M. (2001) *Home Zones: A Planning and Design Handbook*. Bristol: The Policy Press.

Bird, R. N. (2001) Junction design, in Button, K. and Hensher, D. (eds) *Handbook of Transport Systems and Traffic Control*. Oxford: Pergamon.

Boarnet, M. G. and Crane, R. (2001) *Travel by Design: The Influence of Urban Form on Travel*. New York: Oxford University Press.

Brett, M. (1994) The view from Great Linford, in *Architectural Design* profile No. 111, *New Towns*. London: Academy Group.

Brill, M. (1994) Archetypes as a 'natural language' for place making, in Franck, K. and Schneekloth, L. (eds) *Ordering Space: Types in Architecture and Design*. New York: Van Nostrand Reinhold.

Brindle, R. (1995) SOD the distributor! in Brindle, R., *Living with Traffic*, ARRB Special Report 53. Vermont South: ARRB Transport Research Ltd.

Brindle, R. (1996) Road hierarchy and functional classification, in Ogden, K. W. and Taylor, S. (eds) *Traffic Engineering and Management*. Melbourne: Institute of Transport Studies, Department of Civil Engineering, Monash University.

Bristol City Council (2000) *Local Transport Plan*. Bristol: Bristol City Council.

Broadbent, G. (1988) *Design in Architecture*. London: David Fulton.

Brogden, W. A. (1996) The bridge/street in Scottish urban planning, in Brogden, W. A. (ed.) *The Neo-Classical Town: Scottish Contributions to Urban Design since 1750*. Edinburgh: The Rutland Press.

Brown-May, A. (1995) *The Highway of Civilisation and Common Sense: Street Regulation and the Transformation of Social Space in 19th and Early 20th Century Melbourne*, Urban Research Program Working Paper No. 49, April 1995. Australian National University, Research Program of Social Sciences.

Buchanan, C. D. (1958) *Mixed Blessing: The Motor in Britain*. London: Leonard Hill.

Buckwalter, D. (2001) Complex topology in the highway network of Hungary, 1990 and 1998, in *Journal of Transport Geography*, 9, 125–35.

Burdett, R. (1998) Cities in distress – what went wrong in the post-war era? Presentation at the *Urban Design Alliance Annual Conference, Urban Design Makes Better Cities*, London, 15 October 1998.

Butina Watson, G. (1993) The art of building cities: urban structuring and restructuring, in Hayward, R. and McGlynn, S. (eds) *Making Better Places: Urban Design Now*. Oxford: Butterworth Architecture.

Calthorpe, P. (1993) *The Next American Metropolis: Ecology, Community and the American Dream*. New York: Princeton Architectural Press.

Campbell, K. and Cowan, R. (2002) *Re: Urbanism*. London: Urban Exchange.

Carmona, M. (1997) The need for innovation in the control of residential design, in *Urban Design Quarterly*, 62, 17–20.

Carmona, M. (1998) Design control – bridging the professional divide, Part I: a new framework, in *Journal of Urban Design*, 3(2), 175–200.

Carmona, M., Punter, J. and Chapman, D. (2002) *From Design Policy to Design Quality: The Treatment of Design in Community Strategies, Local Development Frameworks and Action Plans*. London: Thomas Telford.

Carter, E. J. and Goldfinger, E. (1945) *The County of London Plan [as explained by E. J. Carter and Ernö Goldfinger]*. London: Penguin Books.

Cervero, R. (1996) Traditional neighborhoods and commuting in the San Francisco Bay Area, in *Transportation*, 23, 373–94.

Chatwin, J. (1997) Brindleyplace implementation, in *Urban Design Quarterly*, 62, 12–15.

Chorlton, E. (2003) Designing streets for people, in *Urban Design Quarterly*, 85, 18–19.

Clark, C. (1958) Transport – maker and breaker of cities, in *The Town Planning Review*, 28(4), 237–50.

Clifford Culpin and Partners (1969) *Mosborough Master Plan*. Sheffield: Sheffield Corporation.

Colin Buchanan and Partners (1968) The South Hampshire study, in Lewis, D. (ed.) *Urban Structure*, Architectural Yearbook 12. London: Elek Books.

Conzen, M. R. G. (1969) *Alnwick, Northumberland: A Study in Town Plan Analysis*. Publication No. 27. London: Institute of British Geographers.

Cooke, C. (2000) Cities of socialism, technology and ideology in the Soviet Union in the 1920s, in Deckker, T. (ed.) *The Modern City Revisited*. London: Spon Press.

Cowan, R. (1995) *The Cities Design Forgot: A Manifesto*. London: Urban Initiatives.

Cowan, R. (1997) *The Connected City*. London: Urban Initiatives.

Cowan, R. (2002) *Urban Design Guidance: Urban Design Frameworks, Development Briefs and Master Plans*. London: Thomas Telford.

Crane, R. (1996) Car drivers and the new suburbs, in *Journal of the American Planning Association*, 60(1), 51–65.

Crane, R. (1998) Travel by design? in *Access*, 12, 3–6.

Crane, R. and Crepeau, R. (1998) Does neighborhood design influence travel?: A behavioral analysis of travel diary and GIS data, in *Transportation Research Part D: Transport and Environment*, 3(4), 225–38.

Crawford, J. H. (2000) *Carfree Cities*. Utrecht: International Books.

Culot, M. (1995) *Percevoir – Concevoir – Rechercher. La Ville Durable. Une Tétralogie Européene. Partie IV. Esthétique, Fonctionalité et Désirabilité de la Ville Durable*. Luxembourg: Office des Publications Officielles des Communautés Européennes.

Davies, N. (1997) Building on the fringe, in *Urban Design Quarterly*, 62, 27–31.

Dawkins, R. (1991) *The Blind Watchmaker*. Harmondsworth: Penguin.

Deckker, S. (1998) *Mews Style*. London: Quiller Press.

Dennett, D. (1996) *Darwin's Dangerous Idea: Evolution and the Meanings of Life*. Harmondsworth: Penguin.

DETR (1998a) *Places, Streets and Movement: A Companion Guide to Design Bulletin 32, Residential Roads and Footpaths*. London: Department of the Environment, Transport and the Regions.

DETR (1998b) *A New Deal for Trunk Roads in England*. London: Department of the Environment, Transport and the Regions.

DETR (2000) *By Design. Urban Design in the Planning System: Towards Better Practice*. London: Thomas Telford Publishing.

Diamond, J. (1998) *Guns, Germs and Steel: A Short History of Everybody for the Last 13,000 Years*. London: Vintage.

Dickinson, R. E. (1961) *The West European City: A Geographical Interpretation* (2nd edn). London: Routledge and Kegan Paul Ltd.

Dimitriou, H. (1995) *A Developmental Approach to Urban Transport Planning: An Indonesian Illustration*. Aldershot: Avebury.

DoE (1994) *PPG13. Planning Policy Guidance: Transport*. London: HMSO.

DoE/DoT (1992) *Design Bulletin 32. Residential Roads and Footpaths: Layout Considerations* (2nd edn). London: HMSO.

DoE/DoT (1995) *PPG13. A Guide to Better Practice: Reducing the Need to Travel Through Land Use and Transport Planning*. London: HMSO.

DoT/IHT (1987) *Roads and Traffic in Urban Areas*. London: HMSO.

Dotterer, S. (1987) Portland's arterial streets classification policy, in Moudon, A. V. (ed.) *Public Streets for Public Use*. New York: Van Nostrand Reinhold.

DTLR and CABE (2001) *By Design: Better Places to Live. A Companion Guide to PPG3*. London: Thomas Telford.

Dunnett, J. (2000) Le Corbusier and the city without streets, in Deckker, T. (ed.) *The Modern City Revisited*. London: Spon Press.

Dupree, H. (1987) *Urban Transportation: The New Town Solution*. Aldershot: Gower.

Dupuy, G. and Stransky, V. (1996) Cities and highway networks in Europe, in *Journal of Transport Geography*, 5(2), 107–21.

Easterling, K. (1999) *Organization Space: Landscapes, Highways, and Houses in America*. Cambridge, Mass. and London: MIT Press.

Echenique, M., Crowther, D. and Lindsay, W. (1972) A structural comparison of three generations of New Towns, in Martin, L. and March, L. (eds) *Urban Space and Structures*. Cambridge: Cambridge University Press.

Engwicht, D. (1993) *Reclaiming Our Cities and Towns: Better Living with Less Traffic*. Philadelphia: New Society Publishers.

Engwicht, D. (1999) *Street Reclaiming: Creating Livable Streets and Vibrant Communities*. Gabriola Island, British Columbia: New Society Publishers.

Erickson, B. (2001) The 'armature' and 'fabric' as a model for understanding spatial organisation, in Roberts, M. and Greed, C. (eds) *Approaching Urban Design: The Design Process*. Harlow: Longman.

Essex County Council (1973) *A Design Guide for Residential Areas*. Chelmsford: Essex County Council.

Essex County Council (1980) *A Design Guide for Residential Areas: Highway Standards*. Chelmsford: Essex County Council.

Essex Planning Officers' Association (1997) *The Essex Design Guide for Residential and Mixed Use Areas*. Chelmsford: Essex County Council and Essex Planning Officers Association.

Evans, D. I., Lee, P. M. and Sriskandan, K. (1986) M25 London Orbital Motorway, in *Highways and Transportation*, 33(11), 6–28.

Evans, R. (1996) Joining things up, paper presented at PTRC seminar *Street Pattern and Town Form*, London (February 1996).

Ewing, R. (1996) *Pedestrian- and Transit-Friendly Design*, report prepared for the Public Transit Office, Miami. Miami: Florida Department of Transportation.

Farby, B. A. and Murchland, J. D. (1967) Towards an evaluation of road system designs, in *Regional Studies*, 1(1), 27–37.

Fowler, D. (2003) Designs on streetwise training, in *Transportation Professional*, December 2003.

Franck, K. (1994) Types are us, in Franck, K. and Schneekloth, L. (eds) *Ordering Space: Types in Architecture and Design*. New York: Van Nostrand Reinhold.

Frey, H. (1999) *Designing the City: Towards a More Sustainable Urban Form*. London: Routledge.

Friedman, A. (1998) Design for change: flexible planning strategies for the 1990s and beyond, in *Journal of Urban Design*, 2(3), 277–96.

Fyfe, N. (ed.) (1998) *Images of the Street*. London: Routledge.

Garland, K. (1994) *Mr. Beck's Underground Map*. Harrow Weald: Capital Transport Publishing.

Garreau, J. (1992) *Edge City: Life on the New Frontier*. London: Anchor Books.

Gehl, J. (1998) The form and use of public space, in *PTRC European Transport Conference Proceedings of Seminar B, Policy Planning and Sustainability*, Volume 1, 193–98.

Gerosa, P. G. (1978) *Le Corbusier – urbanisme et mobilité*. Basel and Stuttgart: Birkhäuser.

Gibberd, F. (1967) *Town Design* (5th edn). London: The Architectural Press.

Gold, J. R. (1997) *The Experience of Modernism: Modern Architects and the Future City, 1928–53*. London: E. & F. N. Spon.

Gold, J. R. (1998) The death of the boulevard, in Fyfe, N. (ed.) *Images of the Street*. London: Routledge.

Goodwin, P. (1995) *The End of Hierarchy? A New Perspective on Managing the Road Network*. London: Council for the Protection of Rural England.

Gordon, G. (1984) The shaping of urban morphology, in Reeder, D. (ed.) *Urban History Yearbook 1984*. Leicester: Leicester University Press.

Gosling, D. and Maitland, B. (1984) *Concepts of Urban Design*. London: Academy Editions.

Greenberg, E. and Dock, F. (2003) Design guidance for great streets: addressing context sensitivity for major urban streets. Paper presented at TRB Second Urban Streets Symposium, July 2003 (www.cnu.org).

Greenberg, K. (1997) Making choices, in *Streets*, 11(2), 14–21.

Groth, P. (1981) Streetgrids as frameworks for urban variety, in *Harvard Architectural Review*, 2(2), 68–75.

Hacking, I. (1983) *Representing and Intervening: Introductory Topics in the Philosophy of Natural Science*. Cambridge: Cambridge University Press.

Haggett, P. and Chorley, R. J. (1969) *Network Analysis in Geography*. London: Edward Arnold.

Hall, P. (1992) East Thames Corridor: the second golden age of the garden suburb, *Urban Design Quarterly*, 43, 2–9.

Hall, P. (1999) *Cities in Civilization: Culture, Innovation and Urban Order*. London: Phoenix Giant.

Hall, P. (2002) *Urban and Regional Planning* (4th edn). London and New York: Routledge.

Hall, P. (forthcoming) Can planning reduce traffic problems? Goals, role and effectiveness of planning 1963–2020. *Proceedings of the Institution of Civil Engineers: Transport* (in press).

Hall, P., Marshall, S. and Lowe, M. (2001) The changing urban hierarchy in England and Wales: 1913–1998, in *Regional Studies*, 35(9), 775–807.

Handy, S. (1992). Regional versus local accessibility: neotraditional development and its implications for non-work travel, in *Built Environment*, 18(4), 253–67.

Hanson, J. (1989) Order and structure in urban space: a morphological history of the City of London. Unpublished PhD Thesis, University College London.

Harwood, D. (1992) Traffic and vehicle operating characteristics, in Pline, J. (ed.) *Traffic Engineering Handbook* (4th edn).

Hathway, G. (1985) *Low-Cost Vehicles: Options for Moving People and Goods*. London: Intermediate Technology Publications.

Hayward, R. (1993) Talking tissues, in Hayward, R. and McGlynn, S. (eds) *Making Better Places: Urban Design Now*. Oxford: Butterworth Architecture.

Hazel, G. McL. (1997) The environmental debate, paper presented at the Institution of Highways and Transportation conference *The Future of Transport in the Urban Environment*, University of Cambridge, June.

Hazel, G. McL. (2003) Urban streets, in *Urban Design Quarterly*, 85, 20–21.

Hebbert, M. (1998) *London: More by Fortune than Design*. Chichester: John Wiley & Son.

Hebbert, M. (2003) New Urbanism: the movement in context, in *Built Environment*, 29(3), 193–209.

Hilberseimer, L. (1944) *The New City: Principles of Planning*. Chicago: Paul Theobold.

Hill, D. (1996) *A History of Engineering in Classical and Medieval Times*. London: Routledge.

Hillier, B. (1987) The morphology of urban space: the evolution of a syntactic approach [La morphologie de l'espace urbain: l'évolution de l'approche syntactique], in *Architecture and Behaviour*, 3(3), 205–16.

Hillier, B. (1996) *Space is the Machine*. Cambridge: Cambridge University Press.

Hillier, B. (1999) The hidden geometry of deformed grids: or, why space syntax works, when it looks as though it shouldn't, *in Environment and Planning B: Planning and Design*, 26, 169–91.

Hillier, B. and Hanson, J. (1984) *The Social Logic of Space*. Cambridge: Cambridge University Press.

Hillier, B., Hanson, J., Peponis, J., Hudson, J. and Burdett, R. (1983) Space syntax. A different urban perspective, in *The Architects' Journal*, 30 November 1983, 47–63.

Hillier, B., Penn, A., Hanson, J., Grajewski, T. and Xu, J. (1993) Natural movement: or, configuration and attraction in urban pedestrian movement, in *Environment and Planning B: Planning and Design*, 20, 29–66.

Hoogma, R., Kemp, R., Schot, J. and Truffer, B. (2002) *Experimenting for Sustainable Transport: The Approach of Strategic Niche Management*. London: Spon.

Houghton-Evans, W. (1975) *Planning Cities: Legacy and Portent*. London: Lawrence and Wishart.

Howard, E. (1904) *Tomorrow: A Peaceful Path to Real Reform*, reprinted as Volume 2 of LeGates, R. and Stout, F. (eds) (1998) Early Urban Planning series, London: Routledge/Thoemmes Press.

ICE (1994) *Managing the Highways Network*. London: Institution of Civil Engineers.

ICE (1996) *Which Way Roads?* London: Thomas Telford Publishing on behalf of the Institution of Civil Engineers.

ICE (2002) *The 2002 Designing Streets for People Report*. London: Institution of Civil Engineers.

IDC (1971) *Irvine New Town Plan*. Irvine: Irvine Development Corporation.

IHT (1997) *Transport in the Urban Environment*. London: Institution of Highways and Transportation.

ITE Transportation Planning Council Committee SP-8 (1999) *Traditional Neighborhood Development Street Design Guidelines*. Washington, DC: ITE.

Jacobs, A. (1993) *Great Streets*. Cambridge, Mass.: MIT Press.

Jacobs, A. B., Macdonald, E. and Rofé, Y. (2002) *The Boulevard Book: History, Evolution, Design of Multiway Boulevards*. Cambridge, Mass.: MIT Press.

Jacobs, A., Rofé, Y. and Macdonald, E. (1995) *Multiple Roadway Boulevards: Case Studies, Designs and Design Guidelines*. University of California Transportation Center Working Paper No. 300. Berkeley: University of California.

Jacobs, J. (1961) *The Death and Life of Great American Cities*. London: Jonathan Cape.

Jakle, J. A. (1987) *The Visual Elements of Landscape*. Amherst: The University of Massachusetts Press.

Jamieson, G. B., Mackay, W. K. and Latchford, J. C. R. (1967) Transportation and land use structures, in *Urban Studies*, 4(3), 201–17.

Jefferson, C., Rowe, J. and Brebbia, C. (2001) *The Sustainable Street. The Environment, Human and Economic Aspects of Street Design and Management*. Southampton and Boston: Wessex Institute of Technology.

Jenkins, E. (1975) Highway hierarchy – or please don't bring your car into the living room, in *The Highway Engineer*, 22(11), 117–22.

Jiang, B., Claramunt, C. and Batty, M. (1999) Geometric accessibility and geographic information: extending desktop GIS to space syntax, in *Computers, Environment and Urban Systems*, 23, 127–46.

Johansson, B. (2003) Transportation fuels – a system perspective, in Hensher, D. A. and Button, K. J. (eds) *Handbook of Transport and the Environment*, Handbooks in Transport Volume 4. Oxford: Elsevier.

Jones, I. D. (1986) A review of highway classification systems, in *Traffic Engineering and Control*, 27(1), 27–30.

Kansky, K. J. (1963) *Structure of Transportation Networks: Relationships between Network Geometry and Regional Characteristics*. University of Chicago Department of Geography Research Paper No. 84. Chicago: University of Chicago.

Katz, P. (1994) *The New Urbanism: Toward an Architecture of Community*. New York: McGraw-Hill.

Keeble, L. (1969) *Principles and Practice of Town Planning* (4th edn). London: The Estates Gazette Limited.

Keeble, L. (1983) *Town Planning Made Plain*. London and New York: Construction Press.

Kemp, R. and Simon, B (2001) Electric vehicles: a socio-technical scenario study, in Feitelson, E. and Verhoef, E. T. (eds) *Transport and Environment. In Search of Sustainable Solutions*. Cheltenham: Edward Elgar.

Khare, M. and Sharma, P. (2003) Fuel options, in Hensher, D. A. and Button, K. J. (eds) *Handbook of Transport and the Environment*, Handbooks in Transport Volume 4. Oxford: Elsevier.

King, A. D. (1994) Terminologies and types: making sense of some types of dwellings and cities, in Franck, K. and Schneekloth, L. (eds) *Ordering Space. Types in Architecture and Design*. New York: Van Nostrand Reinhold.

Kostof, S. (1991) *The City Shaped. Urban Patterns and Meanings Through History*. London: Thames and Hudson.

Kostof, S. (1992) *The City Assembled: The Elements of Urban Form Throughout History*. London: Thames and Hudson.

Krieger, A. and Lennertz, W. (1991) *Andres Duany and Elizabeth Plater-Zyberk: Towns and Town-making Principles*. New York: Rizzoli International Publications.

Krier, L. (1993a) Poundbury Masterplan, in *New Practice in Urban Design* (*Architectural Design* series). London: Academy Editions.

Krier, L. (1993b) Poundbury, Dorset, in *Architecture in Arcadia* (*Architectural Design* series). London: Academy Editions.

Krüger, M. T. J. (1979) An approach to built-form connectivity at an urban scale: system description and its representation, in *Environment and Planning B: Planning and Design*, 6, 67–88.

Kulash, W. M. (1990) Traditional neighbourhood development: will traffic work? Paper presented at the Eleventh International Pedestrian Conference, Bellevue, WA.

Kulash, W. M. (2001) *Residential Streets* (3rd edn). Washington, D.C.: Urban Land Institute.

Lang, J. (1994) *Urban Design: The American Experience*. New York: Van Nostrand Reinhold.

Larkham, P. J. and Jones, A. N. (1991) *A Glossary of Urban Form*. Historical Geography Research Series No. 26. London: Institute of British Geographers.

Laurini, R. and Thompson, D. (1992) *Fundamentals of Spatial Information Systems*. London: Academic Press.

Le Corbusier (1951) *The Modulor: A Harmonious Measure to the Human Scale Universally applicable to Architecture and Mechanics*. London: Faber and Faber.

Le Corbusier (1955) *Œuvre Complète 1946–1952*. Zürich: Editions Girsberger.

Leccese, M. and McCormick, K. (eds) (2000) *Charter of the New Urbanism*. New York: McGraw-Hill.

Leleur, S. (1995) *Road Infrastructure Planning. A Decision-Oriented Approach*. Lyngby, Denmark: Polyteknisk Forlag.

Lerner-Lam, E., Celniker, S. P., Halbert, G. W., Chellman, C. and Ryan, S. (1992) Neo-traditional neighborhood design and its implications for traffic engineering. *ITE Journal*, January 1992, 17–25.

Lillebye, E. (2001) The architectural significance of the street as a functional and social arena, in Jefferson, C., Rowe, J. and Brebbia, C. (eds) *The Sustainable Street. The Environmental, Human and Economic Aspects of Street Design and Management*. Southampton and Boston: Wessex Institute of Technology Press.

Llewelyn-Davies (2000) *Urban Design Compendium*. Prepared in association with Alan Baxter and Associates for English Partnerships and the Housing Corporation. London: English Partnerships.

Llewelyn-Davies, R. (1968) Town Design, in Lewis, D. (ed.) *Urban Structure*, Architectural Yearbook 12, London: Elek Books.

Lock, D. (1994) The long view, in *New Towns* (*Architectural Design* series). London: Academy Editions.

Lord, E. A. and Wilson, C. B. (1984) *The Mathematical Description of Shape and Form*. Chichester: Ellis Horwood.

Lowe, J. C. and Moryadas, S. (1975) *The Geography of Movement*. Boston: Houghton Mifflin.

LTT [Local Transport Today] (1998) New residential road design guidelines bid to put places and people before cars, 24 September 1998, 8–9.

Lynch, K. (1962) *Site Planning*. Cambridge, Mass.: MIT Press.

Lynch, K. (1981) *[A Theory of] Good City Form*. Cambridge, Mass.: MIT Press.

Lynch, K. (1990) *City Sense and City Design: writings and projects of Kevin Lynch*, edited by Banerjee, T. and Southworth, M. Cambridge, Mass.: MIT Press.

MacCormac, R. (1996) An anatomy of London, in *Built Environment*, 22(4), 306–11.

Macpherson, G. (1993) *Highway and Transportation Engineering and Planning*. Harlow: Addison Wesley Longman.

March, L. and Steadman, J. P. (1971) *The Geometry of Environment. An Introduction to Spatial Organization in Design*. London: RIBA Publications.

Mars, T. (1992) Little Los Angeles in Bucks, in *Architects' Journal*, 15 April 1992, 22–26.

Marshall, A. (2000) *How Cities Work. Suburbs, Sprawl and the Road Not Taken*. Austin: University of Texas press.

Marshall, S. (2001) Public transport orientated urban design, in Feitelson, E. and Verhoef, E. (eds) *Transport and Environment: in search of sustainable solutions*. Cheltenham: Edward Elgar.

Marshall, S. (2002a) *A First Theoretical Approach to Classification of Arterial Streets*. ARTISTS Deliverable D1.1. London: University of Westminster.

Marshall, S. (2002b) *Methodological Framework for Compatibility Analysis*. TRANSPLUS Deliverable D4.2. London: Bartlett School of Planning, University College London.

Marshall, S. (2003a) Transport and the urban pattern, in *Town and Country Planning*, 73(2), 106–108.

Marshall, S. (2003b) Traffic in Towns revisited, in *Town and Country Planning*, 72(10), 310–12.

Marshall, S. (ed.) (2003c) TRANSPLUS Deliverable Report D.4: Barriers, Solutions and Transferability. London: Bartlett School of Planning, University College London.

Marshall, S. (2004) The future evolution of urban transport: towards a new modal fit, paper for presented at July World Conference on Transport Research, Istanbul, forthcoming.

Marshall, S. (forthcoming) *Cities Design and Evolution*.

Martin, L., March, L. and others [sic] (1972) Speculations, in Martin, L. and March, L. (eds) *Urban Space and Structures*. Cambridge: Cambridge University Press.

McCluskey, J. (1992) *Road Form and Townscape* (2nd edn). Oxford: Butterworth Architecture.

McGlynn, S. (1993) Reviewing the rhetoric, in Hayward, R. and McGlynn, S. (eds) *Making Better Places: Urban Design Now*. Oxford: Butterworth Architecture.

McKean, C. (1996) The incivility of Edinburgh's New Town, in Brogden, W. A. (ed.) *The Neo-Classical Town: Scottish Contributions to Urban Design since 1750*. Edinburgh: The Rutland Press.

McNally, M. G. and Ryan, S. (1993) A comparative assessment of travel characteristics for neotraditional developments, in *Transportation Research Record*, 1400, 67–77.

Ministry of War Transport (1946) *Design and Layout of Roads in Built-up Areas: Report of the Departmental Committee set up by the Minister of War Transport.* London: His Majesty's Stationery Office.

Mitchell, W. J. (1990) *The Logic of Architecture: Design, Computation, and Cognition.* Cambridge, Mass.: MIT Press.

MKDC (1974) *Central Milton Keynes: Area Plan.* Milton Keynes: Milton Keynes Development Corporation.

Moholy-Nagy, S. (1968) *Matrix of Man: An Illustrated History of Urban Environment.* London: Pall Mall Press.

Moore, J. N. (1996) *The Maps of Glasgow. A History and Cartobibliography to 1865.* Glasgow: Glasgow University Library.

Morlok, E. (1967) *An Analysis of Transport Technology and Network Structure.* Evanston, Illinois: the Transportation Center, Northwestern University.

Morris, A. E. J. (1994) *History of Urban Form: Before the Industrial Revolutions* (3rd edn). Harlow: Longman Scientific and Technical.

Morris, W. and Kaufman, J. A. (1998) The New Urbanism: an introduction to the movement and its potential impact on travel demand with an outline of its application in Western Australia, in *PTRC European Transport Conference Proceedings of Seminar B, Policy Planning and Sustainability*, Volume 1, 199–222.

Morrison, A. (1966) Principles of road classification for road maps, in *Cartographic Journal*, 3(1), 17–30.

Morrison, A. (1981) Using the Department of Transport's Road Network Databank to produce route planning maps, in *Cartographic Journal*, 18, 91–95.

MoT (1963) *Traffic in Towns.* London: HMSO.

MoT (1966) *Roads in Urban Areas.* London: HMSO.

Moudon, A. V. (ed.) (1987) *Public Streets for Public Use.* New York: Van Nostrand Reinhold.

Moudon, A. V. (1997) Urban morphology as an emerging interdisciplinary field, in *Urban Morphology*, 1, 3–10.

Moudon, A. V. and Untermann, R. K. (1987) *Grids Revisited*, in Moudon, A. V. (ed.) *Public Streets for Public Use.* New York: Van Nostrand Co.

Moughtin, C., Oc, T. and Tiesdell, S. (1995) *Urban Design: Ornament and Decoration.* Oxford: Butterworth Architecture.

Moughtin, J. C. (1992) *Urban Design: Street and Square.* Oxford: Butterworth Architecture.

Mumford, L. (1961) *The City in History. Its Origins, its Transformations, and its Prospects.* San Diego: Harcourt, Brace and Company.

Mumford, L. (1964) *The Highway in the City.* London: Secker and Warburg.

Murrain, P. (1993) Urban expansion: look back and learn, in Hayward, R. and McGlynn, S. (eds) *Making Better Places: Urban Design Now.* Oxford: Butterworth Architecture.

Newman, P. and Kenworthy, J. (1999) *Sustainability and Cities. Overcoming Automobile Dependence.* Washington, DC: Island Press.

Njenga, P. and Davis, A. (2003) Drawing the road map to rural poverty reduction, in *Transport Reviews*, 23(2), 217–41.

Norberg-Schulz, C. (1975) *Meaning in Western Architecture*. London: Studio Vista.

O'Flaherty, C. A. (1986) *Highways. Volume 1. Traffic Planning and Engineering* (3rd edn). London: Edward Arnold.

O'Flaherty, C. A. (1997) Evolution of the transport task, in O'Flahery, C. A. (ed.) *Transport Planning and Traffic Engineering*. London: Arnold.

Oc, T. and Tiesdell, S. (1997) *Safer City Centres: Reviving the Public Realm*. London: Paul Chapman.

Odani, M. and Yamanaka, H. (1997) The practice of improving the neighbourhood street environment through traffic calming in Japan, in Tolley, R. (ed.) *The Greening of Urban Transport*. Chichester: John Wiley and Sons.

Oglesby, C. H. and Hicks, R. G. (1982) *Highway Engineering* (4th edn). New York and Chichester: Wiley.

Penn, A., Hillier, B., Banister, D. and Xu, J. (1998) Configurational modelling of urban movement networks, in *Environment and Planning B: Planning and Design*, 25, 59–84.

Potter, S. (1976) *Transport and New Towns. Volume 2. The Transport Assumptions Underlying the Design of Britain's New Towns. 1946–1976*. Milton Keynes: Open University, New Towns Study Unit.

Potter, S. (1977) *Transport and New Towns. Volume 3. Conflicts and Externalities in New Town Transport Plans*. Milton Keynes: Open University, New Towns Study Unit.

Potter, S. (2003) Transport, energy and emissions: urban public transport, in Hensher, D. A. and Button, K. J. (eds) *Handbook of Transport and the Environment*, Handbooks in Transport Volume 4. Oxford: Elsevier.

Pressman, N. (1985) Forces for spatial change, in Brotchie, J., Newton, P., Hall, P. and Nijkamp, P. (eds) *The Future of Urban Form*. London: Croom Helm.

Prince Charles (1987) Speech to the Corporation of London Planning and Communication Committee's Annual Dinner, Mansion House, London (1 December 1987).

Punter, J. (1996) Urban design theory in planning practice: the British perspective, in *Built Environment*, 22(4), 263–77.

Punter, J. and Carmona, M. (1997) *The Design Dimension of Planning*. London: E. & F. N. Spon.

Rapoport, A. (1977) *Human Aspects of Urban Form: Towards a Man-environment Approach to Urban Form and Design*. Oxford: Pergamon.

Richards, B. (1969) *New Movement in Cities*. London: Studio Vista.

Richards, B. (2001) *Future Transport in Cities*. London and New York: Spon.

Rickaby, P. A. (1987) Six settlement patterns compared, in *Environment and Planning B: Planning and Design*, 14, 193–223.

Rietveld, P. (1997) Policy aspects of networks, an introduction, in Capineri, C. and Rietveld, P. (eds) *Networks in Transport and Communications: A Policy Approach*. Aldershot and Brookfield: Ashgate.

Ritter, P. (1964) *Planning for Man and Motor*. Oxford: Pergamon Press.

Robbins, E. (2000) The New Urbanism and the fallacy of singularity, in *Urban Design International*, 3(1 & 2), 33–42.

Roberts, J. (1990) The use of our streets, in *Urban Design Quarterly*, 35, 9–13.

Roberts, M. and Lloyd-Jones, T. (2001) Urban generators, in Roberts, M. and Greed, C. (eds) *Approaching Urban Design: The Design Process*. Harlow: Longman.

Roberts, M., Lloyd-Jones, T., Erickson, B. and Nice, S. (1999) Place and space in the networked city: conceptualising the integrated metropolis, in *Journal of Urban Design*, 4(1), 51–66.

Rook, A. (2003) Streets and the community, in *Urban Design Quarterly*, 85, 26–29.

Rosenkrantz, V. and Abraham, M. (1995) Integrating transport and urban structure – why it matters and how it works. Paper prepared for New South Wales Department of Transportation, Sydney.

Ross, P. (1997) Hulme Development Guide, in *Urban Design Quarterly*, 62, 20–23.

Rudofsky, B. (1969) *Streets for People: A Primer for Americans*. New York: Doubleday.

Russell, J. (1988) Traffic integration and environmental traffic management in Denmark, in *Transport Reviews*, 8(1), 39–58.

Ryan, S. and McNally, M. G. (1995) Accessibility of neotraditional neighborhoods: a review of design concepts, policies, and recent literature, in *Transportation Research Part A – Policy and Practice*, 29(2), 87–105.

Rykwert, J. (1978) The street: the use of its history, in Anderson, S. (ed.) *On Streets*. Cambridge, Mass.: MIT Press.

Sabey, D. L. and Baldwin, K. (1987) Planners' view of highways and transportation, in *Highways and Transportation*, 34(5), 13–19.

Satoh, S. (1998) Urban design and change in Japanese castle towns, *in Built Environment*, 24(4), 217–34.

Scargill, D. I. (1979) *The Form of Cities*. London: Bell and Hyman.

Schurch, T. W. (1999) Reconsidering urban design: thoughts about its definition and status as a field or profession, in *Journal of Urban Design*, 4(1), 5–28.

Scully, V. (1994) The architecture of community, in Katz, P., *The New Urbanism: Toward an Architecture of Community*. New York: McGraw-Hill.

Sheffi, Y. (1985) *Urban Transportation Networks. Equilibrium Analysis with Mathematical Programming Methods*. Englewood Cliffs, NJ: Prentice-Hall.

Simmonds, R. (1993) The built form of the new regional city: a 'radical' view, in Hayward, R. and McGlynn, S. (eds) *Making Better Places: Urban Design Now*. Oxford: Butterworth Architecture.

Sitte, C. ([1889] 1945) *The Art of Building Cities: City Building According to its Artistic Fundamentals*. New York: Reinhold.

Smailes, A. E. (1944) The urban hierarchy in England and Wales, in *Geography*, 29, 41–51.

Smith, G. P. and Freer, G. (1999) Mixed-use main streets: managing traffic within a sustainable urban form, in *The Sustainable Urban Neighbourhood*, 9, 4–5.

Smith, R. D. P. (1968) The changing urban hierarchy, in *Regional Studies*, 2, 1–19.

Smithson, A. and Smithson, P. (1967) *Urban Structuring*. New York: Studio Vista: Reinhold.

Smithson, A. and Smithson, P. (1968) Density, interval and measure, in Lewis, D. (ed.) *Urban Structure*, Architectural Yearbook 12. London: Elek Books.

Soria y Mata, A. (1892) The Linear City, translated by M. D. Gonzalez, in LeGates, R. and Stout, F. (eds) (1998) *Selected Essays*. London: Routledge/Thoemmes Press.

Sorkin, M. (1993) *Local Code: The Constitution of a City at 42 N Latitude*. New York: Princeton Architectural Press.

Southworth, M. (1997) Walkable suburbs? An evaluation of neotraditional communities at the urban edge, in *Journal of the American Planning Association*, 63(1), 28–44.

Southworth, M. (2003) New Urbanism and the American metropolis, in *Built Envrionment*, 29(3), 210–26.

Southworth, M. and Ben-Joseph, E. (1997) *Streets and the Shaping of Towns and Cities*. New York: McGraw-Hill.

Southworth, M. and Owens, P. (1993) The evolving metropolis: Studies of communities, neighborhood, and street form at the urban edge, in *Journal of the American Planning Association*, 59(3), 271–87.

Sperling, D. (2003) Cleaner vehicles, in Hensher, D. A. and Button, K. J. (eds) *Handbook of Transport and the Environment*, Handbooks in Transport Volume 4. Oxford: Elsevier.

Spreiregen, P. (1965) *Urban Design: The Architecture of Towns and Cities*. New York: McGraw-Hill.

Steadman, J. P. (1998) Sketch for an archetypal building, in *Environment and Planning B: Planning and Design*, 27, Anniversary Issue, 92–105.

Stones, A. (1997) The New Essex Design Guide, in *Urban Design Quarterly*, 62, 31–35.

SUNI [Sustainable Urban Neighbourhood Initiative] (1997) The model sustainable urban neighbourhood, in *The Sustainable Urban Neighbourhood*, Issue 4 (Spring/Summer).

Taylor, M. A. P. (2000) Using network reliability concepts for traffic calming: permeability, approachability and tortuosity in network design, in Bell, M. G. H. and Cassir, C. (eds) *Reliability of Transport Networks*. Baldock: Research Studies Press Ltd.

Taylor, N. (1998) *Urban Planning Theory since 1945*. London: SAGE.

Terzaghi, K. and Peck, R. (1948) *Soil Mechanics in Engineering Practice*. New York: John Wiley & Sons; London: Chapman & Hall.

Thompson, D. W. (1948 [1917]) *On Growth and Form*. Cambridge: University Press.

Thompson-Fawcett, M. (2000) The contribution of urban villages to sustainable development, in Williams, K., Burton, E. and Jenks, M. (eds) *Achieving Sustainable Urban Form*. London, E. & F. N. Spon.

Thorne, R. and Filmer-Sankey, W. (2003) Transportation, in Thomas, R. (ed.) *Sustainable Urban Design: An Environmental Approach*. London: Spon Press.

Trancik, R. (1986) *Finding Lost Space: Theories of Urban Design*. New York: Van Nostrand Reinhold.

Tripp, H. A. (1942) *Town Planning and Road Traffic*. London: Edward Arnold.

Tripp, H. A. (1950 [1938]) *Road Traffic and its Control*. (2nd edn). London: Edward Arnold.

TRL (1997) *Urban Design Considerations in Transport Planning: A Guide for Planners and Engineers*. Crowthorne: Transport Research Laboratory.

Tunnard, C. (1970) *The City of Man: A New Approach to the Recovery of Beauty in American Cities*. New York: Charles Scribner's Sons.

Tunnard, C. and Pushkarev, B. (1963) *Man-made America: Chaos or Control?* New Haven and London: Yale University Press.

Turner, T. (1996) *City as Landscape: A Post-postmodern View of Design and Planning*. London: E. & F. N. Spon.

Unwin, R. (1920 [1909]) *Town Planning in Practice: An Introduction to the Art of Designing Cities and Suburbs* (2nd edn). London: Bern.

Urban Task Force (1999) *Towards an Urban Renaissance*. London: DETR/E. & F. N. Spon.

Vaughan, R. (1987) *Urban Spatial Traffic Patterns*. London: Pion.

Vickerman, R. (2001) The concept of optimal transport systems, in Button, K. J. and Hensher, D. A. (eds) *Handbook of Transport Systems and Traffic Control* (Handbooks in Transport 3). Oxford: Pergamon.

Wackernagel, M. and Rees, W. (1996) *Our Ecological Footprint: Reducing Human Impact on the Earth*. Gabriola Island: New Society Publishers.

Walker, F. A. (1996) The emergence of the grid: later 18th century urban form in Glasgow, in Brogden, W. A. (ed.) *The Neo-Classical Town: Scottish Contributions to Urban Design since 1750*. Edinburgh: The Rutland Press.

Western Australia (1997) *Liveable Neighbourhoods: Community Design Code*. Perth: State of Western Australia.

White, P. (1995) *Public Transport. Its Planning, Management and Operation* (3rd edn). London: University College London Press.

Whitehand, J. W. R. (ed.) (1981) *The Urban Landscape: Historical Development and Management: Papers by M.R.G. Conzen*. IBG Special Publication No. 13. London: Academic Press.

Wilford, J. N. (2000) *The Mapmakers*. New York: Vintage.

Wood, C. (1994) *Street Trams for London*. London: Centre for Independent Transport Research.

Wright, P. H. (1996) *Highway Engineering*. New York: John Wiley.

INDEX

ABCD typology 84–6, 144, 174–6
access constraint 162, 172, 178, 202, 291
access road – *see* road and street type
Alexander, C. 3, 221, 249; *A Pattern Language* 53; A city is not a tree 159, 186; *New Theory of Urban Design* 222, 254
analogies of road system: arteries 184–5; backbone 6; canal system 65–7; corridors 48–9, 186, 194; engineering structure xii, 165; leaf veins 66; sea or river system 13, 63, 181, 184, 186; tree 159, 162–4, 167, 186
arterial (route) – *see* road and street types
arterial network 64–5, 291
arteriality 60, 68, 162, 175, 178, 184, 170–1; as basis for ranking street type 64–5, 67, 184–5, 212–3; definitions 61–2, 291; *see also* transit-oriented arteriality
articulated route hierarchy 208–10, 217, 231, 233, 291

Bayswater 121, 127, 140–1, 149, 172, 174
Bentham, J. 70, 243
bicycles – *see* modes
block type 238–40

Buchanan, C. 4–5, 69, 192, 211
Buchanan Report – *see Traffic in Towns*
buses – *see* modes

cars – *see* modes
car orientation, structure of 178, 180–2, 187, 217, 294
car-free cities 238, 254
characteristic pattern or structure – *see* patterns
Ciudad Lineal 92, 149, 151, 225, 284–5
classification: by designation 54–8, 68; by form 54–5, 58–9; functional 24, 34–5, 56, 58, 68; geographical basis 65; problems with 50, 67–8, 74; by relation 54–6, 58, 60, 124, 131; subjectivity 63, 68; themes 54, 57; by use 54–5, 59–60; *see also* hierarchy, typology
coding 10, 222, 242–3, 248–9, 251; *see also* constitutional code
complexity xiii, 147–9, 152, 282
composition 86–90, 166–9, 175, 291
configuration 86–90, 164, 166–9, 175, 177, 292
conjoint constitution 172–3, 179, 292
connectivity 88, 108, 114, 138, 292

connector – *see* road and street
  types
constitution 160, 165, 166–9, 175,
  177, 292
constitutional approach 222–3, 226–8,
  232, 241–8, 253–4
constitutional archetype 229–35, 257,
  292
constitutional code 228–9, 241–9
continuity 120, 292
Craig Plan 36–7, 150, 221, 225, 264;
  constitutional graph 288
crossroads 3, 38, 96, 100, 117–18,
  130, 154, 232, 234, 247
cul-de-sac 27, 31, 38–9, 41, 98,
  100–1, 143, 154, 164

dendritic constitution 172, 177–8,
  180, 183, 186, 292
depth 112, 120, 293
design debate 16, 22, 27, 41, 223
design guidance 21, 23, 27–41, 61,
  221–2, 224, 232–3, 250–2; *see also*
  coding
design standards 12, 17, 27–9
distributor roads – *see* road and
  street type
distributory 84–5, 177
disurban creation 9, 27, 46, 50, 191;
  structure of 183–7, 217, 294

economic considerations 194–6
Edinburgh New Town 46, 53–4,
  176–8, 186, 224; *see also* Craig
  Plan
environmental considerations 193–5,
  198, 211

Fitzrovia 1, 3, 10, 49, 186, 211,
  246–8
Fitzroy Square 194, 211, 248
flow – *see* traffic flow
functional classification – *see*
  classification
future 245, 254, 258

Glasgow grids 149–50
graph theory 108; constitutional graph
  286–8, 292
grids – *see* patterns

hetgram 148–9; properties 282
hierarchical layout or network 28, 37,
  143, 150, 162, 171–2
hierarchy – *see* modal hierarchy, road
  hierarchy, social hierarchy, urban
  hierarchy
highway engineering: criticism of
  11–12, 28, 191, 261; design
  standards 12, 17
Hilberseimer's *New City* 135, 138,
  151, 285
Hillier, B. 40, 111, 113–14, 250

interchange 179
inverse relationship (mobility and
  access) 4, 50, 67–8, 184, 187, 212,
  246, 293
irregularity 79, 133, 147–8

Jacobs, J. 3, 221, 254
joint 115–6, 277, 282, 293

Kansky, K. J. 15, 131

land use zoning – *see* zoning
Le Corbusier 45–6, 67–9, 237, 264
link 6, 28–9, 60, 115–16, 130, 277,
  282
local routes and networks 64–5
London – *see* Bloomsbury, Fitzrovia,
  Thamesmead, Tottenham Court
  Road
Lynch, K. 29, 75, 77, 240;
  classifications 265, 272

mixed-use blocks 238–41
modal hierarchy 179, 193, 197–8,
  204, 206–8; *see also* transport
  modes, road hierarchy
modegram 198–9
modes 25, 49, 192, 252–3; and
  accessibility 199, 255; animal
  power 192, 200; and arteriality
  178; bicycles 9, 25, 192–4, 204,
  256; buses 3, 49, 67, 179, 191–4,
  204; cars 191, 193–4, 198–9,
  204, 252, 255; coaches 204;
  future modes 192, 254–5; goods
  vehicles 194, 204; horses 1, 15,
  54, 192; human powered modes

200, 256; minibuses 179; public transport 25, 38, 49, 67, 178–81, 198–9, 204, 206–8, 252–3; and scale 199, 204, 206–8, 255; trains 193, 204; trams, 179, 256; walking and pedestrian system 9, 25, 38, 49, 66–7, 178, 180, 192, 198–9, 252–3, 256; *see also* modal hierarchy, modegram, railways, segregation

Modernism xi, 9–10, 133; cataclysm of 3, 183; effect on traditional street 4, 6, 22; schism of 7, 11; and transport 6, 8

Morrison, A. 16, 61; classifications 265

Mosborough Master Plan 79–82, 92, 154, 272

neo-traditional urbanism 9, 22, 28, 36, 38–9, 113, 133, 154, 221–3, 225, 227; *see also* New Urbanism

netgram 140–1; conventions 283; properties 282

netspace 145, 284

network analysis 108, 117, 167; *see also* representation

network function, of a road 60, 65, 204

New Urbanism xi, 9, 21, 28, 38, 92; *see also* neo-traditional urbanism

node 29, 100, 116, 130, 277

nodegram 100–1

organic patterns or processes 38–9, 221–2

patterns 27, 36, 293; characteristic 151–5, 222, 291; desired 29, 36; elemental 81; fractal 148, 285; grids 31–2, 36–9, 41, 78–9, 84–5, 92, 94–6, 100, 102, 144, 146, 149–50, 152, 174, 177, 224, 245; and hierarchy 36; pattern of roads on atlas 59–62; street-pattern-shape 145–6, 152, 154–5; tartan grids 236, 256; tree-like patterns 29, 36, 38, 90; tributary 31, 36, 143–4, 149–50, 152, 294; typologies 75, 78, 271–6

pedestrian – *see* modes, segregation

permeability 38, 88–9; *see also* connectivity

Poundbury 20, 33–4, 39, 145, 154, 174–6; typology 53, 59

professional roles and relationships 6, 7, 10, 13, 22–3, 68, 248; *see also* highway engineering

public transport – *see* modes

railways 3, 4, 179, 237; shinkansen 204;

recursivity 148, 282

reference line 278

regularity 79

representation 108–11, 116–18, 130

reseau 278

rhumb line 278

road and street types 264–9; access road 25, 48–51, 64, 206; arterial 50–1, 64–5, 291; boulevard 22–4, 45, 52, 170, 202, 216, 239, 246, 249, 256; connector 26–7, 53, 128, 145, 292; distributor roads 21, 25, 34, 48–51, 64–5, 67, 207; sub-arterial 64–5; trunk road 24, 59, 159, 169–79, 294; *see also* classification, route type

road hierarchy 10, 21, 24–5, 33, 36, 159, 165–6, 242–3, 251–2, 293; 'bad' hierarchy 35, 50, 183–4, 186, 218; as basis of constitutional approach, 223; of distributors 48–50, 64, 66, 169; examples 47, 53, 264–9, 288, 292; 'good' hierarchy 35, 176–7, 186; Le Corbusier's 45–6, 67–9; and pattern 36; principles 46–8; structure 159–65; *see also* articulated route hierarchy, modal hierarchy, street-based constitution, transit-oriented hierarchy

Roman practice 13, 39, 46, 264

route 115, 277, 282, 293

route structure 115, 155, 293

route structure analysis 293; conventions 277, 282

route type 115, 123, 128, 131, 279

routegram 125, 278

safety 3, 12, 15, 47–8, 63, 68, 172, 191–2, 201, 213, 217, 252
scale: and definition of road type 64–6, 68, 184; structures at different scales 92; and transport modes 199, 204, 206–8; and urban status 211–12
segregation 47–9, 66–7, 178, 180, 200
social considerations 194–5, 198
social hierarchy 53, 150
space syntax 111–15, 130
speed 180, 191, 196, 200–6, 247
strategic contiguity 62, 171, 293
stratification 172, 178–9, 293
stratified hierarchy 178–9; stratification by speed 202–6, 217; constitutional graph 288
street: as access road 21, 25; definitions 22, 293; roles of traditional streets 3, 22–3, 25; street type and classification 23–4, 26, 34, 52, 54, 64–6, 170, 169–71, 229–30; as 'twig' 159, 169; as urban place 15, 22, 48, 211–13; see also classification, road and street types
street-based constitution 228–35, 241–3, 248–9
structural conditions 160–4
structure 107, 133, 159, 164–5, 293; constitutional structure 172–4, 292; hierarchical structure 159–65; tree structure 162, 164–5, 169; see also analogies
sustainability 9, 10, 193; sustainable development xi; sustainable transport 192–3, 198

T-junction 38, 96–8, 100, 102, 143–4, 154
taxonomy 90, 294
Thamesmead 127, 150, 172, 174–5
topology 13–14, 87, 90, 108, 114, 117, 253; see also configuration
Tottenham Court Road 1, 3, 10, 185, 244–8

town planning 8, 240, 242, 253–4, 258
traffic calming 9, 255
traffic flow 3, 6, 8, 180, 191, 195–7, 210
Traffic in Towns xiv, 1–3, 5, 10, 15, 48–9, 64, 257, 264; constitutional graph, 287; constitutional types 170; and environment 211, 216, 247–8; hierarchy of distributors 48–50, 64–5, 159, 184–6; and transport modes 191–2; tree analogy 159, 184–5; Venice 65–7, 185–6
transit-oriented arteriality 206–8, 214–17, 229, 253, 294; constitutional graph 288
transit-oriented hierarchy 204, 206–8, 217, 253, 257
transport: and land use 10, 13–14, 252; and urban design xi, 10–15
transport modes – see modes
transport policy 9, 14, 252–3, 255
tree 153, 294 – see also patterns, structure
tributary – see patterns
Tripp, H. A. 1, 4–6, 48, 56, 65, 192; classifications 264, 271
typology 33, 90, 294; see also ABCD typology; block type; constitutional type; patterns; road and street type

unchallenged truths 15, 50, 245
urban code – see coding
urban design 1, 3, 9–10, 15, 21, 25–7, 40, 191, 216, 221, 242, 248–9: and transport xi, 10–15
urban destruction 8, 46, 50
urban hierarchy 68, 211–12
urban place 22, 211–13, 246
urban revolution 3, 6, 259; counter-revolution 9, 15, 257

Venice 65–7, 185–6

walking – see modes

zoning 240, 253, 258